RESEARCH IN URBAN POLICY   VOLUME 11

CAN TOCQUEVILLE KARAOKE? GLOBAL CONTRASTS OF CITIZEN PARTICIPATION, THE ARTS AND DEVELOPMENT

United Kingdom – North America – Japan
India – Malaysia – China

Emerald Group Publishing Limited
Howard House, Wagon Lane, Bingley BD16 1WA, UK

First edition 2014

Copyright © 2014 Emerald Group Publishing Limited

Reprints and permission service
Contact: permissions@emeraldinsight.com

British Library Cataloguing in Publication Data
A catalogue record for this book is available from the British Library

ISBN: 978-1-78190-736-8
ISSN: 1479-3520 (Series)

ISOQAR certified
Management System,
awarded to Emerald
for adherence to
Environmental
standard
ISO 14001:2004.

Certificate Number 1985
ISO 14001

INVESTOR IN PEOPLE

COAUTHORS

Peter Achterberg   Centre for Rotterdam Cultural Sociology (CROCUS), Erasmus University, Rotterdam, the Netherlands

Chad D. Anderson   Department of Public Administration, Incheon National University, Incheon, South Korea

Miree Byun   Department of Future and Social Policy Research, Seoul Institute, Seoul, Korea

Filipe Carreira da Silva Institute of Social Sciences, University of Lisbon, Lisbon, Portugal and Selwyn College, University of Cambridge, Cambridge, UK

Terry Nichols Clark   Department of Sociology, University of Chicago, Chicago, IL, USA

Daniel J. DellaPosta   Department of Sociology, Cornell University, Ithaca, NY, USA

Arkaida Dini   University of Paris, Paris, France

Susana L. Farinha Cabaço Department of Government, University of Essex, Colchester, UK

Wonho Jang   University of Seoul, Seoul, Korea

Seokho Kim   Department of Sociology, Sungkyunkwan University, Seoul, Korea

Yoshiaki Kobayashi   Faculty of Law, Keio University, Tokyo, Japan

Jong Youl Lee   Department of Public Administration, Incheon National University, Incheon, Korea

Cristina Mateos Mora   Centre for Local Political Sociology and
                          Policies, Universidad Pablo de Olavide,
                          Seville, Spain

Clemente J. Navarro   Centre for Local Political Sociology and
   Yáñez   Policies, Universidad Pablo de Olavide,
                          Seville, Spain

María Jesús   Centre for Local Political Sociology and
   Rodríguez-García   Policies, Universidad Pablo de Olavide,
                          Seville, Spain

Stephen Sawyer   Department of History, The American
                          University of Paris, Paris, France

Daniel Silver   Department of Sociology, University of
                          Toronto at Scarborough, Toronto, Canada

Di Wu   Management School, University of Chinese
                          Academy of Sciences, Beijing, P.R. China

Joseph E. Yi   Political Science, Hanyang University,
                          Seoul, Korea

CONTENTS

INTRODUCTION

Terry Nichols Clark

ABSTRACT

This volume outlines a new framework for analysis of democratic participation and economic growth. The new framework joins two past traditions. Their background histories are clearly separate. Democratic participation ideas come mostly from Alexis de Tocqueville, while innovation/bohemian ideas driving the economy are largely inspired by Joseph Schumpeter and Jane Jacobs. New developments building on these core ideas are detailed in the first two sections of this volume. But these chapters in turn show that more detailed work within each tradition leads to an integration of the two: participation joins innovation. This is the main theme in the book's third section, the buzz around arts and culture organizations, and how and why they are critical drivers for the new democratic politics and cutting edge economies. Buzz enters as a new resource, with new rules of the game. It does not dominate; it parallels other activities which continue.

Keywords: Citizen participation; economics; arts; culture; comparative politics

Can Tocqueville Karaoke? Global Contrasts of Citizen Participation, the Arts and Development
Research in Urban Policy, Volume 11, 1–14
ISSN: 1479-3520/doi:10.1108/S1479-352020140000011013

Are you skeptical about the importance of arts and culture, especially about their possible impact on politics and the economy? That they can drive us so far is a new idea. The chapters in this volume explore how these new patterns work around the world. As authors, many of us were surprised at the significance of the findings here, as they contradict much of what we learned. The young are classically most in sync with the latest styles, clothes, music, and lifestyle. Most of us form lifestyles at about age 20. We continue our main lifestyle patterns as we grow older, and these sometimes clash with new practices. This is common with innovations – from the emergence of factories, computers, feminism, or environmental movements, intellectual understandings overlap and interpenetrate political ideologies – and economic interests. But this resistance is not new or unique to arts and culture; it is classic. Dramatic shifts in paradigms take years to diffuse and even after innovations enter their homes and shift their personal lifestyles, many observers deny the changes. Again, this is classic.

We start with two parallel and interrelated processes. First, the dynamics of Tocquevillian citizen participation (sometimes) leads to democracy, legitimacy, and trust. Second, we analyze the sources of economic growth, building on the tradition from Joseph Schumpeter, Jane Jacobs, and others, which stress innovation as an economic driver and citizens as implementers in distinctive, decentralized ways. Both these Western-generated theories ostensibly failed when we pursued them initially in China, Korea, and Japan. This volume traces how emergence of a new conceptualization evolved from initial contradictory results to a more subtle reformulation incorporating global dynamics.

Tocqueville made a critical point about democracy in stressing civic participation, but later work, such as that of Robert Putnam, Sidney Verba (This Introduction omits detailed references, most of which are in later chapters.), and contemporary citizen politics studies by political scientists, has understandably simplified and focused on measuring participation. Tocqueville discussed many aspects of context in his *Democracy in America*. But he wrote as a traveler/journalist, a century before most social science, and did not frame his observations or articulate their contexts with abstract terms like expressive or hierarchical. Raymond Aron revived Tocqueville in France in the 1960s, but it was Robert Putnam's *Bowling Alone* that sparked broad rereading. Tocqueville seemed relevant to Americans due to the decline of civic groups and the concern with selfish individualism captured in Putnam's title. But globally and among European and Latin American intellectuals, the bigger issue was probably the decline of Marxism after the Berlin Wall fell in 1989. This left an intellectual and ideological void. Public intellectuals, policy advisors, and journalists from Budapest to Beijing to Buenos Aires dug out Tocqueville to add democratic theorizing to their array of ideas. They needed specifics about democracy to discuss more than abstractions like neoliberalism or postcommunism. This led to new ideas like the third way, the new political culture (NPC), Bobos, and other political transformations discussed globally especially since 1989.

Robert Putnam's *Bowling Alone* was a major invitation to explore Tocqueville, but unfortunately it largely omitted values and context. This is ironic as Putnam's earlier book *Making Democracy Work* was a highly innovative (thus also highly controversial) introduction of context into Italian political analysis. He showed that democratic forms had emerged centuries earlier in city-states like Venice, Trieste, and Florence and were reflected in the present dramatic regional differences in how citizens and local politicians related to one another. By contrast, the southern parts of Italy had turbulent conquests and developed minimal democratic traditions; the civic void was sometimes filled by the Mafia. The key driver in *Making Democracy Work* was still citizen participation, but Putnam was articulate about how it varied by regional context, and how these regional/ historical differences continued in specific political cultures. Yet, most of this sensitivity to context was lost in *Bowling Alone*. Many social scientist followers/researchers have ignored the context and meaning surrounding citizen participation.

As we move internationally and ask how well Tocqueville travels, we confront paradoxical inconsistencies if we ignore culture and context. One goal of this volume is to sensitize the reader and analyst to the contextual variations sometimes labeled political culture, and how these work in practice to shift local dynamics. Several chapters help build a neo-Tocquevillian framework for analyzing citizen participation, economic change, and the arts, by adding institutions, context, and values. Sometimes we term these scenes as this emphasizes the contextual salience and value content of them to the key participants.

Section I of this volume thus reformulates the basic model of civic participation from Tocqueville/Putnam to stress the context and rules of the game within which local participants operate. As we look at more precise comparative data from many countries, we find that participation often fails to work as theorized by Tocqueville and documented by Putnam. Still, rather than rejecting the positive idea that citizen participation increases leadership skills and legitimacy among citizens, we ask where and why this may still happen, or not. Many theorists frame such issues as what are the underlying assumptions of this model that may not hold. We do too, but rather than asking this question in abstract, and focusing on assumptions, we stress particular contexts where the actual values and rules of the game differ. We contrast nations, thousands of postal codes in the United States and Canada, communes in France and Spain, and small neighborhood areas in Korea. We find old and new, and variations of each in these many different contexts. But in comparing the results, collaborators in this volume seek to use key common concepts, permitting specific contrasts of participation patterns, as well as aspects of contexts that vary globally. When we add the arts and culture, we can then see how they operate in terms of these interrelated factors. Some of our findings are solid and clear; others are new and tentative. And some new interpretations in the following pages are not yet tested empirically.

Perhaps in part as its roots were in the era after the 1960s, when cultural interpretations were less in favor, recent citizen participation work has largely omitted values and issue specificity. This is most clear in the work of Putnam in *Bowling Alone* and the Verba–Nie–Brady tradition of citizen participation studies. These largely ignore value differences, even distinct configurations of value patterns in most of their formulations, or leave them implicit – assuming a quasi-New England Tocquevillian perspective, largely unvarying. Or they looked for more versus less participation, and seemed to assume that more participation was consistently joined with more legitimacy and confidence, as in Tocqueville. Their key work was in the United States, and they did not generally seek to look for patterned differences in these processes across subgroups or nations in a systematic way. When they formerly had looked beyond the United States, in their own works (Italy for Putnam, Almond and Verba, and Verba–Nie–Kim in international books) they changed their interpretation and results dramatically. Putnam found Northern and Southern Italy to be drastically different in their political cultures and citizen participation patterns. Almond and Verba was the foundational work for much cross-national comparison. Verba, Nie, and Kim in cross-national work found that workers in countries with strong unions linked to left parties turned out to vote at higher rates than more upper status persons (e.g., in Korea and Yugoslavia). Putnam elaborated such variations in later books like *Better Together* and *Democracies in Flux*.

They are obviously talented researchers, so we point out this narrowness because it continued in many other studies which they inspired. There are many nuances and subtleties in recent work on citizen participation, but much of it is more social psychological than socio-cultural-contextual, in the broad Michigan tradition of politics research. We thus focus on the core paradigm passed on in the key works of Putnam and Verba et al. and the many who continue it. As we develop below, the core results shift dramatically when we analyze not only the total participation but also (1) to distinguish types of participation in separate issue areas like religion, the environment, or arts and culture and (2) consider differences by subgroups. Then both key past findings change as we move to multiple countries and contexts, concerning: (1) the decline in participation in recent decades stressed in *Bowling Alone* and (2) the "normal" pattern of Verba et al. that more educated and older persons participate more.

Our effort has been to codify these inconsistencies in results and build a more coherent theory, stressing context. This illustrates and continues work labeled local or neighborhood effects which has become distinctly important in recent years in several subfields from health to crime to citizen participation and voting. Sensitivity to such local variations has been made possible by richer data, cross-nationally and digging deeper for more microdata than in past work on one nation or state/regional studies. There are so many accumulated inconsistent results from different studies that it is high time to codify and build more coherent propositions about how the disparities may help deepen our understanding of the core processes at work. Similarly, inconsistent results emerged in the adjacent subfield of New Social Movements, which spurred a paradigm shift stressing context, specifically using concepts like opportunity structure, framing, and movement mobilization (with the work of Mario Diani, Donatella Della Porta, Dieter Rucht, Hanspeter Kriesi, and Doug McAdam). We propose a similar reframing of citizen participation and local development. Many of these foundational points also hold in the rest of the volume, which make possible building a new framework that can span and join at least the three subfields of citizen participation, innovation in economic development, and arts and cultural activities.

Section II of this volume extends a second line of theorizing that stresses not only citizen participation but also how economic development is increasingly driven by innovations in ideas, and how these innovations are often generated by persons and cities where there are more tolerant, non-traditional, and sometimes Bohemian residents. These ideas were stressed in the Schumpeter, Jane Jacobs tradition and pursued further by Richard Florida, Edward Glaeser, Richard Lloyd, Elizabeth Currid, and Michael Fritsch among others. The core idea is that a bohemian neighborhood and lifestyle encourages or at least reflects more tolerance which in turn encourages in-migration by creative persons and more risk-taking innovation. This in turn leads to outcomes such as patents, inventions and in turn drives economic growth in these locations. That such persons comprise a creative class has been articulated by Richard Florida but critiqued by many social scientists. Yet if one looks at his footnotes, it is clear that Florida's key ideas are a synthesis of many subfields from patent research to neighborhood organization to social psychology of workgroups to organization theory. Many persons in these and related fields converge around similar ideas about the importance of innovation for productivity.

Most of this work has focused on geographic proximity (e.g., of biomedical firms and research labs/universities) and stressed tolerance of an anti-establishment lifestyle, epitomized by artists and gays. Yet, insofar as decentralization and collegial engagement are key elements of this creativity story, we can develop a convergence with the specifics of the Tocquevillian civic groups. This is part of our rationale for joining here the Tocqueville and Schumpeter traditions, even if few have done so to date. We may be the first.

Related to the bohemia-drives-development thesis are empirical studies of artists, especially by economists and urbanists. A key point is that most of these recent studies of artists and the arts have not included values explicitly. Many analysts, and artists, assume that artists are hip and bohemian, and broadly oppose the traditional establishment, but they often have no direct evidence as to how much this is or is not the case. For instance, Richard Florida has used a Bohemian Index in several studies which is simply the proportion of the labor force that works in arts-related jobs, based on Census data, often for an entire metropolitan area (not a city or neighborhood). Ann Markusen has done several innovative analyses of artists, often using Census data for arts jobs. But the U.S. Census does not ask people if they are Bohemians or other lifestyle, or value questions that might capture values more directly. Thus, Boho in this type of research is imputed from the occupational title. By not articulating a coherent value concept or finding data to measure it, this line of analysis is troubled by the same issue as the Tocqueville/Putnam tradition of citizen participation.[1]

Section III focuses on buzz, arts, and culture, and how they can transform politics, economics, and social life. Citizens have shifted toward the arts and culture. Citizens (in many countries, not everywhere) report in surveys that they join arts organizations more often, that they spend more time on arts and cultural activities, and that these are linked to happiness and good health. This holds when controlling for education, income, occupation, age, and more.

Related, these citizen values have more impact on many political systems, which have grown more populist/media/citizen-focused, especially since 1968 and later after the fall of the Berlin Wall in 1989, with the spread of global organizations involved with human rights, gender roles, and the environment, often undermining traditional political parties that were slow to respond to these new citizen concerns.

Like the political systems, the economies of many countries have been transformed with general increases in income (especially in less-developed countries, although economic growth is clearly uneven) and more critically, with new ways of responding to narrow niche markets. Labels like the iPhone generation illustrate this point, as smartphones can download a set of music, videos, films, and saved photos unique to each person. Detailed surveys of cultural consumption by the French Ministry of Culture document huge growth among young persons in activities of this general sort. Similarly, several studies stress that key firms have grown by implementing better design, not just low cost or technical excellence (Samsung, Apple, and others). Many are hiring MFAs (Masters of Fine Arts) alongside MBAs (Masters of Business Administration) to improve design, aesthetics, and related marketing and advertising. Apple ads feature the cool Apple user versus the square businessman in a suit, who still uses Microsoft Windows. Samsung similarly transformed its brand to stress design as it applied to user lifestyles, not product technology. Small firms have grown in numbers as they are more responsive to niche consumer markets.

These major global changes in politics and the economy have led to more focus on citizens. The concerns of average citizens have thus entered political and economic decisions more actively, via focus groups, citizen surveys, new candidates and political parties, and new organized groups, like environmentalists. Political party programs have faded in impact, or shifted to incorporate more citizen concerns. One such concern, in some locations, has been a rise of the arts and culture. This is documented in several chapters (Clark and Achterberg, da Silva, and so on) More specifically, artists, arts organizers, and arts-related entrepreneurs have helped expand support for theater, concerts, and attention to and sponsorship of arts activities – in some locations. Private business markets have moved in the same direction, dramatically increasing sales of new media, home theater, and other products.

"Buzz" is a valuable symbolic resource generated by arts and cultural activities. It is more emotional, visual, visceral, and, in some issue areas, rises to rival the more classic resources like money and jobs. Buzz is obviously critical among arts and cultural activities and related scenes, but even more. It is a resource, we suggest, that can be wielded, in certain situations and issue areas, to influence political and economic decisions in new ways. "Cultural power" is increasingly a potent factor; it is part of the soft power that international relations analysts have used to extend work on military and economic factors. Often buzz is local and highly personal, but to cite one globally important example, Cool Japan comprised a range of policies coordinated by the Ministry of Economy, Trade, and Industry "to promote cultural and creative industries as a strategic sector under the single long term concept of 'Cool Japan'." In 2011, it had a budget of 19 billion yen, spurred in part to catch up with the Chinese and Koreans whose public spending on culture comprised 0.79% and 0.51%, respectively, of total government spending, compared to Japan's 0.12% (Cool Japan, n.d.). This led to discussions in Japan that the Gross National Cool was too low, and that more sponsorship for pop culture and anime was needed along with establishing culturally distinctive Cool Japan activities in many foreign countries. How to interpret coolness?

Is buzz a trump card resource? Does adding buzz mean dropping all else? Of course not. We live in a multicausal world where dozens of intertwined factors drive most social, political, and economic processes. We just flag buzz as a new arrival. Buzz is a new flag rising with the transformations of arts and culture into a fundamental part of the new economy. It is a symbolic resource analogous to trust and confidence in political leaders, and money in the economy (most forms of money — checks, bank transfers, etc. — are symbolic; bartered physical goods are not money). One can analogously identify inflation and deflation of these symbolic resources as they grow out of proportion to their underlying foundations (elaborated in the chapter by Silver and Clark).

Buzz links leaders and citizens, albeit loosely, outside political parties and classic hierarchical institutions like the strong state and national churches. Buzz may be more general, or specifically related to arts and culture, as we use it here for the most part. It is part of political branding. Eleonora Pasotti in *Political Branding in Cities* analyzed how branding was used in subtle ways in Bogotá, Chicago, and Naples to transform these cities, their citizen politics, and their economies. Most cities around them in their respective countries lag behind. But to understand the dynamics of innovation, it helps to focus on the key leaders who are inevitably far ahead of the pack. Like Bill Clinton playing his sax and Japan's Prime Minister Koizumi singing Elvis songs at Graceland (in Karaoke style), for instance.

Many have sought to build and analyze buzz in domains that reach further than culture and politics. Just to illustrate that these are not only humanistic, consider how leading market economists have focused on symbolic resources related to buzz. George Stigler, Milton Friedman, and Gary Becker all published in professional journals and wrote for the more general public. Friedman and Paul Samuelson were the two best-known economists of their day, and wrote columns on alternate weeks in *Businessweek* magazine. Gary Becker continued writing for *Businessweek*, and even wrote a paper on the concept of buzz, illustrated by a new restaurant which tries to create a long line of would-be customers outside in the street to attract attention from restaurant reviewers and buzz-sensitive foodies. Buzz underlies the main theory informing financial pricing: the efficient market hypothesis or random-walk approach. It holds that what drives stock markets is not just the fundamentals in a material sense like profits, but the information about these specifics in the minds of key market participants. When identical information is widely shared, markets operate efficiently; information in this sense drives markets. A simple version of this idea was phrased by Thomas Friedman as "following the herd" of investors, based on often manipulated information, in his best sellers *The Lexus and the Olive Tree* and *The World is Flat*.

How do buzz and the arts link to this book's stress on how citizen participation and economic innovation vary by context? First, we identify buzz as part of the context, especially the symbols and rules of the game involving arts and culture. Second, by pointing toward arts and culture as distinct resources that can influence other sectors, like the more classic economy and polity. We illustrate these concretely in case studies of Toronto and Chicago (Silver and Clark), both leading cities where the arts brought deep political and economic transformations. Both actively used culture to transform their images and economies since the late twentieth century. Toronto illustrates a rather Tocquevillian dynamic, driven by neighborhood arts groups, while Chicago does not.

Analogous to the NPC of Clark and Hoffmann-Martinot, buzz and the arts are leading-edge drivers of change, but this does not imply that all citizens or countries move in the same direction, or do so evenly. Rather, there are dramatically different contexts within which participants argue openly over priorities. Codifying these is illuminating, and pursued in several chapters.

Buzz, as an articulation of the symbols and rules of the game about the arts, clearly is not monolithic. The concept of spontaneous artistic creativity only emerged in the early nineteenth century, when the book market grew large enough to support popular novelists like Dickens and Balzac. Balzac became a major spokesman for the arts. He articulated the ideology of the independent artist as a driver of ideas and innovation. This theme of the genius driving innovation was new. The arts just a few decades earlier had been primarily seen as a product of patronage, where the prince or bishop would invite an artist to create a church mosaic or music for a new mass. The beauty and glories of Christianity and the Church were classic themes, as interpreted by the specific patron. Only after the French Revolution of 1789 ushered in the ideals of democracy, and major patrons were beheaded by the guillotine, were leading chefs, novelists, musicians, and others forced to follow a broader market logic. They wrote cookbooks, proclaimed manifestos, made symbolic statements − buzz. Some lived together in neighborhoods that took on the label of Bohemia, la boheme. Walter Benjamin articulated some of these themes in *The Arcades Project*, pointing to the flâneur, the consumer of taste, whose decisions drove the dynamics of production. Even if Benjamin used classic Marxist labels to introduce these ideas, he deeply transformed Marxism by stressing not capital and production, but the independent driving forces of the consumer and aesthetics. One of his major sources was Baudelaire who, for instance, held that less affluent young women, who followed fashion buzz closely, could capture more attention by choosing new stylish outfits that surpassed those of the more affluent but less fashion-sensitive. This continual style-changing, and its buzz, he termed Modernism.

Obviously, a large gray area surrounds the arts and buzz-driven dynamics. It explains more, its resources are more valuable, in certain contexts, than others. But the simplest criticism that buzz only works in affluent areas is clearly false. Africa remains the least economically developed continent but any tourist can see the dramatic power and emotional engagement of African music and the arts − illustrated for instance by teenagers waiting for a bus, singing and dancing. Or consider how the traditional religions of Islam, Roman Catholicism, and the Church of England have been deeply challenged by the rousing music and active citizen participation in evangelical churches, which spread across Africa and poorer areas of Latin America and Asia near the end of the twentieth century. Analogously, young persons in low-income areas in much of the world pay great attention to T-shirts, shoes, hairstyles, and the music they dance to, or shun. These are personal identity markers. Certainly, world areas fundamentally differ in political cultures (as analyzed in Chapter 14) from Protestantism and Catholicism to Asian areas. So too do the dynamics of buzz vary. Globalizing forces of television and the Internet encourage local areas to follow global dynamics. Mayors in Chinese villages can be elected using global "buzzwords," even if many voters may not fully grasp their implications (like social networking, electronic cable, wired community). More than half the Chinese population has access to the Internet. And it is rapidly growing. Still, local cultural sensitivities, sharpened by *local* buzz about arts and culture, can resist globalizing tendencies.

These varied examples illustrate how context clearly matters and transforms local dynamics, a major theme pursued in many chapters of this volume. These forcefully indicate that we do not suggest a one cause, deterministic approach. Nor do we propose a simple diffusion approach that one icon will spread everywhere unchanged. Rather, buzz is part of the NPC, which defines changes in key components of contexts – the rise of social issues, more active media, the decline of traditional political parties and unions, and the importance of values and specific scenes. These NPC patterns are not universal but are more niche-like. Still, to observe that there are major niches in the economy, politics, and social life is not to deny that new patterns spread among them – like social media, informal dress styles, or even the popularity of certain icons like soccer heroes or Lady Gaga or Michael Jackson or Psy, the Korean rapper whose video "Gangnam Style," surpassed all past YouTube viewings in 2012. How does buzz work? We are only at the beginning of explaining buzz in terms of social science research. There are bits of theory, such as efforts to interpret how media markets encourage superstars, by the economist Sherwin Rosen in "The Economics of Superstars," inspiring real estate economist Joseph Gyourko to identify "Superstar Cities." They and others have started to theorize symbolic media like glamour and buzz in ways that overlap with the chapters in this volume. We encourage others to join us and go further.

Findings from several chapters show that specific mechanisms by which the arts and culture "work," substantially shift with context, especially the local political culture. Tocquevillian theory was energized by the civil rights movement in the 1960s United States, where marches and protests joined with song. The example continued in New Social Movements, and challenging but nonviolent political protests spread globally. Songs like We Shall Overcome and The Battle Hymn of the Republic stand as powerful classics whose lyrics invoke God and a moral crusade to improve the world. The egalitarian pressures, joined with prayer and sacrifice for progress, are clear and strong. From South Africa to Bangladesh, one finds similar inspiration. By contrast, in more hierarchical and broadly legitimated political cultures, where citizens are not used to such direct personal participation, they may respond more powerfully to time-honored symbols of national pride: military marches, parades of strong political leaders, church music, and paintings of religious icons inspire a duty-based citizenship. More passive arts activities are common, like visiting museums that feature classics. An Asian trope is the proper 20-year-old daughter in a traditional family. She is politically inspired by ironic and teasing social media, blogs, comics, anime films, and videos of rap songs like Gangnam Style. Her participation may be virtual, via blogs or signing petitions, sent from home.

Young persons the world over are transforming their political and social experiences by creating new artistic experiences – like dancing in a public square, building floats, or recording songs and videos. They participate in and mobilize others in concerts as well as in parades or political demonstrations, with political and economic consequences. Some adults also find new inspiration in distinctive arts and cultural experiences – like a new band, star singer, or inspiring film. Video games, smartphones, and the Internet trumpet themes globally.

These experiences are new for political and economic policy makers, and for analysts. The activities often break with past categories and build new combinations. They create passion and ambition, rage and revenge. That is the point. The new buzz has deeper and broader impact precisely since it works in new and powerful ways, creating and engaging vast new audiences. The chapters in this volume map out major contours of this terrain, which is changing our lives, politics, and economy more deeply and faster than we care to admit. Tocqueville can Karaoke too, but he has to practice first.

ORIGINS OF THIS VOLUME

Participants in this volume have worked together as part of international projects that feature local contexts (Fiscal Austerity and Urban Innovation and the Scenes Project). We explore here how cultural patterns vary cross-nationally. There has been continual exchange among the participants over several years (and for some, decades) as we have unearthed some surprising and controversial results. One key result came from Seokho Kim in his Ph.D. on citizen participation. Contrasting some 30 countries, he found that participation worked in Tocquevillian manner in Northwest Europe and North America. But in some other locations, especially Korea, Portugal, Brazil, the former Soviet area, and Eastern Europe, citizen participation had no effect on legitimacy and trust or was sometimes even negative. This dramatic result of course leads one to ask why. This is a key question addressed in the first section of this volume. Our basic answer, stated in abstract, is that it depends on the local rules of the game and values of key participants. For instance, young people in U.S. cities who participate more in gang activities may grow more alienated from society and distrust people more. Gang participation in this example reinforces a sense that the political leadership in the society around them is not trustworthy and does not inspire confidence. This U.S. gang example is one way that our analyses have evolved from exploring comparisons of national averages to identifying subgroups in specific cities as conceptually critical examples, sometimes in case studies. This illustrates how we move back and forth from surveys of citizens across countries to contrasting subgroups by neighborhood. This helps us generalize in a more specific manner about the key ways of classifying values, participation, and related concepts like trust and legitimacy, and to test these ideas with the best available data. We link where possible with standard measures used by others like voter turnout, citizen participation in organized groups, self-reported trust and confidence, and various economic development indicators such as changes in jobs and population overall, by city or neighborhood, and by age and other subgroups.

The innovations in this volume were sparked from: (1) Comparing processes, from neighborhoods to nations; (2) Using multiple methods – from personal participation to case studies of unusual cases (Toronto and Chicago), to citizen surveys (used by Seokho Kim and Clark/Achterberg), to comparing cities and their neighborhoods with census and original data such as downloaded electronic Yellow Pages advertising listings of restaurants and churches (DellaPosta/Clark and Navarro et al.); (3) Looking for and contrasting contexts, from nations to neighborhoods to "issue areas" like voting versus cultural consumption (This led Clark and Achterberg to find the rise of arts and culture participation in international surveys.); (4) Featuring value differences that reshape what seem to be the "same" processes but with quite different meaning in different contexts. Navarro's and da Silva's insights from Southern European Catholic contexts contrast with the more common Northern European/Protestant/North American focus; (5) Collegial teamwork. We coauthors have talked, and argued, for hours and hours over many years, and learned hugely in the process. Tocqueville visited and interviewed key informants. Then he wrote with one coauthor. We, by contrast, keep meeting in conferences, share emails and draft papers, and Skype in global workgroups, often weekly. We have succeeded in engaging some highly talented persons from disparate locations. We regularly have conflicting interpretations, so we discuss them and learn far more from the diversity of interpretations than is possible if just one person sought to interpret it all.

The distinctiveness of Korea and Portugal from Seokho Kim – that citizens in these countries did not develop trust as in other places – encouraged us to dig further into comparing these countries with others to find out more of how they worked. We thus collaborated with Joseph Yi, Wonho Jang, Chad Anderson, Miree Byun, and Jong Youl Lee in Korea, and Filipe Carreira da Silva and Susana L. F. Cabaço from Portugal. Yoshiaki Kobayashi stimulated many of us with his cross-country comparisons and subtle analyses. Their insights are in the following chapters with global implications.

NOTE

1. Our criticism of this tradition of imputing Boho values from census occupations, and the underlying paradigmatic assumptions, is analogous to our critique of the lack of sensitivity to values in the recent citizen participation research tradition. But these are not criticisms of the lead researchers, who in many cases have done other studies that incorporate more sources. For instance, Richard Florida teamed with a survey research group that conducted several unique surveys of citizens in U.S. cities, including values and lifestyle items. These and many other creative studies are reported on Florida's website and in *Atlantic Cities* which he edits.

REFERENCE

Cool Japan. (n.d.). In Wikipedia. Retrieved from http://en.wikipedia.org/wiki/Cool_Japan. Accessed on March 7, 2014.

KARAOKE TOGETHER VS. BOWLING ALONE: SCENES ILLUMINATE HOW WESTERN RULES CAN BE TRANSFORMED TO DRIVE DEVELOPMENT AND DEMOCRACY

Terry Nichols Clark with Chad D. Anderson,
Miree Byun, Wonho Jang, Seokho Kim,
Yoshiaki Kobayashi, Jong Youl Lee,
Clemente J. Navarro Yáñez,
Daniel Silver and Di Wu

ABSTRACT

What drives workplace and political collaboration, democracy, trust, economic and population growth? Or protest against them? The Western models emerging from Putnam, Verba et al., Florida, Glaeser, Lloyd, Scott, and Porter stress variables that sometimes shift dramatically in

Can Tocqueville Karaoke? Global Contrasts of Citizen Participation, the Arts and Development
Research in Urban Policy, Volume 11, 15−30
Copyright © 2014 by Emerald Group Publishing Limited
ISSN: 1479-3520/doi:10.1108/S1479-352020140000011014

Asia. Those relying on individualism and personal initiative, from Tocqueville on — which stress participation as driving legitimacy, and bohemia as innovating — often fail or shift drastically in a new study of related dynamics in China, Korea, and Japan, compared to the United States, Canada, France, and Spain. Karaoke restaurants and bars can play critical roles, reinforcing workplace and family solidarity, while organized groups shift in their dynamics from the West. We are constructing a multilevel interpretative framework specifying how cultural, political, and economic dynamics interpenetrate in distinct but varying combinations. How engaged or alienated are young persons, workers, and the general public shift other processes. Arts and culture can build glamour and charisma, or alienate as transgressive and inauthentic; each varies by context.

Keywords: Bohemia; culture; arts; economic development; democracy; participation

We are entering a more cosmopolitan age where Europe is increasingly the past, the United States is the present, and Asia leads toward the future. Sensitivity to these changes should focus our attention more explicitly on how well our theories generalize from Europe to the United States to Asia. Many talk of globalization and yet it is these broad regional contexts filled with historical specificities, deep histories, and rich detail that are the building blocks of major global linkages and patterns.

To detail these general points, we focus on two social science theories central in the last decade:

1. Citizen participation increases legitimacy in the political system (Alexis de Tocqueville, Robert Putnam, and many more).
2. Innovation is a critical driver of the economy and urban development, and Bohemia is a core component driving innovation (Joseph Schumpeter, Jane Jacobs, Richard Florida, Edward Glaeser, and more economists).

We do not seek to refute but to specify more closely the key components of what makes these dynamics work in some places, not in others, and possibly reverse course or go wildly awry in still other places. But rather than framing the analysis in terms of "assumptions," which may not be met for a theory to hold, as is common, we stress context and scene. Contexts transform the rules of the game and inform specific motivational patterns (from the Protestant or Confucian ethic to discussions of modernism, postmodernism, postmaterialism, to the rise of scenes). We introduce the arts and buzz as scenes elements in the following pages.

These lines of theorizing need sharpening and reformulation if not refutation, if one shifts from Europe to the United States to Asia. We begin with brief summaries of the two theories and then how we extend past work on contexts.

Tocqueville and Putnam's theory draws on cases like Massachusetts town meetings and Northern Italian city-states, where more participation of citizens seems to have increased their trust, and feelings of support and legitimacy about the political system. We term this Model 1. There are innumerable studies that explore this pattern, but we cite just a few distinctive results that help contextualize it. One is Angelika Vetter (2007) who studied citizen participation using international citizen surveys, linking in a theoretically distinctive way the national and the local. She found that citizens who participated more in local organizational activities felt substantially more legitimacy for the national political system. This held strong in many of the Western European countries and the United States. So, participation leads to more trust and legitimacy, local and national in these results.

A second set of studies focuses on areas like Latin America (e.g., Moreno, 2001; Sudarsky, 2002) and shows that civic participation and trust and legitimacy are low in most Latin American countries. This has led many following the Tocqueville/Putnam tradition to search for ways to increase participation, hoping it will engage citizens more broadly, reduce violence, and contribute to public and civic well-being. We could call this Model 2. But it is simply the obverse of Model 1 and does not per se question the causal dynamics of Tocqueville/Putnam (Fig. 1).

CIVIC PARTICIPATION CAN LEAD TO MANY OUTCOMES

But if we shift to certain Asian countries, the quasi-determinism of Models 1 and 2 is called into question. Model 3 is thus posited, where a positive relation between noncivic variables may substitute for the civic participation so stressed in Model 1. That is, civic participation in Japan is low. By some measures, it is even in the range of Latin America. However, contradicting Models 1 and 2, in Japan trust and legitimacy are roughly similar to Western Europe and the United States – as measured by standardized

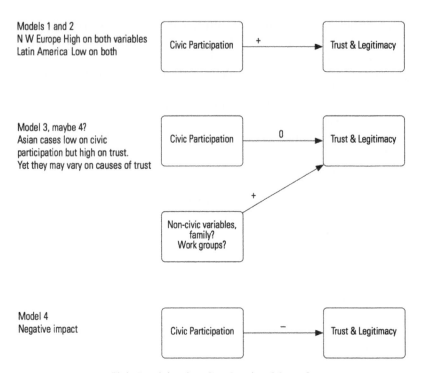

Fig. 1. Civic Participation Can Lead to Many Outcomes.

citizen surveys such as the International Social Survey Programme (ISSP) and World Values Surveys. Seymour M. Lipset, in *American Exceptionalism* (1997), discusses these sorts of results in detail in his last section and appendices with data on Japan; so does Francis Fukuyama in his book *Trust* (1995). However, the highly detailed analysis by Kobayashi (2011) of Japanese citizens questions the depth of this trust, and suggests it is often constrained by traditional leadership in rural localities, clientelist linkages for some citizens, and the strong party allegiance of others. He suggests that the widespread clientelist practices of the Liberal Democratic Party (LDP) are undermining trust for many citizens, especially among younger, more educated, professionals who live in larger cities that have generally elected mayors and governors that are not LDP members. Kobayashi adds substantially more depth and subtlety by combining rich analyses of citizen linkages to parties and leaders, with national and local data in overlapping analyses. He stresses within-country differences and change dynamics. Yet overall, he shows that many of the "normal" practices of North America and Western Europe do not operate as widely assumed (e.g., Inoguchi & Blondel, 2002). Without seeking to detail how and why, we list some major factors that these and other studies of Japan have stressed: the intensity of the family, the social indebtedness which children feel toward parents and authority figures, the tight social relations of work circles in large industries and classrooms for students, the clientelist linkages to traditional leaders which these overlapping, intense social relations enhance and legitimate. In his book on Japanese culture, S. N. Eisenstadt (1995) details how despite continual efforts by foreigners and "modernization" or "reform" over the 20th century, these patterns adapt and continue.

The universality of Tocqueville (Model 1) is more deeply challenged by a provocative recent doctoral dissertation by Seokho Kim (2008) who investigates these patterns by comparing them across 38 countries using the ISSP national survey data for citizen participation, trust, and related items. He finds the expected patterns for much of Northwest Europe and the United States: Model 1 holds, though it reveals some surprising exceptions. The most dramatic results, however, are that in many countries outside Northwest Europe and the United States, civic participation has no impact or reduces trust and support for the political system, shown here as Model 4. This implies, for some citizens at least, even the opposite. That is, the more some Koreans participated, the less they trusted leaders and institutions. Was this unique to Korea? He dug further and found similar patterns in Portugal, Brazil, and Eastern Europe.

This is a dramatic new finding, and important to build on. Look at the Seoul beef protest in 2008, the noted recent example with many historical counterparts as Korean students protested against authoritarian politics. We see analogous protests against authoritarian leaders for centuries around the world, especially by young male students, talented, independent, thoughtful, and critical. Bohemian? Not necessarily. The next logical question: is this specific to Asia? Do we not have student protests, union members, civil rights organizers, and others who actively organized against establishment policies and potentially encourage delegitimizing the establishment through participation in their organized activities? These are widespread, even though they may be a minoritarian variant rather than majoritarian in their impact on trust. This is a quite different conceptual framing, to ask where and why and how much this happens, rather than just link it to names of countries or regions. Can we instead introduce gender, age, living with your family, religiousness, and other factors to help interpret the "Korean effect," that is of participation not building trust? How does context encourage the rise of New New Social movements (NNSMs) which have no formal organization – no officers, board, budget, membership card, or other similar activities? The occupy movements resemble these NNSMs more than New Social Movements (see Chapter 4).

HOW DOES INNOVATION DRIVE THE ECONOMY?

The second key idea is that with the decline in manufacturing and traditional patterns of industrial production, some economists have revisited their theories about what drives the economy. Land, labor, capital, and management efficiency are not enough. One version of the new formulation is innovation or creativity, seen as a critical factor driving economic growth. Some of the most influential theorists here have been Joseph Schumpeter, in *Capitalism, Socialism and Democracy*, which stressed the creative destruction of capitalist entrepreneurs in breaking up old forms of production. Jane Jacobs stressed individual neighborhoods such as New York's Greenwich Village with a distinctly bohemian style as challenging established ways of thinking and acting. The city was more powerful as a personally connected set of streets and neighborhoods, where people could interact in cafés, outdoor bookshops, neighborhood conversations; these could spill into a neighborly sense of distinctiveness and sometimes political action from signing political petitions to marching in demonstrations. She personally helped mobilize opposition to stop construction of some large freeway projects by New York's master planner and builder Robert Moses, because these did not sufficiently incorporate the small human scale. Jacobs transformed many established ideas in planning and later urban economics and parts of sociology and geography, especially through Richard Florida and Edward Glaeser who elaborated her ideas and conducted careful research with their colleagues. Many others followed parallel and overlapping themes making these ideas a major force at the beginning of the 21st century among researchers and policy makers, architects, and urban planners.

But what happens if we shift to areas outside the West, like Asia, and ask, how does this model hold up? The simplest critical point, elaborated below, is that Bohemia is weak to absent in most of Asia, at least as measured using the normal Western indicators of bohemian lifestyle, thinking, and acting. Then how can Japan and Taiwan and Korea be capturing so many patents, generating so many new forms of electronic hardware and software, or recently music and design? And how could many countries across Asia be so phenomenally successful in their economies when Europe was in economic turmoil and the United States sluggish? The first answer is that the simple theory must be wrong. That is the normal (Western) Bohemian cannot be the key source of innovation, or we must find better ways of thinking about Bohemia and innovation.

CONTEXT AS SYNTHESIZER

Since Hegel, the idea of opposing a thesis with an antithesis and then a synthesis transcending both has been an aspiration for many. Marx used it to show how proletarians and capitalists through their class conflicts could generate fundamental historical transformations. Max Weber in turn suggested the Marxian stress on material-based conflicts was incomplete. He added context. Mapping broad but specific areas of the world, and studying them carefully, he showed how a few were successful in developing rational markets, organized industry, distant trading partners, and other components of modern industrial capitalism. Most others failed. Why? His core driver was Calvinist Protestantism, elaborated in *The Protestant Ethic and the Spirit of Capitalism.* Then in subsequent books he probed which critical elements were lacking in India, China, Catholic Southern Europe, and in past Middle Eastern empires surrounding the ancient Jews and Greeks, which crushed their efforts to develop. Weber also added values carried by individuals in their heads and hearts which drove them in a more powerful way than material self-interest. Money alone often led to disloyal followers, an unreliable military, and corrupt government administrators. The concept of legitimacy, even striving toward God and salvation, as a value in the minds of average citizens/consumers/soldiers, was a critical contribution of Weber's to move from an elitist model to a more citizen-driven conception of a modern complex economy and decentralized political system, for which citizens would voluntarily fight wars and sacrifice their lives. Philip Gorski has filled in these more political elements of Weber's analysis with richer historical specifics, especially the role of Calvinism.

As we move from Max Weber's past historical examples through the complexities and increasing flexibility of the early 21st century, specifics like his three components of legitimacy (traditional, charismatic, and bureaucratic) appear insufficient. More generally, education, income, travel,

and information revolutions like the Internet have hugely increased
the sophistication of average citizens. In a few years they helped transform
the simpler (often top-down) theories that ignore these increasing dimensions and the complexities of citizens' values that drive them. We have presented these changes under the general heading of the New Political Culture
in some eight books (e.g., Clark & Hoffmann-Martinot, 1998), stressing
such factors as how heightened citizen resources like education, income, etc.
create new specific contexts which transform simpler past relationships. We
here extend this general logic specifically to the theories of (1) citizen participation, (2) innovation and Bohemia, and (3) reinterpreting conflicts and
inconsistencies in theories 1 and 2 by introducing context via the 15 dimen-
sional classification of the theory of scenes. The scenes perspective can help
us join Asia with the United States and Europe so that we are part of a
world system which can be more coherently interpreted by social scientists,
policy makers, and average citizens. These key points we elaborate here and
in chapters below.

CONTEXTS, VALUES, AND SCENES

The two general propositions about bohemia and civic participation are
transformed by a third idea, the context. The family is one obvious context
that shifts purely individualistic patterns. But scenes are bigger than
families. With the spread of individualism, the "scene" rises in salience, as
it is an open physical space where individuals can freely enter or depart,
driven more by individual preferences than by externally imposed factors
like class, state, church, or family obligations. Think of the teahouse or
walk in a garden as a classic Asian activity within a broader scene. Family
groups can participate in scenes, around restaurants or churches, for
instance. But families go less to the more extreme Bohemian amenities (tattoo parlors, transgressive concerts).

Social scientists and others consider many types of contexts that we
build on in the scenes approach. But if the components have been used previously, we join them together to create a new holistic synthesis. That is a
scene includes (1) *Neighborhoods*, rather than cities, metro regions, states/
provinces, or nations. (2) *Physical structures*, such as dance clubs or shopping malls. (3) *Persons*, described according to their race, class, gender,
education, occupation, age, and the like. (4) Specific combinations of 1–3,
and the *activities* which join them, like young tech workers attending a

local punk concert. (5) These four in turn express *symbolic meanings, values* defining what is important about the experiences offered in a place. General meanings we highlight include legitimacy, defining a right or wrong way to live; theatricality, an attractive way of seeing and being seen by others; authenticity, a real or genuine identity. (6) *Publicness* – rather than the uniquely personal and private, we highlight the scenes projected by public spaces, available to passers-by and deep enthusiasts alike. (7) *Politics and policy*, especially policies and political controversies about how to shape, sustain, alter, or produce a given scene, how certain scenes attract (or repel) residents, firms, and visitors, or how some scenes mesh with political sensibilities, voting patterns, and specific organized groups, such as new social movements. These seven foci are part of a more general effort to retain the sensitivity to local complexity characteristic of ethnographers but disciplined by comparative methods, both quantitative and qualitative.

We particularly stress how scenes are often based on values, which are critical in adding deeper meaning to the participants, and often more emotion which can in turn lead to satisfaction or happiness and more powerful voting and economic decisions.

We distinguish 15 types of scenes in Fig. 2 to illustrate the rising "issue specificity" of people's complex and differentiated social lives and value configurations. We have gathered measures of each of these 15 scenes dimensions from data like electronic Yellow Page listings of churches, restaurants, and associations, census data on small industry types (like business organizations and unions as well as web designers), and survey data from citizen respondents. These data have been assembled by cooperating teams in France, Spain, Germany, Poland, Korea, China, Japan, Canada, and the United States. Several county and city reports have been completed for Paris, Seoul, Chinese cities, Spain, Toronto, Chicago, and the United States.

To build strong theories that can be adapted and extended globally, we must go beyond names of regions like the West, or countries. We thus formulated concepts at the level of generality illustrated by these 15 scenes, which can be combined and weighted in various ways to generate specifics for types like Bohemia or Max Weber's ideal types like peasant or bureaucrat. And to analyze how these multiple components variously combine and generate new meanings with new combinations, it is more empirically rich to dig deeper than nations. We thus drill down to local areas like communes in France or Spain or zip codes in the United States. This provides thousands of cases that vary in more unusual combinations than if we study nations. We still often start with all cities or zip codes in a single nation and then analyze how the patterns that vary within a nation shift when we add other countries. The examples above about the limits of bohemia and Tocqueville illustrate the beginnings of this strategy.

How do Asian scenes differ from one another and from Western scenes? We answer where possible by transcending specific names like Asia or Tokyo, and instead introduce more general dimensions that may be shared more universally, such as stronger families, transgression, self-expression. These in turn we can use to reinterpret the two main propositions above about Tocquevillian democracy leading to legitimacy, and bohemianism driving economic development. Here are components that illustrate this analytical move toward more general concepts that travel further.

SCENES CAN JOIN ART, POLITICS, AND URBAN DEVELOPMENT

Beyond the seven defining characteristics, scenes have emotional power and holism that link to distinct lifestyles. Scenes articulate how these are not totally unique to the individual; many people hold partially overlapping components. Scenes identify the shared building blocks for more unique combinations. But they help codify internal logics and dramas that unfold, for instance, around how to express original feelings rather than pale imitations, stay true to rather than do violence to a tradition, shine glamorously rather than fade into anonymity, project warmth and intimacy rather than distance and aloofness, maintain an authentic and real life rather than a phony existence. We have articulated this internal environment of life in scenes in terms of three broad dimensions that define the qualitative experience of a scene: theatricality, authenticity, and legitimacy (Silver, Clark, & Graziul, 2011). Extending these three dimensions, we further distinguish 15 types of scenes activities which link to the rising "issue specificity" of people's more complex and differentiated social lives and value configurations (Fig. 2).

A Grammar of Scenes: 15 Dimensions

First, the dimension of legitimacy is related to people's decisions about a worthwhile way of life. It is a judgment about what is right and wrong, how one ought to live, structuring the legitimacy of social consumption, shaping the beliefs and intentions of their members. The dimension of

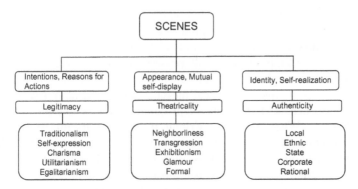

Fig. 2. A Grammar of Scenes: 15 Dimensions.

legitimacy can be divided into five subdimensions: traditional, utilitarian, egalitarian, self-expressive, and charismatic legitimacy.

While many combinations are logically possible, we introduce here just two that illustrate how the 15 dimensions can be combined in distinct ways that link to Asian and Western key differences, and the core dynamics of the two theories about citizen participation and economic development.

Weber used just three dimensions to capture legitimacy, but we add egalitarianism and self-expression. The rise of egalitarian individualism, joined with self-expression and the transgression of bohemia, has spread powerfully from artists to their fans. Fans choose their own scenes. This democratization of cultural participation is a key development informing many changes globally. It contrasts East and West, old and young, traditional and socially liberal. It makes things cool to some, repulsive to others. Whether the analyst personally loves or hates something may not change the world, but analyzing why others embrace different aesthetics is essential to interpret ongoing changes globally. This is all the more the case as the citizens of countries like India and China rise further from poverty and make more complex decisions.

Self-Expressive Legitimacy
Self-expression grounds the legitimacy of a scene in its capacity to actualize an individual personality. The good person is the person who brings her own unique take, her own personal style, her own way of seeing, to each and every one of her actions. This is self-expression as an ethical task, a demand to improvise a response to situations in unscripted and surprising ways. Themes of self-expression run through Herder, Emerson, Thoreau,

and the American Pragmatists. Here is Emerson: "Insist on yourself; never imitate. Your own gift you can present every moment with the cumulative force of a whole life's cultivation; but of the adopted talent of another you have only an extemporaneous half possession." Lady Gaga's theme song "Born This Way" updates Emerson: she told *Vogue*, "I wrote it in ten f.. minutes and it is a completely magical message song. And after I wrote it, the gates just opened, and the songs kept coming. It was like an immaculate conception ... When I started writing it, [it] was meant to be a song about revolution and freedom and lack of prejudice." From *Gagapedia*: http://ladygaga.wikia.com/wiki/Born_This_Way_(song). The global rap blockbuster, "Gangnam Style" by Psy, is a most nontraditional take on his neighborhood, mapped here with scenes indicators for Seoul.

The legitimacy of self-expression continues to be affirmed in improve comedy theaters, rap cyphers, and Karaoke clubs, in the stress on interior and product "design," or in the demand that each person construct a unique music playlist. Daniel Bell suggested that this sort of outlook has come to dominate the contemporary art world from conductors to poets, extending out from there to the general populace. Robert Bellah's (Bellah, Madsen, Sullivan, Swidler, & Tipton, 1996) famous case study in *Habits of the Heart* of a woman named Sheila showed its religious potential – when asked if she believed in God, she replied, yes, I subscribe to Sheilaism.

Transgressive Theatricality
Transgression breaks conventional styles of appearance, shattering normal expectations for proper comportment, dress, and manners, outraging mainstream sensibilities. Much of what counts as transgressive will be determined by what counts as conventional or mainstream. The key is to have recognized the theater of social life and to be ready to violate its scripts. Urban ethnographer Richard Lloyd's *Neo-Bohemia*, on Chicago's arts neighborhood Wicker Park, reveals how crucial this type of theatricality is to sustaining a distinctively powerful yet fragile type of urban ambiance, which he calls "grit as glamour."

> [For Wicker Park's neo-bohemians,] ... [n]avigating the gritty streets involved adopting an "outlaw aesthetic," expressed through both dress and demeanor, that was similar to the persona that Norman Mailer attributed to the "existential hipster" during the 1950s. Such personal styles were intended to mark them as different from mainstream society and to help them blend into the local scene as they experienced it ... To be on "the edge" with all the valences that attach to this term is crucial to neo-bohemian identification. As one West Side gallery owner put it, echoing a familiar bon mot, "If you're not living on the edge, you're taking up too much space."

Amenity indicators of transgression celebrate styles of appearance that break from conventions, like tattoo parlors, strip clubs, body piercing studios, adult entertainment stores, and some contemporary art galleries. Amenities that instead convey the importance of deference and conformity would instead indicate scenes opposed to transgression, from the black business suit to the alb, cincture, and chasuble – professional associations, churches, schools, legal offices, investment firms, and the like.

These brief examples illustrate how forceful legitimation of egalitarianism can lead the citizen to think, for herself, and how some can resonate to diverse scenes (even a mini-scene on her smartphone). These quick examples show how past theories about citizen participation and economic development take on more power when explicitly joined with arts and culture that elaborate and magnify their messages and meanings. Clearly, these self-expressive and transgressive views shock many older and more traditional Americans, Asians, Southern Europeans, and Arabs to the core. Some 9/11 terrorists claimed that such Western self-indulgence drove them to support the Taliban and Al-Qaeda. Russia banned Lady Gaga. When we created indexes for all U.S. local areas of Bobo, Heartland/Bushie (country/tradition), and Blueblood scenes, we found these helped explain party voting, above and beyond the normal factors like race, education, and income. The three-mile downtown area of Chicago, relative to its suburbs, is the fastest growing of any in the entire United States in 25–34 year olds. This area hosts huge concerts and has spawned related entertainment activities that drive Chicago's new economy. Yet other Chicago neighborhoods host staunch conservative scenes, including many immigrants from foreign countries. Neighborhood activists, priests, and bartenders can resist new migrants and their upstart lifestyles. Scenes are more than aesthetic: they can mobilize political conflicts, and encourage or rechannel migration and job growth. Scenes analyses can serve as powerful tools of theory and policy, illustrated in the following chapters.

REPORTS ON SCENES

Seven monographs have been completed on scenes to date, most available from Dropbox. These should open in your browser when you click the address, or paste it into your browser. Or you can choose "Download" in top right of screen and save the file to your hard drive.

U.S./Canada Scenes Book

Silver, D. A., & Clark, T. N. (in process). *Scenes*. Chicago, IL: University of Chicago Press (In production, publication expected in 2014). https://www.dropbox.com/sh/22oa1c97rnphswd/aJBk_iX1n7

Seoul/Tokyo/Chicago

Jang, W., Clark, T., & Byun, M. (2011). *Scenes dynamics in global cities: Seoul, Tokyo, and Chicago* (196 p.). Seoul: Seoul Development Institute (English text quite different from "Seoul Scenes" which is only on Seoul). https://dl.dropbox.com/u/5559963/Seoul%20Dev%20Inst.%20July%202012. 2011-PR-60.pdf

Seoul

Byun, M., Jang, W., Clark, T., & Lee, J. Y. (2011). *"Seoul scenes" and its use for space characterization* (198 p.). Seoul: Seoul Development Institute (Korean language).

Anderson, C. (December 2010). *Urban scenes and urban development in Seoul: Three cases viewed from a scene perspective*. Submitted to the School of Social Sciences of the University of Incheon, South Korea as Part of the Requirements for the Degree of Doctor of Philosophy in Public Administration (in English). https://dl.dropboxusercontent.com/u/5559963/ChadAndersonPhD.Seoul.Korea.2011.Final%20Print.docx.zip

Spain

Step by step explanations of scenes construction and results of the Spanish project on scenes website in English and Spanish:

http://proyectoscspl.nubeando.com/en

Navarro, C. J. (Ed.). (2012). *Las dimensiones culturales de la ciudad* (206 p.). Madrid: Los libros de la catarata.

https://dl.dropbox.com/u/5559963/Navarro.Spanish%20Scenes%20Bk.17243_Las_dimensiones_%283%29.pdf

Paris

Sawyer, S. (Ed.). (2011). *Une cartographie culturelle de Paris-Métropole* (149 p.). Paris: Rapport a la Mairie de Paris.

http://dl.dropbox.com/u/5559963/Paris.May%2019.2011.Rapport%20Final% 20CARTOGRAPHIE%20CULTURELLE%20FINALE%202011.pdf.zip

Video on Paris Scenes, 25 min:

http://joelukawski.wordpress.com/2010/12/17/paris-underground-exploring-urban-scenes/

China

Book:
Wu, D. (2013). *The research on urban residential choice and housing price's spatial difference in China: Based on the theory of scenes.* Beijing: Economy & Management Publishing House. 07. ISBN: 7509625149 (in Chinese with English abstract).

Wu, D., Mao, J., Clark, T. N. (2011). The influence of regional culture and value in sustainable development of Chinese urban residential choice. In *2011 International Conference on Management and Sustainable Development.* 10.1109/APPEEC. 5749091 (EI Index) (English paper summarizing above book). https://dl.dropboxusercontent.com/u/5559963/DiWu%20et%20al. %20THE%20RESEARCH%20OF%20URBAN%20RESIDENTIAL %20SPACE%20IN%20CHINA%20BASED%20ON%20THEORY%20 OF%20SCENES.pdf

REFERENCES

Bellah, R. N., Madsen, R., Sullivan W. M., Swidler, A., & Tipton, S. M. (1996). *Habits of the heart.* Berkeley, CA: University of California Press.
Clark, T. N., & Hoffmann-Martinot, V. (Eds.). (1998). *The new political culture.* Boulder, CO: Westview Press.
Eisenstadt, S. N. (1995). *Japanese civilization.* Chicago, IL: University of Chicago Press.

Fukuyama, F. (1995). *Trust: Human nature and the reconstitution of social order.* New York, NY: Simon and Schuster.

Inoguchi, T., & Blondel, J. (2002). Political cultures do matter: Citizens and politics in Western Europe and East and Southeast Asia. *Japanese Journal of Political Science, 3*(2), 151–171.

Kim, S. (2008). *Voluntary associations, social inequality and participatory democracy from a comparative perspective.* Doctoral dissertation, Department of Sociology, University of Chicago. Available from ProQuest Dissertations and Theses (3300436).

Kobayashi, Y. (2011). *Malfunctioning democracy in Japan: Quantitative analysis in a civil society.* Lanham, MD: Lexington Books.

Lipset, S. M. (1997). *American exceptionalism: A double edged sword.* New York, NY: W. W. Norton & Company.

Moreno, A. (2001). Democracy and mass belief systems in Latin America. In R. Camp (Ed.), *Citizen views of democracy in Latin America* (pp. 27–50). Pittsburgh, PA: University of Pittsburgh Press.

Silver, D., Clark, T., & Graziul, C. (2011). *Handbook of creative cities.* Cheltenham: Edward Elgar.

Sudarsky, J. (2002). Participación, racionalidad colectiva y representación de Bogotá (2001–2003) desde la perspectiva de la acumulación de capital social. Hacia la formación de capital social en Bogotá. Bogotá: sistema político y cultura democrática; Bogotá: Alcaldía Mayor de Bogotá, Departamento Administrativo de Acción Comunal Distrital, Universidad Javeriana.

Vetter, A. (2007). *Local politics a resource for democracy in Western Europe: Local autonomy, local integrative capacity, and citizens' attitudes toward politics.* Lanham, MD: Lexington Books.

SECTION I
TOCQUEVILLE IN CONTEXT: GLOBAL STUDIES IN CIVIC PARTICIPATION

INTRODUCTION TO SECTION I

Where, why, and when does citizen participation have the legitimating impact that Tocqueville posited? The introduction stressed that the Tocqueville/Putnam theory seems more affected by context than has been previously recognized. The next chapters explore how contexts shift participation effects. Kim leads off with an examination of the United States and South Korea, comparing effects of voluntary associational participation in each society. His dramatic findings are that citizens participating more report more civic trust in the United States, but not in Korea (using national samples of citizens surveyed in each country). But why? Americans, he suggests, join associations in a more open manner, based on their beliefs and/or hobbies and are therefore more often exposed to people different from themselves. By contrast in Korea, associational participation is more often restricted to family ties, alumni groups, hometown, and the like. In the Korean context, participation can have no impact on trust or lead in the opposite direction to the Tocqueville/Putnam model, producing individuals who are more segmented in their social relationships and less civic minded. Extending this work, Kim has elsewhere established similar inconsistencies with Tocqueville across some 38 countries.

Jang, Clark, and Byun expand on Kim's results by exploring how voluntary participation differs in the contexts of Seoul, Tokyo, and Chicago. In the West, strongly Bohemian scenes often correlate with voting for socially tolerant issues and new social movements. But in Asian contexts, family and communitarian influences often suppress the relationships of education, tolerance, and individualism with new social movements. Fundamental in Asia are traditional family relationships, which can transform how individuals volunteer or participate in civic groups. This is ignored in many Western models, which assume a stronger individualism. However, younger Asians may still support socially liberal causes in a less overt manner – in voting or through nontraditional (and less visible) forms of activism, like blogging and social media.

Most citizen participation research has not been issue specific; one measure summing all types of participation is common. Showing how issues are critical, Joseph Yi identifies dramatic differences in types of participation by adding the symbols and culture surrounding distinct contexts. He contrasts voluntary organizations in the United States and South Korea in terms of encouraging collaboration and social trust. But by digging deeper to probe some revealing individual organizations, he shows that both nations vary internally. Somewhat counterintuitively, he finds that more authoritarian, rule-following organizations can actually have greater success in fostering social trust and collaboration across lines of diversity, especially strong ethnic and racial backgrounds. Such organizations are most effective when they avoid broader cultural rifts – for instance, "outsider" organizations that have little historical baggage linking them to cultural rifts of income or race (his key examples for the United States are martial arts clubs). The strong leadership of certain Asian organizations continues in their affiliates abroad, like evangelical churches and martial arts clubs, which has helped them achieve success and expand substantially in recent decades, especially among lower status persons in the United States, Latin America, and Africa. The take away is that voluntary participation does not have a uniform or universal effect: local history, culture, the nature of social relationships, and even the structure of individual organization types yield diverse results, even within the same nations and neighborhoods. These sensitive observations come from Yi's two monographs building on years of ethnographic fieldwork as well as national surveys of citizens.

DellaPosta and Clark show how and where civic groups can make a difference by contrasting types of elections. They start with the classic hierarchy of the French state, aligned with left political parties and unions. Its classic enemy was the Roman Catholic Church and conservative political parties, supported by higher status groups. These state/class/work cleavages have long been classic in French voting. What is missing: civic groups, which Tocqueville emphasized, outside France. But patterns have changed with the rise of the European Union (EU), which has consciously sought to change traditional social cleavages. There are many new social movements and lifestyle parties in EU elections, and they find more support among French voters in the same French localities than these splinter parties win in French domestic elections. The main new result in the chapter is that having more local civic groups in a commune does raise turnout for EU elections, while these civic groups are insignificant for French domestic elections. So the Tocquevillian logic may emerge in less hierarchical EU elections, even in a general national context of strong hierarchy that is more like the Asian countries than the Northern European Protestant countries. These broader EU social issues even penetrate into France.

The results parallel those of Kim and Yi in their contrasts of the United States and Korea: all three studies suggest that more general hierarchy suppresses the impact of civic groups. Still, this finding for France is based on more aggregate data than was available for Korea, and demands elaboration.

VOLUNTARY ASSOCIATIONS, SOCIAL INEQUALITY, AND PARTICIPATORY DEMOCRACY IN THE UNITED STATES AND KOREA

Seokho Kim

ABSTRACT

Analyzing the 2004 U.S. General Social Survey and Korean General Social Survey, this chapter attempts to show that even similar climates of associationalism in two countries can lead to differential consequences for participatory democracy, depending on the associations' capacities to foster civic resources. This chapter first examines whether the politically desirable traits of civic virtue and social trust essential to political participation can be developed by associational membership in the United States and Korea. Second, it investigates whether associational membership strengthens, weakens, or leaves unchanged the effects of socioeconomic resources measured by educational attainment and family income on political participation especially among association members in these two countries. The results indicate that voluntary associations in the United States, compared to those in Korea, do a better job of playing the role of civic educator and even of political equalizer.

Can Tocqueville Karaoke? Global Contrasts of Citizen Participation, the Arts and Development
Research in Urban Policy, Volume 11, 37–66
ISSN: 1479-3520/doi:10.1108/S1479-352020140000011016

First, associational membership significantly and positively affects civic virtue and social trust in the United States. Second, associational membership does not affect civic virtue and social trust in Korea. Third, the effects of educational attainment and family income on political participation among members are weak in the United States. Fourth, the effects of educational attainment and family income on political participation among members are strong in Korea. Therefore, this chapter concludes that voluntary associations do not contribute to participatory equality in Korea despite its vibrant group-centered culture, whereas their American counterparts are relatively effective in bringing about the expected outcome.

Keywords: Political participation; voluntary association; social inequality; political disparity; civic virtue; participatory democracy

INTRODUCTION

Voluntary associations improve the quality of representation by bringing those with insufficient resources who are often locked out of politics into political participation. Given that the advantaged with higher education, more income, and higher social standings participate more in politics than the disadvantaged with less education or income, and lower social standing (Verba, Schlozman, & Brady, 1995; Wolfinger & Rosenstone, 1980), voluntary associations are expected to provide their members with psychological resources such as civic virtue and generalized trust, and thus help them overcome a barrier to collective action due to insufficient socioeconomic resources. In short, voluntary associations promise the means for voice for those disfavored by existing distributions of power and money. Accordingly, membership in voluntary associations can reduce the impacts of socioeconomic resources on political participation, thereby leading to greater participatory equality. However, little quantitative empirical evidence exists to support the idea that voluntary associations improve participatory democracy.

This chapter examines the cases found in the United States and Korea. Comparing these two countries is certainly meaningful because of their similarities and differences in associational and political culture. On the one hand, the two countries resemble one another in that they have a tradition of associationalism aimed at solving community problems, and in which joining and forming groups are essential ways of socializing encounters (Ch'oe, 1994; Schlesinger, 1944).[1] On the other hand, they are different in that participatory political culture is incipient and currently expanding in Korea. Furthermore, there still remains a hierarchical Confucian tradition and the legacy of an authoritarian regime (Hahm, 2004; Kim, 2004; Shin, Park, Hwang, Lee, & Jang, 2003; Steinberg, 1997). Unlike Korean society, American society has a long history of liberal democracy and a healthy heritage of associationalism as a vital political tool for disadvantaged groups such as women and ethnic minorities (Burns, Schlozman, & Verba, 2001, pp. 219–238; Polletta, 2002). These similarities and differences make a comparative study of the link between voluntary associations and participatory equality in each country particularly appropriate. At a glance, a common facet of active roles that voluntary associations play in everyday life lets us expect corresponding foundations of participatory equality in two countries. In reality, however, the contextual differences in which the associationalism of each country is embedded may force us to speculate about differential pathways.

In this chapter, I will demonstrate that voluntary associations do not contribute to participatory equality in Korea despite its vibrant group-centered culture, whereas their American counterparts are relatively effective in bringing about the expected outcome. It does not mean that voluntary associations cannot facilitate political participation in Korea. Many studies confirm that members in voluntary associations exhibit more political activity than do nonmembers in Korea (Kim, 1980; Lee, 2006; McDonough, Shin, & Moisés, 1998; Park & Shin, 2005). Instead, it does indicate that voluntary associations may not function as a political equalizer because certain critical factors, "civic resources" or "politically desirable traits," especially civic virtue and social trust or what Tocqueville calls "habits of the heart" cannot be cultivated through associational activities.[2] The underlying assumption here is that similar associational atmospheres can lead to radically varying consequences for participatory democracy depending on their capacity to cultivate civic resources (Krishna, 2002; Letki, 2004; Paxton, 2002; Rosenblum, 1998). If so, why do similarly vigorous associational spheres diverge in this capacity? How is the presence or absence of this capacity related to the role of voluntary associations as a political equalizer? To answer these questions, I direct my attention to the general characteristics of the interpersonal environment that members face in their associations. I treat the properties of interpersonal ties or type of people with whom individuals mainly interact as a key factor creating differential capacities to produce the civic resources and eventually making differing consequences for participatory equality between the United States and Korea.

As M. E. Warren (2001) claims, Americans actively organize and join voluntary associations on behalf of their beliefs, concerns, activities, and hobbies. They come into direct contact with people unlike themselves, and train civic competence for political deliberation in democracy. The civically oriented attitudes engendered by diverse social contacts in turn motivate members to take political action (Dagger, 1997). This may lead to an increase in the political activity of individuals regardless of their social and economic positions, and thus, to some extent, to an equalization of political influence. In short, heterogeneous social contexts likely enhance the level of democratic dispositions and political involvement, thereby reducing the political disparity caused by the differences in socioeconomic resources. Compared to those in the United States, interpersonal ties formed through associational membership in Korea are more likely to be homogeneous, dense, and like-minded. It is because most voluntary associations are built around such primordial affinities as kinship, place of birth, and old boys networks (Chang, 1991; McDonough et al., 1998). In such circumstances, the association members will hardly be equipped with civic resources (Park & Shin, 2005). As a result, they are likely to become isolated from civic affairs or exclusive of others. Thus, their political participation, at best, is directed only toward their particular interests, or is mobilized by political recruiters. In the absence of civic resources, voluntary associations exacerbate rather than mitigate political disparity between the privileged and the disadvantaged. Basically, I believe that the increased political activity via associational membership may actually do more harm than good for democracy, if not elicited by civic resources.

Using General Social Survey (GSS) datasets for both countries, this chapter attempts to shed light on varying consequences of voluntary associations for participatory democracy in socially, politically, and culturally different contexts from a comparative perspective. To this end, this chapter first examines whether the politically desirable traits of civic virtue and social trust essential to political participation can be developed by associational membership in the United States and Korea. Second, it investigates whether associational membership strengthens, weakens, or leaves unchanged the effects of socioeconomic resources measured by educational attainment and family income on political participation especially among association members in these two countries.

CHARACTERISTICS OF SOCIAL NETWORKS IN THE CREATION OF CIVIC VIRTUE AND TRUST

Voluntary associations develop civic virtue and social trust by providing spaces in which individuals can meet people of diverse backgrounds and values, thereby teaching them how to act as democratic citizens (Kornhauser, 1959; Simmel & Wolff, 1950). Tocqueville (2004 [1845]) is often cited for first noting this virtuous relationship. In order to explain how equality and freedom shaped political and civil affairs, in *Democracy in America* (2004 [1845]), he paid attention to secondary associations that stand between the powers of the state and the immediate associations of friends and family. He linked quality of representative democracy to civic habits developed within the associational terrain. Tocqueville claimed that voluntary associations educated individuals about their dependence upon others by drawing them out of primary relations. Voluntary associations stimulate a civic consciousness and displace narrow self-interest with trust of others, a "self-interest rightly understood." Accordingly, for Tocqueville, a healthy democracy results from the cultivation of civic virtues and social trust via associational ties and experiences.

Embracing Tocquevillian tradition, Putnam (2000) argues that voluntary associations provide the most suitable environment for accumulating favorable experiences with others. Intense interaction and repeated cooperative encounter within associations are touted as a necessary condition for those traits to emerge. Consequently, civic virtue and social trust enable individuals to overcome problems of collective action, which in turn helps them to organize politically, pressure governments, and get the things done that "make democracies work" (Putnam, 1993, 2000, pp. 338–339). Putnam (2000) claims that voluntary associations are always effective in solving the collective action problem by playing a role as a "seedbed of civic virtue" or "school for democracy" (Putnam, 2000, pp. 19, 152–154). Participation even in small and informal groups such as card-playing clubs or book-reading groups improves the probability that civic virtue and social trust can thrive (Fleischacker, 1998). Intense interaction and repeated cooperative experience within associations are touted as a necessary condition for those traits to emerge.

However, associational membership is not necessarily followed by the development of such civic resources (Gambetta, 1993; Jackman & Miller, 1998; Newton, 2001; Yamagishi & Yamagishi, 1994). Based on innumerable empirical studies, many scholars criticize Putnam by arguing that dense networks of horizontal relationships within associations do not necessarily cultivate civic virtue and social trust if membership is based on informal and particularistic criteria. The frequent contacts with socially or economically homogeneous and politically like-minded members tend to not only breed private civility and trust among those inside the networks, but also generate antagonistic attitudes and distrust toward those outside the networks (Berman, 1997; Uslaner & Conley, 2003). Coleman (1988) argues that intensely connected networks are likely to foster norms of reciprocity and trustworthiness, but those psychological benefits are likely to be consumed only internally. At worst, they may reinforce hostility and prejudices against others who do not belong to the immediate circle of known people, leading insiders to attempt to institutionalize their exclusive interests (Tilly, 1997). In some cases, therefore, voluntary associations are detrimental to the development of civic virtue and social trust and could be sources of undemocratic dispositions and particularized trust.

In addition, Putnam is faulted for his ambiguous stance about how private civility and in-group trust can be generalized to the larger society (Brown & Uslaner, 2002; Eisenstadt, 2000; Freitag, 2003; Stolle, 1998; Stolle & Rochon, 1998). He tends to support the effectiveness of voluntary associations without specifying the grounds on which private civility and interpersonal trust can be extended to civic virtue and social trust, respectively. Indeed, he seems to overstate the positive aspect of associational membership, neglecting the possibility that intense interaction can cause either generalized or particularized attitudes depending on its interpersonal environment (Levi, 1996). Therefore, contrary to Putnam's assertion, intensely connected social groups whose members are unreasonably and intolerantly devoted to their immediate relationships are less likely to produce civic resources. In such cases, civic attitudes, norms of mutual benefits, and interpersonal trust beyond the realm of the group can scarcely grow (McPherson, Smith-Lovin, & Cook, 2001; Walzer, 2002, p. 37). While the criticism seems to be reasonable, however, it should be also noted that Putnam at least alludes to the conditions under which associations can be facilitative of civic resources. He maintains that civic virtue and social trust could be dominant aspects of association culture if two properties of social networks, density and diversity, are aligned together.[3] By bringing together diverse goals and members, associational activities inculcate skills of cooperation and a sense of shared responsibility for collective endeavors, and build the cross-pressures that result in attitudinal moderation and political tolerance (Putnam, 1993, pp. 89–91). According to him, chances to meet dissimilar people may be obtained from either internal or external sources of associations, that is, either by belonging to crosscutting ones or by performing joint activities with the members of other associations. The problem is that by unconditionally supporting the effectiveness of dense networks in every situation, Putnam has no rigorous viewpoint about how density of network interacts with its diversity to develop civic virtue and social trust.

Accordingly, it is important to clarify when dense networks of social interaction can be connected to the inculcation of civic attitudes in the minds of citizens. In fact, the success of density is contingent on its diversity (Burt, 2005, pp. 112–146; Fennema & Tillie, 1999; Freitag, 2003; Stolle, 1998; Stolle & Rochon, 1998; Uslaner, 2002). The intensely connected networks can be better off only when they are socioeconomically and attitudinally diverse. Members in groups operating with a homophile bias in their networks are likely to possess a shared knowledge and identity, and easily produce mutually respectful attitudes. But, in order for favorable attitudes within groups to be generalized the opportunities for interracial and cross-class contact must be guaranteed (Brown & Uslaner, 2002; Erickson & Nosanchuk, 1990; Mutz, 2002; Rahn, Brehm, & Carlson, 1999). The combination of high density with low diversity is likely to generate clannish or cliquish attitudes and even prejudices (Huckfeldt, Beck, & Levine, 1995; Levi, 1996; Uslaner & Conley, 2003). As Amy Gutmann points out, "The more ethically, economically, racially, and religiously homogeneous the membership of an association is, the less its capacity to cultivate the kind of public discourse and deliberation that is conducive to democratic citizenship" (Gutmann, 1998, p. 25). Therefore, whether private civility and in-group trust can be extended is dependent on the presence of a swirling mix of preferences, views, and social origins in the networks formed from internal and external sources of associations. In Woolcock's and Narayan's (2000) terms, outward-looking, inclusive, and bridging social capital networks spanning diverse social cleavages. In the subsequent section, I will briefly address how the inability of voluntary associations to promote civic virtue and social trust leads to the aggravation of participatory disparity between the privileged and the disadvantaged.

VARYING CONSEQUENCES OF ASSOCIATIONAL MEMBERSHIP FOR PARTICIPATORY EQUALITY IN THE UNITED STATES AND KOREA

In this chapter, the composition of associational memberships among ordinary citizens in the United States and Korea is treated as the most important indicator of the potential for cultivating civic virtue and social trust. Considering that current associational composition reflects historical, social, and political experiences in a given country (Curtis, Baer, & Grabb, 2001; North, 1981; Putnam, 1993; Riley, 2005, pp. 292−296; Wuthnow, 1991), the fact that similarly vigorous networks of voluntary associations have produced different outcomes concerning participatory equality in the United States and Korea can be best explored by examining the overall distribution of membership. Understanding such compositions may allow us not only to conjecture about widespread organizing principles, but also to infer the general pattern of networking around voluntary associations from a comparative perspective (Avritzer, 2002, pp. 69−86). Once they are confirmed, it would be possible to formulate a hypothesis about whether membership can foster civic virtue and social trust and thus restrain the widening political gap between the privileged and the disadvantaged. Therefore, in order to evaluate the role of voluntary associations in mitigating participatory inequality intrinsic in social stratification systems, it is first necessary to see what types of associations prevail in each country.

People in different countries join voluntary associations for different reasons (Anderson, Curtis, & Grabb, 2006; Schofer & Fourcade-Gourinchas, 2001). Voluntary associations also vary in their roles from country to country (Lowry, 2005; Ross, 1988; Wuthnow, 1991). Similar to the United States which is known as a "nation of joiners" (Schlesinger, 1944), Korea too is a nation where people have an unusual proclivity to organize and enter a variety of associations (Ch'oe, 1994). Thus, people in both countries deem the associational life to be a locus for socializing with others. Different are the purposes of associations and general properties of social networks created through associational activity. While most associations in the United States are formed in pursuit of a specific interest, value, religion, race, national origin, or occupation, those in Korea are built alongside primordial affinities such as personal friendships, region, school, and family relationships. Since most people are affiliated with associations with such narrow and particularistic membership bases in Korea, the social networks among members tend to be encapsulated and tightly knit. They are also likely to be composed of homogeneous people of similar backgrounds, position, personality, and way of life (Park & Shin, 2005).[4] It is probable that such interpersonal environments cannot instill civic resources or politically desirable traits. Instead, they may reinforce particularized trust and exclusive identity (Chang, 1991; Fukuyama, 1995). In fact, such associations are often blamed for the spread of a backward political culture characterized by familism, egoism, and exclusivism. In Korea, what associational activity actually encourages is the thick trust of and respect only for one's own people (Kim & Son, 1998).

Compared to Korea, social networks in voluntary associations in the United States are less restricted to particular people and values. That is to say, networks built by memberships are more bridging in the United States than in Korea. These voluntary associations not only underpin the vigorous interaction with in-group members, but also provide members with an opportunity to get acquainted with out-group members. On the one hand, religiously affiliated groups and sport clubs, known as the top two associations embedded in civic affairs, involve their members with diverse kinds of people across racial, religious, and class lines and encourage them to engage in collaborative work inside and outside their local community (Cornwell & Harrison, 2004; M. R. Warren, 2001). On the other hand, the traditionally prevalent forms of associations such as labor unions, professional groups, fraternal groups, veterans' groups, service groups, and religious denominations help their members establish trans-local social networks through locally rooted yet nationally organized chapter-based membership federation systems (Kaufman, 2002; Skocpol, 2003).[5] Thus, voluntary associations are expected to enable multilevel collaborations with diverse people and to enhance the understandings of and tolerance toward those with different socioeconomic origins. In a relative sense, they are more often conceptualized as a breeding ground for democratic norms and order in which the notions of civic virtue, generalized trust, and a sense of responsibility for the common good are nourished (Cohen & Rogers, 1995; Evans & Boyte, 1992; Kymlicka, 1998).[6] Because of these differences and similarities in associational atmospheres, the United States and Korea provide intriguing settings that enable us to compare the roles of voluntary associations in reducing or reinforcing the effects of socioeconomic resources on political participation. In Korea, considering the prevalence of homogeneous networks, exclusive attitudes, and high trust of in-group members but low trust of out-group members, the political participation facilitated by associational membership can be mostly explained as the pursuit of magnifying interest and mobilization of political activists. In general, members neither have far-flung connections outside their groups nor work together for collective goals. Consequently, they tend to be mobilized into political activity through personal ties and individual networks (Song, 2000). Otherwise, they organize themselves and compete with others for the limited resources within the community or in the nation, exclusively pursuing their own interests. Since political actions of members are mostly rooted in inward-looking efforts and political mobilization, the privileged participate more in politics than the disadvantaged. Thus, voluntary associations may aggravate participatory inequality beyond the level that the difference in socioeconomic resources would cause. On the contrary, in the United States, increased political activity by the membership can to some extent be ascribed to enhanced civic resources. Private civility toward and trust of specific others within associations are likely to be converted into a feeling of being part of a community and faith in the broader society because members are given opportunities to contact socially, economically, and attitudinally diverse people. Given these circumstances, we can formulate the hypothesis, at least among association members, that the impact of educational attainment and family income on political participation will be weak in the United States, whereas it will remain strong in Korea, meaning that political disparity between the privileged and the disadvantaged is less likely to be mitigated by a wide range of voluntary associations in Korea than the prevailing model based on practices in the United States would suggest.

Hypothesis 1: Associational membership will significantly and positively affect civic virtue and social trust in the United States.

Hypothesis 2: Associational membership will not affect civic virtue and social trust in Korea.

Hypothesis 3: The effects of educational attainment and family income on political participation among members will be weak in the United States.

Hypothesis 4: The effects of educational attainment and family income on political participation among members will be strong in Korea.

It should be noted that voluntary associations in the United States can amplify the influence of those who have resources because they are able to more effectively associate, which in turn increases their wealth and power (Skocpol, 1999). It is true that the privileged can better organize their political voices and they have more impact on public policy than the disadvantaged. Thus, the unequal political representation due to unequal distribution in socioeconomic resources is likely to be deepened by the superior organizing capacity of the privileged. Note that, however, the focus of this chapter is on political participation and participatory equality among association members. I am not saying that associational membership is equally distributed across socioeconomic lines or that political influence becomes undifferentiated by voluntary associations, but rather that greater participatory equality may prevail at least among association members because their common membership mitigates the effects of socioeconomic resources on political participation.

DATA, MEASURES, METHODS

U.S. data come from the 2004 General Social Survey (U.S. GSS) conducted by the National Opinion Research Center. The 2004 U.S. GSS consists of 2,812 respondents with an overall response rate of 70.2%. The Korean data come from the 2004 Korean General Social Survey (KGSS) conducted by the Survey Research Center at Sungkyunkwan University. The 2004 KGSS data consist of 1,312 respondents with the overall response rate of 66%. Both U.S. GSS and KGSS data include the 2004 International Social Survey Programme (ISSP) citizenship module encompassing various topics about citizens' civic attitudes and political identities as well as their social and political activities.

An index of political participation, which will serve as a dependent variable in the analysis, was constructed by adding the number of self-reported political acts in which respondents engaged at least once in the last twelve months. The 2004 ISSP includes the battery of political acts asking whether a respondent *signed a petition, boycotted products for social or political reasons, took part in a demonstration, attended a political rally, contacted officials or politicians to express one's opinion, donated money, contacted media, or were involved in an Internet political forum in the past year.*[7] Thus, it is an additive index with each counted as one act, an eight-point scale for overall political participation. This index, though not exhaustive, captures essential dimensions of political behaviors derived from private motivations to communal causes. The average number of political acts is 1.42 with 1.65 standard deviations among American respondents and 0.83 with 1.29 standard deviations among Korean respondents. In both countries, those who belong to one or more voluntary associations (members) show more than twice as much political involvement as those who do not belong to any (nonmembers).

The U.S. membership questions consist of 16 different types of voluntary groups originally developed by Sidney Verba and Norman Nie for the American political participation survey in 1967. These include (1) Fraternal

Groups; (2) Service Clubs; (3) Veterans' Clubs; (4) Political Clubs; (5) Labor Unions; (6) Sports Groups; (7) Youth Groups; (8) Social Service Groups; (9) Hobby or Garden Clubs; (10) School Fraternities or Sororities; (11) Nationality Groups; (12) Farm Organizations; (13) Literary, Art, Discussion, or Study Groups; (14) Professional or Academic Societies; (15) Church-Affiliated Groups; and (16) Another Voluntary Association. The KGSS asks whether respondents belong to eight different types of voluntary groups. These groups are (1) Civic Groups; (2) Labor Union, Business, or Professional Associations; (3) Sports, Leisure, or Cultural Groups; (4) Church-Affiliated Groups; (5) Hometown Organizations; (6) Alumni Associations; (7) Fraternity Societies; and (8) Other Groups. The difference between U.S. GSS and KGSS is that the latter offers a more simplified list of voluntary groups by combining similar types of voluntary groups into one category. For example, (5), (12), and (14) in the U.S. GSS are comparable to (2) in KGSS.

The index of civic virtue is constructed by adding the 10 items asking citizens' attitudes about civic duties, liberal virtue, and civility that encourage individual political involvement. Respondents were asked to give a score between 1 (Strongly Disagree) and 7 (Strongly Agree) for each item, so the index ranges from a minimum of 7 to a maximum of 70. The battery of civic virtue questions asks how important each of 10 items is, including *Always vote in elections, Never try to evade taxes, Always obey laws and regulations, To keep watch on the actions of government, To be active in social or political associations, To try to understand the reasoning of people with other opinions, To choose products for political, ethical or environmental reasons, even if they cost a bit more, To help people in our country who are worse off than yourself, To help people in the rest of the world who are worse off than yourself, To be willing to serve in the military at a time of need, to being a good citizen.*[8] *Social trust is measured by a four-point scale asking "How often do you think that people would try to take advantage of you if they got the chance, and how often they would try to be fair?"* The ranges of possible responses are (1) *You almost always can't be too careful in dealing with people*; (2) *You usually can't be too careful in dealing with people*; (3) *People can usually be trusted*; (4) *People can almost always be trusted.*[9]

In the analyses that follow, the measures of civic virtue and social trust are utilized as dependent as well as independent variables. Firstly, by constructing two OLS regression models of civic virtue and social trust, I investigate how they are affected by associational membership, socioeconomic resources, and other demographics. In particular, I compare how effectively voluntary associations foster civic resources in the United States and Korea. Secondly, the measures of civic resources are also considered as independent variables in the negative binomial regression models estimating political acts. In order to show how associational membership modifies the effect of socioeconomic resource on political participation, I split the samples into two groups of respondents who have at least one membership (members) and those who have none (nonmembers), and run a separate negative binomial regression for each group.

RESULTS

Population Distribution of Voluntary Associations

Both Americans and Koreans tend to belong to one or more voluntary association. In the United States, 62.3% of respondents report that they belong to at least one voluntary association while 80.8% of those surveyed do in Korea. Simply comparing the overall membership rate, the United States is less of a "nation of joiners" than Korea. Moreover, the mean number of memberships is also lower in the United States (1.6 per respondent) than in Korea (2.1 per respondent).[10]

The associational compositions in these two countries are quite different. In the United States, it comes as no surprise that church-affiliated groups (32.0%) and sports clubs (17.5%), known as the two most embedded associations in civic affairs, comprise significant portions of all American memberships (Cornwell & Harrison, 2004; Curtis et al., 2001; Schofer & Fourcade-Gourinchas, 2001). It is also worth noting that fraternity groups (6.6%), veterans' clubs (5.2%), school fraternities or sororities (3.8%), and nationality groups (2.8%), often suspected of generating particularized trust and intolerance of out-group members by asserting their superiority to other races or faith, have the lowest prevalence (Kaufman, 2002, pp. 56–84; Rosenblum, 1998, pp. 239–284, 319–348). Meanwhile, occupation-related groups and social or recreational clubs which are also touted as having high potential for developing civic virtue and social trust (M. E. Warren, 2001, pp. 152–154), exhibit only a moderate level of membership rates. In Korea, as described in some studies about Koreans' everyday encounters and conversations (Ch'oe, 1994, p. 99), the majority of associations are composed of socially and economically homogeneous people, exclusive of others, and fragmented. As anticipated, most voluntary associations are based on primordial ties requiring intense identification with one's own circles. More than half of Koreans belong to a fraternal society (56.5%) and an alumni association (54.2%) whereas only less than 10% of Koreans join groups organized by formal relations or political causes such as civic group (2.3%) and occupation-related groups (6.9%). Church-affiliated groups (25.1%) and sports and cultural groups (22.2%) show moderate membership rates in Korea. The supremacy of ascriptive, primary, and informal associations in Korea can be clearly revealed by looking at the proportion of people affiliated with hometown associations (19.7%), placed at the lowest among three primordial associations but three times as common as that of occupation-related groups. In short, togetherness based on primordial criteria is the most common form of associationalism in Korea. Those associations thrive on a sense of exclusiveness or superiority, which injures community-wide unity (Ch'oe, 1994).

In sum, the different compositions lead us to expect that voluntary associations have differential capacities for cultivating civic virtue and social trust in the United States and Korea. Since social networks established through associational activities in the United States are likely to be heterogeneous and bridging, it seems reasonable to posit that they have greater potential for developing civic resources. In contrast, since associational membership likely provides homogeneous and narrowly bounded social networks in Korea, private civility and in-group trust can hardly extend beyond the confines of immediate relations (Chang, 1991; Kim & Son, 1998). An intensely connected interpersonal environment is less likely to teach the lessons that Tocqueville and his intellectual heirs had in mind. It also runs against Putnam's assertion that civic resources are always functions of intense interaction within voluntary associations. Next, I will investigate whether or not membership can inculcate civic virtue and social trust in the United States and Korea.

The Effects of Associational Membership on Civic Virtue and Social Trust

Table 1 shows the results of the OLS regression used to estimate the effects of associational membership, socioeconomic resources, and other control variables on civic virtue and social trust in the United States and in Korea. A striking contrast is found in the effects of associational membership on two dependent variables. Holding other variables constant, membership significantly and positively affects civic virtue and social trust in the United States, whereas it is not related to the development of such politically desirable traits in Korea. The results suggest that members develop politically

Table 1. Coefficients from OLS Regression of Civic Virtue and Social Trust on Associational Membership and Socioeconomic Resources.

	Civic Virtue		Social Trust	
	The United States	Korea	The United States	Korea
Associational membership	1.26 (0.46)***	0.79 (0.66)	0.12 (0.04)***	0.09 (0.05)
Socioeconomic resources				
High school diploma	0.47 (0.71)	−0.13 (0.79)	0.19 (0.06)***	0.15 (0.06)**
Some college	2.34 (0.98)**	−0.33 (0.97)	0.25 (0.09)***	0.16 (0.08)**
College graduate or more	2.25 (0.80)***	−0.17 (0.91)	0.38 (0.07)***	0.20 (0.08)***
Second quartile	1.30 (0.67)*	−0.38 (0.77)	0.14 (0.06)**	0.07 (0.06)
Third quartile	0.52 (0.76)	−0.48 (0.83)	0.13 (0.07)**	0.17 (0.07)**
Top quartile	0.46 (0.76)	−0.49 (0.85)	0.27 (0.07)***	0.17 (0.07)**
Refused/don't know	−0.03 (0.95)	−0.12 (1.33)	0.18 (0.08)**	0.17 (0.11)
Controls				
35–54	1.93 (0.51)***	2.35 (0.69)***	0.12 (0.05)***	−0.09 (0.06)
55–64	2.32 (0.67)***	4.41 (1.05)***	0.14 (0.06)**	−0.09 (0.09)
65 or older	3.95 (0.81)***	3.10 (1.05)***	0.08 (0.07)	0.06 (0.09)
White	0.88 (0.66)	NA	0.25 (0.06)***	NA
Other races	2.49 (1.02)**	NA	0.20 (0.09)**	NA
Female	0.77 (0.43)*	0.68 (0.55)	−0.09 (0.04)**	0.01 (0.05)
Married	−1.25 (0.50)**	1.10 (0.66)*	−0.05 (0.04)	0.01 (0.05)
Working full-time	0.21 (0.54)	−0.91 (0.59)	−0.11 (0.05)**	0.02 (0.05)
Working part-time	0.35 (0.71)	0.00 (0.98)	−0.07 (0.06)	0.00 (0.08)
Protestant	1.85 (0.65)***	1.48 (0.65)**	0.04 (0.06)	−0.10 (0.05)*
Catholic	0.95 (0.71)	2.23 (0.92)**	−0.03 (0.06)	−0.06 (0.07)
Other religion	2.02 (0.84)**	0.55 (0.65)	−0.04 (0.07)	−0.11 (0.05)**
Parental status	0.62 (0.48)	−0.06 (0.63)	−0.05 (0.04)	−0.02 (0.05)
Living in South (Youngnam)	1.34 (0.45)***	−1.04 (0.57)*	−0.05 (0.04)	0.03 (0.05)
Big city	0.98 (0.57)*	0.05 (0.62)	0.06 (0.05)	0.02 (0.05)
Suburbs	1.31 (0.64)**	0.12 (0.62)	0.01 (0.06)	0.04 (0.05)
Constant	48.99 (1.22)	50.95 (1.20)	1.81 (0.11)	2.01 (0.10)
R-squared	0.076	0.059	0.118	0.043
Number of cases	1318	1186	1372	1254

Note: SEs in parentheses.
*$P < 0.1$, **$P < 0.05$, ***$P < 0.01$, two-tailed tests.

important psychological resources and learn how to work together for collective ends when they belong to associations in the United States. In Korea, members have neither greater civic virtue nor higher social trust compared to nonmembers, meaning that voluntary associations do not function as a "school for democracy." Thus, it seems to imply that, if there is any increase in political activity from associational membership in Korea, at least, it is probably not due to enhanced civic virtue or social trust.

The fact that voluntary associations have varying capacities for cultivating civic resources enables us to identify different processes of political participation between American and Korean members. Political activity among Korean members may be mostly rooted in the instrumental pursuits of immediate interest and the mobilization effort by political recruiters, whereas their American counterpart can be accounted for by all three, civic resources, mobilization, and interest pursuit. At a glance, this difference looks trivial, but its consequences for participatory inequality might be huge. Since civic virtue and social trust as well as the other two factors seem to successfully mediate the effect of membership on political participation in the United States, the effects of socioeconomic resources should be constrained. Specifically, educational attainment and family income only have a limited impact on political activity among American members. On the contrary, the participatory inequality should be unchanged or exacerbated among Korean members because most of their political activity is likely to be instrumental and mobilized in the absence of civic resources. Thus, it is expected that the impact of educational attainment and family income on political participation cannot be reduced by associational membership in Korea. Before examining the varying consequences of voluntary associations for participatory equality, it is necessary to examine whether associational membership really increases the level of political activity in either country.

Political Participation in the United States and Korea

Table 2 shows the results of the negative binomial regression used to estimate the number of political acts in which respondents participated in the past year for the United States and Korea. The equations in the first and second columns of Table 2 only estimate the effects of socioeconomic resources and other control variables on political participation in the United States and Korea. The results suggest that pathways through which people come to participate in political activity are quite similar between

Table 2. Coefficients from the Negative Binomial Regression Models of Political Acts on Socioeconomic Resources and Associational Membership.

	Model 1		Model 2	
	The United States	Korea	The United States	Korea
Socioeconomic resources				
High school diploma	0.54 (0.12)***	0.51 (0.15)***	0.40 (0.12)***	0.50 (0.16)***
Some college	0.62 (0.16)***	0.65 (0.18)***	0.44 (0.16)***	0.59 (0.18)***
College graduate or more	1.07 (0.13)***	0.87 (0.17)***	0.77 (0.13)***	0.81 (0.17)***
Second quartile	0.23 (0.10)**	0.19 (0.15)	0.14 (0.10)	0.23 (0.15)
Third quartile	0.28 (0.11)**	0.34 (0.15)**	0.13 (0.11)	0.32 (0.15)**
Top quartile	0.38 (0.11)***	0.47 (0.15)***	0.24 (0.11)**	0.46 (0.15)***
Refused/don't know	0.18 (0.14)	0.40 (0.22)*	0.19 (0.14)	0.48 (0.23)*
Controls				
35–54	0.10 (0.08)	−0.08 (0.11)	0.04 (0.08)	−0.15 (0.11)
55–64	0.26 (0.10)***	−0.53 (0.20)***	0.18 (0.09)*	−0.64 (0.21)***
65 or older	0.03 (0.12)	−1.10 (0.23)***	−0.13 (0.12)	−1.08 (0.24)***
White	0.04 (0.10)	NA	0.00 (0.10)	NA
Other races	−0.49 (0.16)***	NA	−0.60 (0.16)***	NA
Female	0.04 (0.06)	−0.17 (0.09)*	0.02 (0.06)	−0.18 (0.10)*
Married	−0.07 (0.07)	−0.02 (0.12)	−0.08 (0.07)	−0.01 (0.12)
Working full-time	−0.13 (0.08)*	0.00 (0.10)	−0.17 (0.08)**	−0.05 (0.10)
Working part-time	0.02 (0.10)	0.22 (0.16)	−0.05 (0.10)	0.18 (0.16)
Protestant	−0.08 (0.09)	0.01 (0.11)	−0.21 (0.09)**	−0.06 (0.11)
Catholic	−0.27 (0.10)***	0.10 (0.15)	−0.32 (0.10)***	0.13 (0.15)
Other religion	0.09 (0.12)	−0.08 (0.11)	−0.02 (0.11)	−0.05 (0.11)
Parental status	−0.01 (0.07)	0.04 (0.11)	−0.03 (0.07)	0.04 (0.11)
Living in South (Youngnam)	−0.24 (0.07)***	0.06 (0.10)	−0.24 (0.06)***	0.06 (0.10)
Big city	0.08 (0.08)	−0.04 (0.10)	0.05 (0.08)	−0.05 (0.11)
Suburbs	−0.01 (0.09)	−0.16 (0.11)	−0.03 (0.09)	−0.15 (0.11)
Associational membership			0.64 (0.07)***	0.56 (0.13)***
Civic virtue			0.02 (0.00)***	0.02 (0.01)***
Social trust			0.08 (0.04)*	0.07 (0.06)
Constant	−0.46 (0.19)	−0.75 (0.21)	−1.85 (0.30)	−2.18 (0.37)
Over-dispersion alpha	0.45 (0.05)	0.88 (0.10)	0.33 (0.05)	0.80 (0.10)
Number of cases	1386	1265	1327	1180
Likelihood ratio chi-square	217.43	189.76	315.94	198.62
Log likelihood	−2164.2	−1501.9	−2027.6	−1419.3

Note: SEs in parentheses.
*$P < 0.1$, **$P < 0.05$, ***$P < 0.01$, two-tailed tests.

two countries. Regarding the effects of socioeconomic resources, those with higher education and more income, on average, participate significantly more in politics, net of age, race, gender, marital status, working status, religious denomination, parental status, region of residence, and size of place. In the United States, those with a high school diploma reported 0.70 more political acts in the past year compared to those with less than a high school diploma, holding the other variables constant. Those with some college education and those who are college graduates or more report 1.05 and 1.78 more political acts, respectively. In Korea, those with a high school diploma exhibit 0.38 more political acts than those without a high school diploma. Those with some college education and those with more than a bachelor's degree report 0.55 and 0.78 more political acts, respectively, when compared to those without a high school diploma. A slight difference is found in the effect of family income between the two countries. All income groups reveal statistically more significant political activity than the lowest quartile in the United States whereas there is no statistical difference between the second and the lowest quartiles in Korea. In the United States, the numbers of political acts that those in the second, third, and top quartiles reported more political acts in the past year than those in the lowest quartile on family income are 0.32, 0.39, and 0.54, respectively. The corresponding numbers for Korean respondents are 0.14, 0.26, and 0.37.

In order to explore the potential that voluntary associations have for improving participatory equality, the variables of associational membership and civic resources, including civic virtue and social trust, are added to the equations in the third and fourth columns of Table 2. As these variables are controlled, the impact of educational attainment and family income become weaker in the United States. Although all coefficients on education remain statistically significant, the results show that their absolute values decrease remarkably. The decrease in coefficients also occurs on all the income variables. Moreover, the significances of the second and third quartiles on income evaporate after controlling associational membership and civic resources. The weakened effects of socioeconomic resources can be confirmed by looking at the changes in the expected number of political acts calculated from the third column of Table 2. For example, the expected difference in the numbers of political acts between the highest and the least educated decreased from 1.78 to 1.14 after including associational membership and civic resources. On the other hand, the results in the fourth column show that no major changes have been made after introducing those membership-related variables in Korea. The results indicate that the level of coefficients on education and income remains the same and their statistical significances are still alive. Moreover, the expected difference in the numbers of political acts between reference categories and the other categories on education and income does not significantly change even after controlling for associational membership and civic resources.

For instance, the expected difference between the most and the least educated decreased from 0.78 to 0.72, which is much smaller a change than its American counterpart. In sum, the results reveal that associational membership mitigates the influence of socioeconomic resources on political participation more effectively in the United States than in Korea. Though not perfect, the results imply that a vibrant culture of associational life in the United States may contribute to participatory equality better than in Korea.

As shown in the third and fourth columns of Table 2, associational membership itself has a strong and significant influence on political participation both in the United States and in Korea. Those with at least one membership show 0.74 more political acts than those without any membership in the United States. The corresponding number is 0.31 in Korea. Since the membership variable here is constructed to refer to "a mere membership in any voluntary groups," this result suggests that associational membership promotes more political involvement even when the primary purpose of the associations is apolitical (Erickson & Nosanchuk, 1990). Even affiliation with just one group may raise the average level of political participation. It is noteworthy that both civic virtue and social trust are significantly and positively related to political involvement in the United States and only civic virtue in Korea.

Effects of Socioeconomic Resources on Political Participation among Members and Nonmembers in the United States and Korea

It is still unclear how associational membership interacts with the effects of other variables presented in Table 3. What will the effect of socioeconomic resources on political participation look like within a sample containing only associational members? To estimate the interplay of the variables included in the first and third columns of Table 2 with associational membership, I constructed two separate models for members and nonmembers. These models will help us discern more clearly whether membership intensifies or reduces the participatory disparity that one would expect on the basis of the differences in socioeconomic resources. Since the purpose of this analysis is to examine whether the same membership can lead to varying consequences for participatory equality in the United States and Korea, I will mainly focus on the effects of educational attainment and family income on political participation among members in this section. As shown above in Table 2, general features of political participation for the United

Table 3.   Coefficients from the Negative Binomial Regression Models of Political Acts on Socioeconomic Resources by Associational Membership.

	Members		Nonmembers	
	The United States	Korea	The United States	Korea
Socioeconomic resources				
High School diploma	0.22 (0.15)	0.44 (0.16)***	0.63 (0.23)***	0.85 (0.55)
Some college	0.03 (0.19)	0.56 (0.19)***	0.96 (0.28)***	0.82 (0.63)
College graduate or more	0.55 (0.15)***	0.77 (0.18)***	1.17 (0.26)***	1.04 (0.61)*
Second quartile	−0.07 (0.12)	0.25 (0.16)	0.43 (0.19)**	0.13 (0.47)
Third quartile	−0.10 (0.13)	0.34 (0.16)**	0.57 (0.22)***	−0.04 (0.50)
Top quartile	0.10 (0.13)	0.43 (0.16)***	0.47 (0.22)**	0.82 (0.53)
Refused/don't know	0.08 (0.18)	0.18 (0.25)	0.46 (0.25)*	1.58 (0.62)**
Controls				
35–54	0.11 (0.09)	−0.09 (0.12)	0.00 (0.16)	−0.43 (0.36)
55–64	0.16 (0.11)	−0.52 (0.21)**	0.21 (0.19)	−2.06 (1.15)*
65 or older	0.09 (0.13)	−0.88 (0.25)***	−0.57 (0.26)**	−2.26 (0.87)***
White	−0.05 (0.11)	NA	0.26 (0.22)	NA
Other races	−0.51 (0.18)***	NA	−0.66 (0.35)*	NA
Female	0.07 (0.07)	−0.12 (0.10)	−0.21 (0.13)	−0.80 (0.33)**
Married	−0.07 (0.08)	−0.03 (0.13)	−0.05 (0.14)	−0.18 (0.45)
Working full-time	0.07 (0.09)	0.01 (0.11)	−0.72 (0.15)***	−0.16 (0.35)
Working part-time	0.17 (0.11)	0.28 (0.17)*	−0.44 (0.22)**	−0.45 (0.71)
Protestant	−0.16 (0.10)	−0.03 (0.12)	−0.26 (0.17)	−0.32 (0.46)
Catholic	−0.35 (0.12)***	0.09 (0.16)	−0.26 (0.19)	−0.04 (0.47)
Other religion	0.03 (0.13)	0.01 (0.12)	−0.17 (0.23)	−0.62 (0.36)*
Parental status	−0.12 (0.08)	0.04 (0.11)	0.26 (0.15)*	0.28 (0.39)
Living in South (Youngnam)	−0.23 (0.07)***	−0.01 (0.10)	−0.37 (0.14)***	0.56 (0.36)
Big city	0.06 (0.09)	0.00 (0.11)	0.13 (0.18)	−0.23 (0.35)
Suburbs	0.01 (0.10)	−0.15 (0.11)	0.05 (0.19)	0.17 (0.38)
Civic virtue	0.02 (0.00)***	0.02 (0.01)***	0.03 (0.01)***	0.03 (0.02)*
Social trust	0.05 (0.05)	0.04 (0.07)	0.15 (0.09)*	0.24 (0.22)
Constant	−0.61 (0.34)	−1.55 (0.38)	−2.95 (0.61)	−2.89 (1.25)
Over-dispersion alpha	0.27 (0.05)	0.72 (0.10)	0.36 (0.12)	0.88 (0.36)
Number of cases	841	963	486	217
Likelihood ratio Chi-square	125.37	123.71	115.69	67.04
Log likelihood	−1456.4	−1244.8	−536.4	−157

Note: SEs in parentheses.
*$P < 0.1$, **$P < 0.05$, ***$P < 0.01$, two-tailed tests.

States and Korea are quite similar with one another when the entire samples are considered. Yet, Table 3 shows that the differences between two countries in relation to the effects of socioeconomic resources on political participation are far more salient than are the similarities when the sample is divided into members and nonmembers.

The results in the first and third columns of Table 3 imply that voluntary associations play a role as equalizing forces more effectively in the United States than in Korea. Among American members, educational attainment and family income have little impact on political participation. All coefficients on education and income variables are not statistically significant except for the most educated (vs. the least educated). All else being equal, neither those with a high school diploma nor those with some college education exhibit more political activity compared to those with less than a high school diploma. Only those with a college degree or higher education are more likely to participate in politics than the least educated. Furthermore, no significant difference exists in political activity across all income levels among American members. Neither those located in the top income quartile, those in the third quartile, nor those in the second quartile show more political involvement than those at the lowest quartile. Although it was predicted by my corollary above, the minor explanatory linkage between education and political participation is especially astonishing, considering that almost all studies over the past several decades have identified formal education as the most consistent and critical determinant of political behavior in the United States. In sum, Table 3 clearly lends some credence to my hypothesis that associational membership decreases the impact of socioeconomic resources on political participation in the United States. The disparity in political influences originating from the unequal distribution of socioeconomic resources disappears once people are affiliated with voluntary associations. Although the perfect conditions for participatory equality might be impossible, voluntary associations in the United States seem to provide, to some degree, a space where individuals are able to express their political preferences regardless of their socioeconomic status.

This pattern is totally reversed for Korean members. The results in the third column of Table 3 suggest that voluntary associations exacerbate rather than mitigate participatory inequality in Korea. All coefficients on socioeconomic resources are significant at the 95% confidence level except for the second quartile on family income (vs. the lowest quartile). Holding other variables constant, all categories of educational attainment are more likely to get involved in politics than are those with "less than a high school diploma." The third and highest income quartiles show more political involvement than the lowest quartile. The results imply that those from the upper echelons of society tend to take advantage of whatever is offered to them through associational activities, thereby amassing their political influences in the policy-making process. Knowledge, political skills, time, social standing, and money help the privileged to acquire more political opportunities, which in turn enable them to use their available resources to secure political leverage in the polity. Put differently, it is uncommon for the disadvantaged to speak their political voices even though they join voluntary associations in Korea. Members with less education and income are likely to be separated from political affairs not only because they do not receive requests to participate, but also because they have neither the right channels nor any instrumental reasons to do so. The results seem to support the notion that associational membership leads to either getting involved in or to withdrawal from politics depending on the level of socioeconomic resources where associational membership is based on particularistic and exclusive criteria. Due to their inability to function as a civic educator, voluntary associations ironically seem to intensify the gap in political influence between the privileged and the disadvantaged in Korea. In Verba's terms, political voices may be at the center of a virtuous circle of capabilities for the advantaged, but a vicious circle of incapabilities for the disadvantaged.

Turning to nonmembers in both countries, the patterns of influences by socioeconomic resources are quite different from the ones found among members. The results in the second column of Table 3 show that political participation is completely contingent on socioeconomic resources for nonmembers in the United States. All else being equal, those in all higher education and higher income levels are more likely to take political action than are those with less than a high school diploma and those in the bottom quartile, respectively. The well-educated and the rich are more likely to be politically active than the less educated and poorer. The results imply that in the United States political disparity between the privileged and the disadvantaged is intensified in the absence of institutional forces, such as voluntary associations. In contrast, none of the socioeconomic variables except for the most educated are significant among nonmembers in Korea. However, it would be misleading if we take this to mean that participatory equality is conspicuous among Korean nonmembers. Rather, it seems to be more appropriate to think that socioeconomic resources cannot be converted into political action without associational ties in Korea.[11] For example, formal political channels, such as political parties, which are supposed to articulate the voices of their supporters and connect them to the policy-making process, do not function properly at all (Kim, 2003, pp. 101–103). As such, voluntary associations are the most effective channels for systematically exposing ordinary citizens to political opportunities. Consequently, nonmembers hardly get the chance to participate in politics. The relatively minor degree of political activity among Korean nonmembers can be easily revealed when compared to that of American nonmembers. As a result, the difference in political participation due to the difference in educational attainment and family income barely exists among them.

CONCLUSION

In this chapter, I have demonstrated that even similar climates of associationalism in different societies can lead to differential consequences for participatory equality, depending on the associations' capacities to cultivate civic resources among citizens. I showed that associational membership effectively, though not completely, cancels some effects of social inequality on political inequality in the United States, while it deepens them in Korea. Voluntary associations in the United States successfully inculcated civic virtue and social trust. Such politically desirable traits, in turn, reduce the degree in which education and income influence political participation. In Korea, being a member of a voluntary association neither produces civic resources nor outweighs the effects of education and income on political activity. Among association members, the more educated and the more affluent get involved in politics more. Based on these results, I concluded that voluntary associations in the United States, compared to those in Korea, do a better job of playing the role of civic educator and even of political equalizer. Political participation through membership is not structured around social divisions of income and education in the United States, whereas it is mostly shaped by them in Korea.

I attributed the divergent capacities of similarly vibrant associational cultures in developing civic resources to the characteristics of interpersonal environments that voluntary associations generally create. Despite their comparable importance in the citizens' social lives, voluntary associations in the United States and Korea take totally contradictory paths to participatory democracy because of the different properties of social networks in each country. The majority in the United States has a higher likelihood of being exposed to a far more diverse group of people, while the majority in Korea is mostly composed of people who share socially significant attributes. From the comparative perspective, I contended that heterogeneous social contexts operate as more structural opportunities for participatory democracy by making association members civically motivated to work for collective ends irrespective of their socioeconomic resources in the United States. On the other hand, homogeneous social contexts in Korea are more likely to become structural constraints for participatory democracy, because they tend to make members particularistic and less tolerant toward others with different backgrounds and values. Thus, political activity through associational membership is mainly encouraged by strategic political mobilization and the pursuit of immediate self-interest. Consequently, voluntary associations are found to exacerbate political disparities between the privileged and disadvantaged in Korea. In conclusion, the findings in this chapter confirmed my skepticism about the long-standing belief in the social sciences that voluntary associations function in all contexts as a school for democracy, a civic organizer, and an agent of participatory equality.

Although the contrast between the United States and Korea is remarkable, it would be a large jump to generalize that American associational culture is exemplary for participatory democracy in other societies, or that the Korean counterpart is inferior. Note that this chapter only reveals a relative advantage of political consequence that American associational membership has over the Korean one. Namely, it is possible that voluntary associations in Korea can emulate or overwhelm those in the United States in other aspects of the political arena. For instance, homogeneous and particularistic social networks can be effective in producing norms of reciprocity and trust between the leaders and the led, thereby making sensitive political decisions easier for the leadership. It eventually raises efficiency and lowers transaction costs in the decision-making process. Thus, the relative weakness of Korean membership in this chapter should be taken as just another side of the same coin. In a similar vein, it would also be a little unsafe to rely fully on the existence or absence of civic resources from associational experiences to explain the cross-national variations in the role of voluntary associations in improving political equality.

The limited availability of data seems problematic. First, it calls for caution in accounting for how associational membership alters the effects of socioeconomic resources on political participation. Remember that overall network homogeneity or heterogeneity among members in terms of education, income, social standing, race, and age is presumed to be the main cause of differences in the capacity to produce civic virtue and social trust and to achieve participatory equality. Unfortunately, detailed information about network properties among association members is not identified for both the American and Korean GSSs. The results could be different if the actual network measures are controlled in the equations (Gould, 1991; McAdam & Paulsen, 1993; McClurg, 2003, 2005; Sampson, McAdam, MacIndoe, & Weffer-Elizondo, 2005; Snow, Zurcher, & Ekland-Olson, 1980; Weatherford, 1982). Second, the information about association-level characteristics such as the objectives of associations, internal structure, years of establishment, size of association, existence of regular meeting, and number of lodges or branches is also absent. These structural characteristics are certainly wound together around the cultivation of civic resources and the equalization of political influences (Stolle, 2001). Third, despite the fact that political mobilization and the instrumental pursuit of political interests operate as important mechanisms for associational memberships to deepen political inequality among members in Korea, there is no way to examine whether they really cause this. Future research should sort out these potential problems with more comprehensive data. However, I do not think that the limited availability of such information harms the reliability of findings and implication in this chapter. I believe that this chapter can enrich our knowledge about the role of voluntary associations in politics and their sociological consequences in different societies.

NOTES

1. By associationalism, I mean "the propensity of individuals to form and join a wide range of organizations spontaneously" (Berman, 1997, pp. 402–403).

2. By "civic resources" and "politically desirable traits," I mean the attitudinal attributes such as civic virtue and social trust relevant to participation in civic and political affairs. On the one hand, trusting citizens will be less likely to engage in opportunistic behavior, rather, they are more likely to participate in politics to enrich their surroundings because they comply with the requirements of democratic practice based on the belief that others will also comply (Cohen & Rogers, 1995; M. E. Warren, 2001). On the other hand, virtuous citizens will be the ones who regard political participation as a necessary contribution to the good of the community (Dagger, 1997, p. 197; Kymlicka, 1998). I will use both terms interchangeably in this chapter.

3. Apparently, the aggregated social context and an individual's immediate social network are different from one another and they may have independent

effects on political desirable traits and political participation. Nevertheless, the strict distinction between two concepts is not applied in this chapter.

4. It should be noted that not all associations are homogeneous, small-sized, and tightly knit in Korea. Some voluntary associations have hundreds of local branches with thousands of members and may maintain high levels of socioeconomic diversity. Members in those associations neither have intense face-to-face interaction nor frequently meet. Nevertheless, those associations cannot make their members establish diverse social ties and learn civic virtue because they are likely to be composed of factions formed around informal and particularistic criteria. Factions in any social organizations are said to be the basic unit of social and political interaction in Korea. Actually, these factional cleavages exist in every corner of Korean society (Kim, 2003, pp. 27—28). Even formal social organizations such as political parties, firms, schools, and the military also are factionalized. Accordingly, interpersonal ties formed through such factionalized voluntary associations also are centered on primordial criteria involving blood, school, and local ties. Thus, members are likely to hold exclusive and particularistic attitudes toward others outside their factions.

5. Moreover, even newly proliferating advocacy groups, those that rely on a private foundation for funding, an expert staff of researchers and lobbyists, and direct-mail and mass media for recruitment increasingly try to combine local roots with a much broader reach and expose their members and supporters to various values and concerns (Skocpol, 2003, pp. 265—276).

6. It is true that some traditional associations such as fraternal orders, nationality groups, and fundamentalist religious groups may pursue goods defined in opposition to others and are likely to cultivate particularized trust (M. E. Warren, 2001, pp. 151—152). However, I do not scrutinize this issue because it is sufficient for the purpose here to underscore the relative superiority of American voluntary associations in providing heterogeneous social contexts and in developing civic resources over their Korean counterparts.

7. Employing an additive scale for overall political participation as a dependent variable rather than constructing eight different models for individual political acts would be more appropriate in the interest of conducting a comparative study because some concepts of the same political act vary in meaning across countries.

8. Among Korean respondents, mean and standard deviation of civic virtue index are 54.03 and 8.67, respectively. The Cronbach's Alpha for 10 items is 0.801. Among American respondents, mean and standard deviation of this index are 56.86 and 7.69, respectively. The Cronbach's Alpha for 10 items is 0.714.

9. Among Korean respondents, mean and standard deviation of social trust are 2.25 and 0.73, respectively. Among American respondents, mean and standard deviation of social trust are 2.43 and 0.72, respectively.

10. The difference in overall membership rate between the two countries could be larger if we consider the tendency that number of membership answers increases with the number of voluntary group questions asked in the survey. Note that there are 16 types of voluntary membership asked in the United States, whereas only 8 are inserted in Korea.

11. This is also just a possibility. Another possibility is that the effects of socioeconomic resources on political participation disappeared because the standard errors of coefficients increased due to the small number of Korean nonmembers.

REFERENCES

Anderson, R., Curtis, J., & Grabb, E. (2006). Trends in civic activity in four democracies: The special case of women in the United States. *American Sociological Review, 71*, 376–400.

Avritzer, L. (2002). *Democracy and the public space in Latin America.* Princeton, NJ: Princeton University Press.

Berman, S. (1997). Civil society and the collapse of the Weimar Republic. *World Politics, 49*, 401–429.

Brown, M., & Uslaner, E. M. (2002). Inequality, trust, and political engagement. Presented to 2002 American Political Science Association, Boston, MA, September.

Burns, N., Schlozman, K. L., & Verba, S. (2001). *The private roots of public action: Gender, equality, and political participation.* Cambridge, MA: Harvard University Press.

Burt, R. S. (2005). *Brokerage and closure: An introduction to social capital.* New York, NY: Oxford University Press.

Chang, Y. S. (1991). The personalist ethic and the market in Korea. *Comparative Studies in Society and History, 33*, 106–129.

Ch'oe, C. (1994). *Han'gugin ŭi sahoejŏk sŏngkyŏk.* [Social Characteristics of Koreans]. Sŏul: Hyŏnŭmsa.

Cohen, J., & Rogers, J. (1995). *Associations and democracy.* London: Verso.

Coleman, J. (1988). Social capital in the creation of human capital. *American Journal of Sociology, 94*, 95–120.

Cornwell, B., & Harrison, J. A. (2004). Union members and voluntary associations: Membership overlap as a case of organizational embeddedness. *American Sociological Review, 69*, 862–881.

Curtis, J. E., Baer, D. E., & Grabb, E. G. (2001). Nations of joiners: Explaining voluntary association membership in democratic societies. *American Sociological Review, 66*, 783–805.

Dagger, R. (1997). *Civic virtues.* New York, NY: Oxford University Press.

Eisenstadt, S. N. (2000). Trust and institutional dynamics in Japan: The construction of generalized particularistic trust. *Japanese Journal of Political Science, 1*, 53–72.

Erickson, B. H., & Nosanchuk, T. A. (1990). How an apolitical association politicizes. *Canadian Review of Sociology and Anthropology, 27*, 206–219.

Evans, S. M., & Boyte, H. C. (1992). *Free spaces: The sources of democratic change in America.* Chicago, IL: University of Chicago Press.

Fennema, M., & Tillie, J. (1999). Political participation and political trust in Amsterdam: Civic communities and ethnic networks. *Journal of Ethnic and Migration Studies, 25*, 703–726.

Fleischacker, S. (1998). Insignificant communities. In A. Gutmann (Ed.), *Freedom of association* (pp. 273–313). Princeton, NJ: Princeton University Press.

Freitag, M. (2003). Social capital in (dis)similar democracies: The development of generalized trust in Japan and Switzerland. *Comparative Political Studies, 36*, 936–966.

Fukuyama, F. (1995). *Trust: The social virtues and the creation of prosperity.* New York, NY: The Free Press.

Gambetta, D. (1993). *The Sicilian mafia: The business of private protection.* Cambridge, MA: Harvard University Press.

Gould, R. V. (1991). Multiple networks and mobilization in the Paris commune, 1871. *American Sociological Review, 56*, 716–729.

Gutmann, A. (1998). *Freedom of association.* Princeton, NJ: Princeton University Press.

Hahm, C. (2004). Disputing civil society in a confucian context. *Korea Observer, 35*, 433–462.

Huckfeldt, R. E., Beck, R. D., & Levine, J. (1995). Political environments, cohesive social groups, and the communication of public opinion. *American Journal of Political Science, 39*, 1025–1054.

Jackman, R. W., & Miller, R. A. (1998). Social capital and politics. *Annual Review of Political Science, 1*, 47–73.

Kaufman, J. (2002). *For the common good? American civic life and the golden age of fraternity.* Oxford: Oxford University Press.

Kim, C. L. (1980). Political participation and mobilized voting. In C. L. Kim (Ed.), *Political participation in Korea* (pp. 119–141). Santa Barbara, CA: Clio Books.

Kim, H. R. (2004). The paradox of social governance: State, civil society, NGOs in South Korean reform politics. *Korea Observer, 35*, 417–432.

Kim, S. H. (2003). Civil society in democratizing Korea. In S. H. Kim (Ed.), *Korea's democratization* (pp. 81–106). Cambridge: Cambridge University Press.

Kim, Y. H., & Son, J. S. (1998). Trust, cooperation and social risk: A cross-cultural comparison. *Korea Journal, 38*(Spring), 131–153.

Kornhauser, W. (1959). *The politics of mass society.* New York, NY: The Free Press.

Krishna, A. (2002). Enhancing political participation in democracies: What is role of social capital? *Comparative Political Studies, 35*, 437–460.

Kymlicka, W. (1998). Ethnic associations and democratic citizenship. In A. Gutmann (Ed.), *Freedom of association* (pp. 177–213). Princeton, NJ: Princeton University Press.

Lee, J. H. (2006). Trust and civil society: Comparative study of Korea and America. *Korean Journal of Sociology, 40*(5), 61–98 (in Korean).

Letki, N. (2004). Socialization for participation? Trust, membership and democratization in East-Central Europe. *Political Research Quarterly, 57*, 665–679.

Levi, M. (1996). Social and unsocial capital: A review essay of Robert Putnam's making democracy work. *Politics & Society, 24*, 45–55.

Lowry, R. C. (2005). Explaining the variation in organized civil society across states and time. *The Journal of Politics, 67*, 574–594.

McAdam, D., & Paulsen, R. (1993). Specifying the relationship between social ties and activism. *The American Journal of Sociology, 99*, 640–667.

McClurg, S. D. (2003). Social networks and political participation: The role of social interaction in explaining political participation. *Political Research Quarterly, 56*, 448–464.

McClurg, S. D. (2005). The mobilization of core supporters: Campaigns, turnout, and electoral composition in the United States. *American Journal of Political Science, 49*, 689–703.

McDonough, P., Shin, D. C., & Moisés, J. A. (1998). Democratization and participation: Comparing Spain, Brazil, and Korea. *The Journal of Politics, 60*, 919–953.

McPherson, L., Smith-Lovin, L., & Cook, J. M. (2001). Birds of a feather: Homophily in social networks. *Annual Review of Sociology, 27*, 415–444.

Mutz, D. C. (2002). Cross-cutting social networks: Testing democratic theory in practice. *American Political Science Review, 96*, 111–126.

Newton, K. (2001). Trust, social capital, civil society, and democracy. *International Political Science Review, 22*, 201–214.

North, D. C. (1981). Structure and change in economic history. New York, NY: W. W. Norton & Company, Inc.

Park, C. M., & Shin, D. C. (2005). Social capital and democratic citizenship: The case of South Korea. *Japanese Journal of Political Science, 6,* 63–85.

Paxton, P. (2002). Social capital and democracy. *American Sociological Review, 67,* 254–277.

Polletta, F. (2002). *Freedom is an endless meeting: Democracy in American social movements.* Chicago, IL: University of Chicago Press.

Putnam, R. D. (1993). *Making democracy work: Civic traditions in modern Italy.* Princeton, NJ: Princeton University Press.

Putnam, R. D. (2000). *Bowling alone: The collapse and revival of American community.* New York, NY: Simon & Schuster.

Rahn, W. M., Brehm, J., & Carlson, N. (1999). National elections as institutions for generating social capital. In T. Skocpol & M. Fiorina (Eds.), *Civic engagement in American democracy* (pp. 111–162). Washington, DC: Brookings Institution.

Riley, D. (2005). Civic associations and authoritarian regimes in interwar Europe: Italy and Spain in comparative perspective. *American Sociological Review, 70,* 288–310.

Rosenblum, N. L. (1998). *Membership and morals: The personal uses of pluralism in America.* Princeton, NJ: Princeton University Press.

Ross, M. H. (1988). Why complexity doesn't necessarily enhance participation: Exit, voice and loyalty in pre-industrial societies. *Comparative Politics, 21,* 73–89.

Sampson, R. J., McAdam, D., MacIndoe, H., & Weffer-Elizondo, S. (2005). Civil society reconsidered: The durable nature and community structure of collective civic action. *American Journal of Sociology, 111,* 673–714.

Schlesinger, A. (1944). Biography of a nation of joiners. *American Historical Review, 50,* 1–25.

Schofer, E., & Fourcade-Gourinchas, M. (2001). The structural contexts of civic engagement: Voluntary association membership in comparative perspective. *American Sociological Review, 66,* 806–828.

Shin, D. C., Park, C. M., Hwang, A. R., Lee, H. W., & Jang, J. H. (2003). The democratization of mass political orientations in South Korea: Ascertaining the cultural dimension of democratic consolidation. *International Journal of Public Opinion Research, 15,* 265–284.

Simmel, G., & Wolff, K. (Ed.). (1950). *The sociology of Georg Simmel.* Glencoe, IL: The Free Press.

Skocpol, T. (1999). Advocates without members: The recent transformation of American civic life. In T. Skocpol & M. P. Fiorina (Eds.), *Civic engagement in American democracy* (pp. 461–509). Washinton, DC: Brookings Institute Press.

Skocpol, T. (2003). *Diminished democracy: From membership to management in American civic life.* Norman, OK: University of Oklahoma Press.

Snow, D. A., Zurcher, L. A., & Ekland-Olson, S. (1980). Social networks and social movements: A microstructural approach to differential recruitment. *American Sociological Review, 45,* 787–801.

Song, H. K. (2000). Analysis of participants in the new social movements in Korea: Mobilization and networks. *Korea Journal, 39*(Autumn), 95–130.

Steinberg, D. (1997). Civil society and human right in Korea: On contemporary and classical orthodoxy and ideology. *Korea Journal, 37,* 145–165.

Stolle, D. (1998). Bowling together, bowling alone: The development of generalized trust in voluntary associations. *Political Psychology, 19*(3), 497–525.

Stolle, D. (2001). Clubs and congregations: The benefit of joining organizations. In K. Cook & D. Stolle (Eds.), *Trust in society*. New York, NY: Russell Sage Foundation.

Stolle, D., & Rochon, T. R. (1998). Are voluntary association alike? *American Behavioral Scientist, 42*, 47−65.

Tilly, C. (1997). *Durable inequality*. Berkeley, CA: University of California Press.

Tocqueville, A. D. ((2004) [1845]). *Democracy in America*. New York, NY: Vintage Books.

Uslaner, E., & Conley, R. S. (2003). Civic engagement and particularized trust. *American Politics Research, 31*, 331−360.

Uslaner, E. M. (2002). *The Moral foundations of trust*. New York, NY: Cambridge University Press.

Verba, S., Schlozman, K. L., & Brady, H. E. (1995). *Voice and equality civic voluntarism in American politics*. Cambridge, MA: Harvard University Press.

Walzer, M. (2002). Equality and civil society. In Chambers & Kymlicka (Eds.), *Alternative conceptions of civil society* (pp. 34−49). Princeton, NJ: Princeton University Press.

Warren, M. E. (2001). *Democracy and association*. Princeton, NJ: Princeton University Press.

Warren, M. R. (2001). *Dry bones rattling: Community building to revitalize American democracy*. Princeton, NJ: Princeton University Press.

Weatherford, M. S. (1982). Interpersonal networks and political behavior. *American Journal of Political Science, 26*, 117−143.

Wolfinger, R. E., & Rosenstone, S. J. (1980). *Who votes?* New Haven, CT: Yale University Press.

Woolcock, M., & Narayan, D. (2000). Social capital: Implications for development theory, research and policy. *The World Bank Research Observer, 15*, 225−249.

Wuthnow, R. (1991). *The voluntary sector in comparative perspective*. Princeton, NJ: Princeton University Press.

Yamagishi, T., & Yamagishi, M. (1994). Trust and commitment in the United States and Japan. *Motivation and Emotion, 18*, 9−66.

CITIZEN PARTICIPATION IN SEOUL, TOKYO, AND CHICAGO

Wonho Jang, Terry Nichols Clark and Miree Byun

ABSTRACT

In this chapter, we review how scenes theory can be related to civic participation and how the relationship differs across Seoul, Tokyo, and Chicago. The discussion begins with the major Western theory of Tocqueville/Putnam that participation drives legitimacy. However, it can be briefly relativized by introducing alternative paths. These ideas link to results from Kim (Kim, S. 2008) that show different paths for legitimacy and trust according to different political development and different cultural structure in the society. As shown in Fig. 1 of Chapter 2, most of Northwest Europe and North America supports Model 1: more participation leads to more trust. Obversely, Latin Americans have such low participation and trust that even if participation "works" for a few it misses the great majority. However, the model grows more complex when we shift to Korea, Portugal, and Eastern Europe, as the participation to trust path coefficient falls to zero: no impact. For some subgroups, the coefficient even becomes negative (Model 4). How can we codify these results and link them to our cumulative theorizing? This question cannot be answered with a simplistic generalization. Instead, we

Can Tocqueville Karaoke? Global Contrasts of Citizen Participation, the Arts and Development
Research in Urban Policy, Volume 11, 67−78
ISSN: 1479-3520/doi:10.1108/S1479-352020140000011017

need to introduce a different conceptual framing to ask where and why and how much this happens.

In this chapter, we try to suggest various propositions to explain differences in civic participation in the three cities by using various concepts related to scenes.

Keywords: Participation; urban; culture; politics; Asia

COMMUNITARIAN SCENES AND CIVIC PARTICIPATION

Where families are stronger, family members are constrained more by family-related, consensual organizational participation, some of which they can pursue as a family group, such as participation in neighborhood associations, festivals, folk music, attending religious services, participation that welcomes people of all ages and educational levels. Related are local amenities like restaurants and parks, where families can eat, exercise, walk, and relax as a family unit. Active families fill this space that is filled by civic groups in a Tocquevillian civic model, or in a more individualized world by bowling or blogging alone.

By contrast, such familial participation leads to choosing activities that can be broadly shared by all family members. This discourages more specific, demanding, extreme, ideological activities that may appeal to only one family member. The sole family member may pursue such individual preferences alone, but general family strength and time engagement should suppress the volume of such activities.

Thus, Asians generally and Koreans in particular should be less active in New Social Movements (NSMs, women or gay and lesbian movements) than in other countries and the effects of socioeconomic status on NSM activism and impact should be less, especially for children living with parents. Age effects should be greater than in more socially individualistic societies, especially for groups reacting against older/established persons. However, these relations may not appear in reported participatory activities as they may be held internally as privately antiestablishment or anti-authoritarian views that may only be partially expressed in organized activities. They may surface more in blogs.

Environmental organizations that can engage entire families, like recycling or neighborhood clean ups, should be more supported in stronger family areas, but not the extreme political environmentalism more common in the 1970s and 1980s (sometimes "terrorist" − like sinking whaling boats, putting nails in trees to destroy loggers chainsaws, etc.).

The strong family proposition is testable globally as families vary in strength and breadth over generations, household sharing, mutual support, and related dimensions. However, it combines in Asia with the religious base of Buddhism/Confucianism that adds more legitimacy than in world areas like Latin America, the Middle East, and Africa where legitimacy is weaker.

Widely publicized tragedies mobilized Asian youths from the 1990s onward into new civic-organized volunteer activities: floods, tsunami, hurricanes, and the Japanese nuclear disaster. These substantially raised the levels of membership, funding and volunteering activities of social service and environmental support organizations in Taiwan, China, Korea, and Japan (Kallman, Clark, & Xia, 2011). These generally fit with a state-supported, consensual form of (more classically Asian) activism, rather than the Western establishment − challenging type of NSMs.

There are often dramatic age differences here − younger people tend to be more open to change than their parents and grandparents. Indeed, the work of Ronald Inglehart (1997) and others suggests that most citizens form their views about political participation, ideology, their identities, and related general conceptions of civic and political and social engagement as young adults, somewhere between ages 18 and 25. After this, though they may change the specifics, their fundamental political and social commitments are seldom deeply transformed. This implies that, for instance, societies that have been drastically changed by war or an economic shock may have serious value commitments that differ by age group. This seems to be partially the case in China and more explicitly the case in South Korea where the younger generation has grown up in a fairly open democratic political system and is deeply in conflict with older people in political speeches, Internet debates, and elections.

Young people in Korea are much more active in individualized or invisible associations and many people have suggested that this sort of involvement is more common because young Koreans fear sanctions from their parents and grandparents for other kinds of political participation. That is, Koreans have more often been involved in blogs, Internet sites, and other associations wherein the individual is anonymous. This has been interpreted by some to be related to a fear of reprisal, combined with an age conflict and a conflict over parental power and authority. This pattern has also been linked to the religious traditions of Buddhism and Confucianism, the latter of which encourages deference to elders and both of which seek to avoid personal confrontation. This joint tradition contrasts with the western Protestant tradition, especially Calvinism, which encourages more confrontation.

An analogous case to the story of "invisible" Korean social movements is the flash mob — a group that is organized for one particular purpose, i.e., it descends as a "flash" — which performs a brief action and disseminates rapidly afterward. These flash mobs are more often than not assembled via text message, instant message, and other means of rapid communication and generally are the purview of the young; the phenomenon is closely linked to the availability of instant information transfer technologies.

Still, this Internet-oriented, "invisible" style of public engagement has spread worldwide since 2000 and can be a very powerful force. We could interpret this as illustrating a new form of New New Social Movement (NNSM) political engagement. The difference between NSMs and NNSMs is that the NNSMs do not have any formal organization — they lack a president, a board, a budget, formalized membership card, a fundraising program, or other similar activities. Rather, they permit individuals to be much more anonymously engaged and only to the degree that they choose. Larger activities and meetings have been described in these terms as well, such as the protests against the World Trade Organization and international financial agencies that occurred in cities where these organizations meet. People travel, individually or through organizational coordination, to places like Seattle, making substantial commitments of time and money to fly, often halfway around the world, in order to participate in street-like activities. Quite unlike earlier protests over race or the environment or human rights, many of these NNSMs have been highly disorganized, dispersed, uncoordinated, and filled with dozens and dozens of individual small organizations and many individuals who do not identify with any organization. The occupy movements are often NNSMs.

Further, social movement activity has been seeking to incorporate actions and activities that engage the participants and audience in an explicitly emotional manner. For instance, they may use makeup, costuming, dancing, or other symbols designed to attract a television camera or photographer that can in turn show some drama to others who were not present at the event. The preparations for these demonstrations are a focal point for recruitment of new members, although in many cases there is no organization: it is more of a diffuse movement of people who come together as they feel justified and interested in participating. They increasingly involve music, art, and dancing in part as these seem to engage more emotion among the participants – who may lack any official structure – and communicate powerfully to others via mass media. They help create what we have analyzed as "scenes," which energize associations.

Just as the NSMs in the 1970s were seen as external, noninstitutionally engaged, improper organizations by the established political parties as well as the social scientists and journalists writing about them, so these NNSMs have not even been recognized as political movements or social movements by many of the participants, organizers, or analysts. NNSMs are seen as too individualized or fragmented to really "count," but more recent global analyses are beginning to show that they can be numerous and powerful indeed.

BOHEMIAN SCENES AND CIVIC PARTICIPATION

The bohemian concept has been widely discussed since Balzac. Near the end of the twentieth century, a new version appeared that was very tolerant on social issues yet fiscally cautious about taxes and government spending. We termed it The New Political Culture (NPC) in several books, and documented it in some 20 countries. Bobo is a similar label, short for bohemian/bourgeois. A similar pattern in Korea is the "386 generation." In much of our past research, and in other chapters of this book, we report many quantitative analyses that cover similar terrain to what we discuss here. But to assess the validity and coherence of an interpretation, it is classic to compare it to others conducted totally independently, by other persons with other methods. As social scientists specialize ever more, their colleague-specialists in the next alcove or faculty office increasingly ignore each other. At the same time, the "general public" grows ever more distant from the mainstream journals like the *American Political Science Review* or *American Sociological Review*. Journalists and communications professionals of all sorts have moved in to help fill the void left by synthesizing social science – of the Max Weber, Talcott Parsons sort. Two of the most talented contemporary generalists are the *New York Times* writers Thomas Friedman and David Brooks. We introduce them here as they illustrate how talent and social sensitivity led them to cover some of the same terrain as this chapter and to come to essentially similar conclusions on major issues. To compare results from books by social scientists and journalists is a dramatically different form of evidence than comparing two tables both using statistically sophisticated modeling. It also parallels a revival in the interest in "ethnography," at least among sociologists and anthropologists and parallels the biographies and country-specific histories that political scientists and historians have written for decades, partially with the general public in mind. How do Bobo's compare to the NPC?

Brooks (2000) charts a broader version of the cultural themes that join in the NPC in his book *Bobos in Paradise*. Bobos are an amalgam of the bourgeois wealth of the 1980s and the hip, counter-culture of the 1960s – illustrated for instance by Bill Clinton and many stereotypical Young Urban Professionals (Yuppies). Brooks shows sensitively how a new set of values and norms has emerged, especially in the United States, but with many global counterparts, especially in Western Europe: in aesthetics (peasant simple replaces aristocratic elegance in dress, home furnishings and more), social movements (gender egalitarianism replaces the elite social club), career aspirations (top college, meritocratic promotion across multiple jobs replace inheritance or long-term loyalty to one big firm). Meanwhile, in politics, traditional left and right are replaced by an NPC that includes all seven of our definitional elements in the NPC (Clark & Hoffmann-Martinot, 1998). Although there are no footnotes in the book, Brooks' (2004) next book, *On Paradise Drive* pushes this further and directly cites a wide range of studies of values and culture that he seeks to join in a manner that parallels our more scholarly efforts. The *Drive* is an auto tour across the American social landscape that locates multiple subcultures (Bohemian, traditional small town conservative, Bobo and more). It characterizes the emergence of new subcultures in the metaphors of new suburbs, brand name stores (Ben and Jerry's is an ice cream company with its own foreign policy, etc.) and types of sport-utility vehicles (SUV) driven by their proud owners. People increasingly change suburbs in order to find political, as well as social, counterparts that heighten socioeconomic fragmentation. This parallels our work in *The City as an Entertainment Machine* (Clark, 2004, 2011), which shows how NPC politics parallels issue-specific consumption patterns. For instance, individualistic lifestyle and egalitarianism in dress can lead to resistance to traditional Veblenesque conspicuous consumption in a manner that becomes an active political statement. How? To bring your own mug to McDonalds rather than despoiling the forests by using a paper cup is a daily green attack on the Establishment, more pervasive and appealing than voting for distant party candidates who are seen as unresponsive to core concerns of lifestyle-defined subcultures. The rise in importance of subcultures, for lifestyle and politics, is a direct extension of our general NPC point about issue-specific politics replacing traditional party politics and general social movements on broad issues. Issue-specificity is heightened by the Internet, blogs, NGOs, chat groups, and related developments. It also joins politics, production and consumption in what appears as "mere play" to some outsiders.

Another highly popular work is Richard Florida's *Rise of the Creative Class* and his follow up books, like *Cities and the Creative Class*. They detail the new individualism of creative people, especially young, who move from job to job easily and are attracted to new cities by lifestyle and amenities, which interpenetrates their work. The young illustrate a "big morph" away from traditional left and right, Bohemian and bourgeois, building on Brooks and the NPC. They are an explicit critique of Robert Putnam's *Bowling Alone*, which Florida suggests is a carry-over of communalism from a past that is less dynamic than the individualistic creative class. Normatively, Florida suggests that Putnam's lauded communalism is stultifying creativity and leads to conformity and rebellion.

Hypotheses emerging from above comments: in Asia, especially Korea, given the dynamics of the family, Confucianism, lack of neighborhood segregation of amenities, cohabitation of children with generations of parents and grandparents, we should find weaker correlations between the factors linking Bohemia and NSMs, but maybe not voting. This can be partially proven by the comparison of liberal voting by the Bohemian neighborhood. As shown in Fig. 1, those areas with higher Bohemian scene scores show higher proportion of voting for liberal parties.

At the individual level, the expected boho/left voting pattern usually holds as well. However, how much this varies, especially in Asia, and why demands elaboration. Too many recent studies have only been of politics, narrowly and traditionally conceived or of lifestyle or of the economy. We need to join politics and lifestyle and the economy to understand how they are interrelated and deeply changing in some locations. This can help interpret the occasional success of extreme political candidates and Internet use as these choices may be private and/or segmented across generations. They may also serve as a means to let some of the private seething dissent emerge into actions of distinctive sorts.

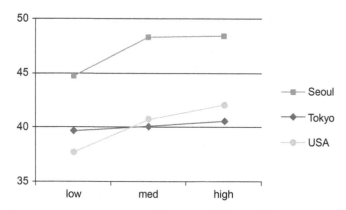

Fig. 1. Seoul and the United States Show More Bohemian Voting than Tokyo. *Note*: The horizontal axis is the bohemianism score (high, medium, low). The vertical axis is the percent left-liberal party votes. Units are the neighborhoods for Seoul and Tokyo, while the USA units are all the U.S. counties, since data was hard to access in smaller units for national elections.

ASIAN TRADITIONS AND SHARP CONTRASTS

When Terry Clark presented some observations on associations and democracy to a meeting of the Japanese Political Science Association soon after 2000, several political scientists commented, "we have no democratic tradition in Japan." They recounted a story of Japanese peasants who circulated a petition requesting a small reform, which one person would then place in the carriage of the Emperor when he passed through the village. The petitioner was assassinated, following the tradition that a courier who challenges must be dispensed with. It was considered improper for a peasant to request change from higher authorities. In many instances, the administrative staff implemented those very reforms regardless. However, it was considered the responsibility of the administrators to make this judgment, based on administrative review, not on the process of citizen consultation. Of course this is the opposite of the de Tocqueville/Calvinist story. Max Weber's books on ancient Judaism, India, and China (Weber, 1968; Weber, 1967) as contrasted with Calvinism and the Protestant ethic are classic sources codifying these background contexts. They point to the core elements of culture and subcultures.

Still even if traditions of these sorts help explain the background against which socioeconomic changes have developed around the world, we should not assume them to be unchanging. The dramatic transformations in China in the last few decades are one of the most powerful testimonies as to how rapidly change can occur. From the strong political egalitarianism model to the spread of market principles and then the global integration with other economies, China has shown the world how forcefully a nation can craft such a change. With other transformations underway around the globe, increasingly since the fall of the Berlin Wall in 1989, the concepts of capitalism and socialism as competing worldviews are no longer such helpful guides to interpret many specific policies. More specific elements, like those debated around Tocqueville or Calvinism, grow more salient.

The third-sector organizations that in many Asian contexts are linked with the national government often have service provision as a principal concern. That is, the service recipient is the main focus: the poor person, the elderly person, the child. Many organizations, such as small clinics, were thus seen as a useful alternative and a more efficient mode for providing a service than the national government. These are smaller and more nimble (and often less expensive and more efficient) agencies. In some cases, citizens even "coproduce" the service (e.g., citizen volunteers tutor at-risk children after school). Having citizens more actively engaged clearly generates a higher-quality and lower-cost service. In some cases, private groups can better handle these delicate social projects than the bigger state agencies.

Over time some of these third-sector organizations have developed linkages with other third-sector organizations internationally, or have seen other new kinds of organizations develop alongside them. This development of the third sector generally has led to a questioning of what these organizations are as a whole, and what their impact might be as a whole, and how and when they can complement one another. Some of these questions are purely technical. Similarly, there are possibly economies of scale in some areas, but the "possibility," even in more technical service areas often falls short of the technical expectations. Many small organizations, Non-Profit Organizations (NPOs) with a technical focus, were created separate from the state that would provide and sell these services. This has been studied in detail in Eastern Europe and compared internationally, after 1989, when many governments were reviewing all services and considering privatization. The Hungarian-American George Soros funded a large number of studies of this process and Soros himself wrote books (Soros, 2004) on how important the third sector was for changing the economic and political systems in authoritarian areas like Eastern

Europe and Russia. Yet, the ambivalence of results reported about the implementation of such privatization was often due to the providers working in a bureaucratic/political context where patronage or offering contracts to personal supporters undercut the idealized technical estimates (Hermann, 1999).

More generally, there has been a move away from an emphasis on the more technical or production of service for a single type of recipient. Rather, we have seen an increased emphasis on the participants themselves (the providers and recipients of services) working with and within organizations and associations. This question is one with which we are uniquely concerned – what is the impact of these associations on participating citizens? Do they trust one another more? Do they trust the state more? Does the quality of life improve when citizen participation improves? Does this vary across the United States, Europe, and Asia? What are the regional differences?

A central tenet of this NPC is the role of associations and organizations. There are two main points of particular concern for us for the NPC. First, in an NPC context, we see citizen concerns becoming less about production and more about consumption. This transformation is heightened by higher income and more education, as citizens as well as consumers want and expect more subtlety in the ways they are addressed by employers and salespeople seeking to market to them. In China, the production of large quantities of standardized products at low cost was seen as increasing the economic wellbeing of most citizens in a powerful way, for decades. As new levels of income, education, media exposure, Internet penetration and the like are reached, citizens and consumers grow more sophisticated in their demands for products and services. Income alone no longer dictates specific consumer practices ipso facto. That is, the consumer has become more critical and distinct from the producer. Suddenly, the citizen is more than his or her work: participation, lifestyle, and consumption practices take on increasing importance and merge with identity. This in turn leads to the development of what we have termed "issue specificity" (Clark & Hoffmann-Martinot, 1998). Organization is no longer based on one sole factor (like a neighborhood), but rather on multiple ones.

In conjunction with the rise of thinking on social capital worldwide, a veritable explosion of NPOs and activities began in the late 1980s and continued well into the 1990s. This was simultaneous with the spread of the NPC and a populist, egalitarian, citizen-empowered kind of political development.

The rapid expansion of the third sector joined a sense of moralism and concern for the disadvantaged to the prevalent political discourse. Additionally, governments across the world began to outsource services to the third sector (Clark, Kallman, with Lin & Wu, 2012). This was driven by concern for traditional economic issues (that had previously been the purview of technical administrators), as well as a sense that they sometimes were more agile than government agencies and nearly always cheaper. In many instances, international NPOs filled the gaps in countries where central administrations were particularly bureaucratic or otherwise dysfunctional. These organizations, often British and American-led, number in the thousands, particularly in "developing" countries. Recently, there has been a heated discourse about the role of foreign third-sector organizations working in those "developing" countries and the social and cultural impacts of such work.

Beginning in the 1960s, government financing of nonprofits in the United States increased sharply, fueled by extensive federal spending on social and health programs; government support prior to this point had been largely restricted to child welfare or high-profile institutions. This rate of funding again increased in the 1980s and went on to address other urgent public needs through NPOs, such as low-income housing and immigrant assistance (Smith, 2006, p. 221). The overall rise and diversification in government funding of the third sector spurred growth of NPOs during this time and since. The U.S. National Center for Charitable Statistics reports that the number of 501(c)(3) organizations grew from 535,888 in 1996 to 822,817 in 2004. The number of social welfare agencies has more than tripled since 1980 (p. 224). For policymakers, this was a positive phenomenon, because it brought services and decisions closer into the local communities that those organizations served – as noted by Frumkin (2005). Interestingly, this shift represents a dramatic diversion from, for example, the Japanese model, wherein nonprofits began as state partners and gradually diversified their interests.

Within little more than a decade, nonprofits became the principle vehicle for government-financed human services in the United States and perhaps unsurprisingly, the government had also become the largest financer of human service NPOs.

Ironically, these results suggest that in recent years while U.S. nonprofits have moved toward the Asian model of state-support, the Asian states have variously moved toward granting more autonomy to various forms of civic and social groups. Yet inside most every country we find substantial differences among subsectors, illustrating the issue-specificity that is a hallmark of the NPC.

REFERENCES

Brooks, D. (2000). *Bobos in paradise: The new upper class and how they got there.* New York, NY: Simon and Schuster.

Brooks, D. (2004). *On paradise drive: How we live now and always have in the future tense.* New York, NY: Simon & Schuster.

Clark, T. N. (Ed.). (2004). *The city as an entertainment machine, Research in Urban Policy,* Vol. 9, Oxford: JAI/Elsevier. Lantham, MD: Lexington Books, 2011 (Paperback).

Clark, T. N., Kallman, M., & Xia, J. (2011). *On the development of community social organizations: Experiences from China and abroad.* Beijing: Ministry of Civil Affairs. Published in Mandarin. Available from Chinese Amazon.com. English draft: https://dl.dropbox usercontent.com/u/5559963/China%20Report.Version.35.2.Feb.2011.PLUS.Appendix. doc.zip

Clark, T. N., & Kallman, M. with assistance from Lin, J., & Wu, Z. (2012). The third sector: New roles for community service organizations, non-profits, and the new political culture. Presented to Midwest Political Science Association, Annual Meeting, Chicago, April 12, 2012. Session 5–12. Section: Comparative Politics: Transitions Toward Democracy. Retrieved from http://www.mpsanet.org/Conference/ConferencePaper Archive/tabid/681/year/2012/p/12/Default.aspx?q = Special + Interest + Partisanship + The + Transformation + of + American + Political + Parties

Clark, T. N. (Ed.). (2011). *The city as an entertainment machine.* Lantham, MD: Lexington Books.

Clark, T. N., & Hoffmann-Martinot, V. (Eds.). (1998). *The new political culture.* Boulder, CO: Westview Press.

Frumkin, P. (2005). *On being nonprofit: A conceptual and policy primer.* Cambridge, MA: Harvard University Press.

Hermann, Z. (1999). *Allocation of local government functions: Criteria and conditions: Analysis and policy proposals for Hungary.* Washington, DC: The Fiscal Decentralization Initiative for Central and Eastern Europe.

Inglehart, R. (1997). *Modernization and postmodernization: Cultural, economic, and political change in 43 societies.* Princeton, NJ : Princeton University Press.

Kim, S. (2008). Voluntary associations, social inequality and participatory democracy from a comparative perspective. Doctoral dissertation, Department of Sociology, University of Chicago. Available from ProQuest Dissertations and Theses (3300436).

Smith, S. R. (2006). Government financing of nonprofit activity, In *Nonprofits & government: collaboration & conflict.* Washington, DC: The Urban Institute.

Soros, G. (2004). *The bubble of American supremacy: Correcting the misuse of American power.* New York, NY: Public Affairs.

Weber, M. (1967). Ancient Judaism. In H. H. Gerth & D. Martindale (Trans. & Ed.). New York, NY.

Weber, M. (1968). *Economy and society.* In G. Roth & C. Wittich (Eds.) (Vol. 3). New York, NY: Bedminster Press.

FROM BOWLING ALONE TO KARATE TOGETHER (USA TO ASIA): PRELIMINARY CLAIMS AND FINDINGS

Joseph E. Yi

ABSTRACT

From Egypt to South Korea, traditional institutions and sources of authority are being challenged as never before. To survive and prosper, organizations and institutions adapt to the changing values and needs of people in a modern, globalizing world. This essay discusses how some organizations adapt traditional, hierarchical authority to the challenges of a dynamic, diversifying society. It presents three claims. First, modernizing, liberalizing societies generate a tendency to separation and indifference. Second, "authoritative" organizations that stress obedience to a set of beliefs and practices partly counter these atomizing tendencies and attract many, diverse persons. Third, the formation of diverse, authoritative communities is more likely among newcomers or outsiders less attached to historic, societal divides. I illustrate this

Can Tocqueville Karaoke? Global Contrasts of Citizen Participation, the Arts and Development
Research in Urban Policy, Volume 11, 79–89
ISSN: 1479-3520/doi:10.1108/S1479-352020140000011018

with some preliminary findings and observations, mostly in USA but also in South Korea.[1]

Keywords: Authority; comparative politics; culture; inclusion; Korea

LIBERAL DEMOCRACY: DYNAMICS OF INDIFFERENCE

I begin with Alexis de Tocqueville's analysis of American liberal democracy (*Democracy in America*). In the 1830s, Tocqueville described the USA as the first significant manifestation of liberal modernity, a polity whose dominant culture and institutions are shaped by the principles of individualism, equality, voluntarism, and empiricism. "Democracy" referred not only to representative government, but also to the larger culture of individualism and equality.

In a traditional, feudal society, such as prerevolutionary France, each person has his fixed station, and is bound by relations of obligation and duty to those above and below him. "Aristocracy links everybody, from peasant to king, in one long chain" (Tocqueville, 1969, p. 508). In contrast, "democracy," or a predominantly individualist, egalitarian society, breaks the chain and frees each link.

In the absence of traditional hierarchies, free persons retreat into private, isolated circles, indifferent to the larger society. Alternately, individuals may seek affirmation in socially homogeneous groups, that is, "their fellows" (p. 435) or "those who are like themselves."[2] Americans generally prefer to associate with "people like themselves," where they can find shared "meaning and belonging" (Emerson & Smith, 2000, pp. 136–137). In the USA, people largely define likeness in racial and economic terms. Middle-class whites mostly prefer homogeneous neighborhoods, schools, congregations, and other voluntary organizations.

Progressive organizations, such as the Episcopal Church and the Girl Scouts, proclaim the ideals of social and racial diversity, but are often racially and economically homogeneous (Emerson, 2006; Weisinger & Salipante, 2005).[3] Some mainline denominations attempt to diversify local, predominantly white and older, congregations by bringing in minority-race pastors and staff; however, the members resist these top-down efforts at racial integration (Emerson, 2006, p. 61). Elite universities actively recruit students of diverse ethnic backgrounds; once on campus, students gravitate to narrower circles, such as black graduate students or Singaporean undergraduates. After graduation, people mostly sort themselves into racially and economically homogeneous neighborhoods and organizations.

DYNAMICS OF INCLUSION: AUTHORITATIVE COMMUNITIES

In a diverse society, individual choices often lead to ethnically or economically homogeneous clusters. Conversely, *less* choices, or greater obedience to particular rules, practices, and persons, can promote broad, crosscutting ties. I use the term *authoritative* to describe organizations that stress obedience to a particular set of rules and practices. Under certain conditions, authoritative organizations attract many, diverse persons. To go back to Tocqueville, a fluid, egalitarian culture fosters individual isolation or narrow, homogeneous clusters. It also stimulates individuals to join authoritative organizations that exemplify collective unity and discipline, such as the Catholic Church (Tocqueville, 1969, p. 450). More-authoritative communities offer a sense of collective unity, solidarity, and trust, or *bonding* social capital (Putnam, 2007), which is often lacking in less-authoritative communities. Authoritative organizations also develop hierarchical structures to encourage and monitor obedience among members as they become larger.

Among Protestant congregations, racial diversity is more common among evangelical and conservative churches with core, biblically based teachings than among the doctrinally loose, liberal mainline churches (Dougherty & Huyser, 2008; Putnam & Campbell, 2010; Yi, 2009, 2012).[4] Racial diversity is particularly robust among rapidly growing, "megachurches," which offer intensive outreach, small-group Bible studies, and one-to-one mentoring (Emerson, 2006, p. 58; Marti, 2009).[5]

Similarly, the U.S. Army, with its detailed rules of conduct and hierarchical, command structures, generates more positive racial interactions than do the more individualist, elite universities. Moskos and Butler (1996, p. 108) report that black students at Northwestern University were twice as likely to report worse relations (18 percent) than better relations (9 percent) since matriculation. In contrast, black soldiers in the Army were five times more likely to report better race relations (25 percent) than worse relations (5 percent).

Direct selling organizations (e.g., Amway, Mary Kay Cosmetics) promote a distinct code of professional conduct and a socially conservative lifestyle through their vertical networks of distributors (Biggart, 1989). One distributor, Ms. Susie Kim, a Korean-American immigrant in her early 50s, sold (or "distributed") Cutco knives, pots, and pans to all races and classes, including Chinese waitresses and Hispanic grocery workers. Kim said, "I am very 'hal-ba-reh' (active). Selling Cutco products give me great motivation to go out there and meet different kinds of people."

In a globalizing era, organizations representing alternative religious and ethical traditions, such as Asian-style martial arts, also recruit enthusiasts across gender, racial, and economic boundaries (Guthrie, 1995; Krucoff, 1999; Yi, 2009). Martial arts students are linked by a finely graded system of belts, from white to black to master, each with distinct status and obligations. In many cases, the hierarchical relations of the school extend beyond class hours, with students expected to bow and defer to higher-ranked practitioners even in informal meetings on the street or in restaurants. The hierarchy of belts provides an effective mechanism to incorporate diverse persons. In the Chicago Park District, martial arts classes frequently include students of various races, ages, sexes, and economic backgrounds; they are one of the few settings where women (senior belts) hold positions of authority and respect among young males.

Paradoxically, authoritative communities show the most positive *or* negative relationships with social inclusion (bridging social capital). Organizations with high levels of moral and social cohesion often resist potential changes that could threaten such cohesion. Many religiously conservative congregations are ethnically homogeneous (e.g., white, black, or Korean), and resist opening up to new groups. To the extent that communities require mutual trust and solidarity, the less welcoming it is to out-groups (Taylor, 1998).

On the other hand, some of the fastest-growing organizations combine traditional authority with diverse outreach. Highly disciplined organizations, such as religious and military, unleash human energies[6] that can be channeled to recruit and integrate diverse persons. In the early twentieth century, the Latter Day Saints (LDS) (Mormons) and the U.S. Army strictly excluded or separated the different races. However, in the latter twentieth century, the leadership of these organizations rapidly mobilized their members to the task of racial outreach as essential to their missions.

Stark and Iannaccone (1997, p. 152) argue, "Religious movements will succeed to the extent that they sustain strong internal attachments, while remaining an open social network, able to maintain and form close ties to outsiders." In authoritative organizations, obedience to a set of beliefs and practices potentially facilitate social ties among different people; but for this potential to be actualized, the beliefs and practices also need to adapt to the different needs and values of new members. In dynamic, diversifying organizations, one sees a continuous dialectic of both obedience to and contestation of authority. The communal organization both asks obedience and is open to the claims and challenges of newcomers.

Both the LDS and the U.S. Army, for example, revised some core doctrines and practices (e.g., opening upper ranks to nonwhites) to meet the claims of equal participation among blacks and other races; in the process, they solidified the allegiance of both newcomers and (most) old members. In the USA, the largest Protestant congregation is the evangelical, Lakewood Church in Houston, with 43,500 weekly attendants. Lakewood has grown fivefold in the past decade, with at least half the members visibly "people of color" (Putnam & Campbell, 2010, p. 308). It boasts small groups and activities for every demographic category, from Hindi/Urdu speakers to single parents to rock climbers. Still, the church stresses core, biblical teachings and connects small group activities with larger ones (e.g., weekly congregation-wide services). In summary, new groups do not simply conform to the existing community culture, but continually help remake and expand it, with varying degrees of resistance from and negotiation with older groups.

NEWCOMERS AND OUTSIDERS

The ability of organizations to combine obedience and contestation, and to bring different groups together, often depends on the larger, social context. Organizations that are *framed* (Goffman, 1974) as new or "outsiders" to prevailing societal cleavages are oftentimes more likely to bring together members of different groups than are more-established actors. Conversely, a new, *"frontier"* environment allows actors to leave behind old patterns and to create new ones.

Powerful, disciplined organizations, such as Tocqueville's Catholic Church, would attract more converts if they did not attract external, political animosities. In the 1830s, the Catholic Church was embroiled in the political divides between liberal-democratic reformers and the political establishments in Europe and between Anglo Protestants and Catholic immigrants in the USA. Tocqueville writes, "If Catholicism could ultimately escape from the political animosities to which it has given rise, I am almost certain that ... it would make great conquests [i.e. converts]."[7]

Analogous to Catholicism in the 1830s, religiously and socially conservative organizations today (e.g., Evangelical churches, Boy Scouts) are caught in "culture war" controversies. Since the 1960s, Americans have become sharply divided over the influence of Judeo-Christian traditions in our public laws and institutions (Hunter, 1991; Wilson, 2006). The Supreme Court banned religious prayers in public schools (e.g., *Lemon v. Kurtzman*, 1971, http://en.wikipedia.org/wiki/Lemon_v._Kurtzman), local governments (e.g., New York, Philadelphia) have expelled the Boy Scouts from public facilities for its ban on gay scout leaders, and Christian student groups are excluded from mainstream campus activities (Kim, 2006; Yi, 2009). A significant number of persons, especially college-educated, seek social and moral alternatives to traditional Christianity, and have embraced artistic and environmental groups and even various forms of Asian spirituality (Hansen, 2011; Heelas & Woodhead, 2005).

Interestingly, one disciplined, authoritative institution that largely remains aloof from culture war controversies is Asian-style martial arts. Like conservative churches, martial arts schools stress obedience to a set of beliefs and practices, which in turn facilitate social ties among different people. *Unlike* conservative churches, martial arts are typically framed as outsiders and newcomers to American society, including its post-1960 cultural divide between religious conservatives and secular-minded progressives. The Asian martial arts share some similarities with Christian religions, such as disciplined structure and conception of supernatural cosmic energy (e.g., "chi"). By not being *framed* as a religion, however, they avoid potential opposition from both conservative and progressive elites.[8] Martial arts not only bring together different races, but also attract educated progressives, including Jewish and secular intellectuals, who desire a sense of moral community but who would not enter a conservative Christian church. Large tournaments draw practitioners of all ages, races, educations, and religions.

With the partial de-legitimation of traditional Christianity, outsider traditions, from Aikido to Yoga, help rebuild a common, popular, and civic culture. We can make an analogy with Rousseau's alien legislator, whose outsiderness places him above the messy disputes internal to a society and allows a new set of rules acceptable to all (Rousseau, 1978). In sharply divided societies, actors representing new or outsider traditions offer neutral settings for different people to communicate and to forge common norms and practices.

Organizations that are part of the old establishment in one social context can become like "new/outsider" in another. A new, "frontier" environment allows individuals and groups to leave behind historic sentiments and patterns, to experiment with new combinations, and consequently to remake themselves and their surroundings (Turner, 1893/1935). In East Asia, Confucian traditions are often rejected by liberal reformers as part of the biased patriarchal past. In the USA, Confucian ethics ("traditional" Asian values) are reinterpreted by martial arts practitioners as a dynamic tradition that is open to all, including women and racial minorities.

To give another example, the LDS (Mormons) are the historic, and until recently racially exclusive, religious establishment in Salt Lake City; but they are relative newcomers in the immigrant enclaves of New York City. Until 1978, the LDS Church excluded people of African descent from the priesthood. Since then, the LDS has opened up to, and actively recruit, all races. Because of their antiblack legacy, Mormons are often viewed with greater wariness among black Americans than among nonblacks or new immigrant groups. In other words, Mormons are framed as new/outsiders among Hispanics, less so among Black Americans. Among immigrant enclaves, and among developing countries overseas, the Mormons operate in a relatively "frontier" context, less encumbered by their racist legacy.

SOUTH KOREA

The dual patterns of indifference and inclusion are visible in other diversifying democracies. France is notorious for the spatial and social isolation of Muslims of North African descent. However, Catholic schools and a direct selling organization helped one such immigrant child, Rachida Dati, rise in French mainstream society. Ms. Rachida Dati, daughter of a Moroccan father and Algerian mother, was educated in a Catholic parochial school and became Avon's top saleswoman in the Burgundy region; she later became France's first justice minister of Muslim faith (2007–2009) during the Sarkozy government.

To detail another example: South Korea (hereafter termed Korea), a historically homogeneous, closed society, has rapidly globalized and diversified. In the past decade, the number of foreigners increased nearly sevenfold from 210,000 (2000) to more than 1.4 million (2012), and more than a tenth of marriages are international (nonKorean spouse). However, as in the USA, this transformation has largely happened without substantive, public discussion on how natives and foreigners can relate to each other on regular, daily basis. Government agencies, universities, public schools, and other bureaucracies spend significant monies and efforts to provide welfare benefits, education, and other assistance to foreigners and migrants; however, these costly, "multicultural" programs engender strong resentments among natives and provide little motivation for personal interaction.

For much of the populace, relations tend to be *instrumental* and *indifferent*. Koreans invite foreigners for instrumental reasons, such as to teach English, to work in factories, or (in the case of American soldiers) to provide military security, but reserve their primary, intimate relations mostly with coethnics. This is especially the case in a country that stresses primary, affective ties more than other countries (Lew, Chang, & Kim, 2003). Koreans generally avoid living or studying with lower-income migrants, such as those in the Chinese-dominated, factory town of Ansan (south of Seoul).

Recently, leaders stress the need to connect temporary expats, longer-term immigrants, and especially "multicultural" families (i.e., nonKorean spouse, mixed-race children) with Korean natives, not just with welfare professionals. In 2013, the Korean military officially recruited young men from multicultural, mixed-race families, and changed its members' pledge of allegiance from the Korean "race" (*Min-Jok*) to the more inclusive "citizenry" (*Shi-Min*). Universities and some public schools sponsor "multicultural" or international festivals to share the national cultures of expatriates with each other and with other Koreans.

Aside from these government-funded entities, a wide variety of private organizations connect expats, immigrants, and native Koreans. Seoul houses more than 169 officially registered "Meetup.com" groups for specific activities, from books to language-exchange to volunteering. Language-exchange (or Language-Cast), especially English, is the most popular (200—300 in weekly meetings), but it tends to draw a transient, youthful crowd that participates sporadically. More durable participation is found in authoritative organizations, which — like the Korean Army — combine familial, hierarchical bonds with modern ideals of diversity.

For example, the 2,000-member New Harvest Ministry (NHM — affiliated with the 60,000-member Sarang mega-church) includes an equal mix of native Koreans, overseas Koreans (mostly Korean-Americans), and nonKoreans. One member, Raymond, Korean-born but adopted into a white-American family, was a life-science graduate student at Hanyang University. He was not fluent in Korean language and felt distant from the materialistic South Korean culture. Still, NHM provided a strong spiritual home and solid friends from around the world.

If I wasn't in church, I would have left [Korea] long time ago. They are like having a new family and it permitted me to grow a lot about and with God. I am feeling that God wants me here.

During our interview (2013), Raymond had received an ideal job offer from a fellow church member to work at a private, English kindergarten, teaching sports, cooking, and science. If the offer is actualized, Raymond may stay in Korea for the foreseeable future. From his Seoul base and with his academic degree, Raymond also plans to serve as a visiting lecturer in other countries (including North Korea) and to share the gospel.

As a relatively new ministry not dominated by native Koreans, NHM offered a welcoming, open environment for newcomers and native Koreans alike. I suggest similar dynamics among martial arts clubs: relatively new/ outsider clubs, such as Brazilian Jiu-Jitsu or Japanese Aikido, would be more open to a variety of ethnic groups than more established, domestic clubs (e.g., Hapkido, Taekwondo) dominated by native Koreans.

NOTES

1. The claims and observations are part of an ongoing research project on the dynamics of indifference and inclusion in liberal democracies, mostly in the USA but also starting in South Korea. It has produced one book (Yi, 2009) and several articles published, forthcoming, or under review (e.g., Yi, 2013a, 2013b).
2. Tocqueville (1899).
3. In the Girl Scouts (USA), interethnic ties were concentrated among the professional staff and top echelon leaders, not among the general members (Weisinger & Salipante, 2005).
4. Dougherty and Huyser (2008) find that other-race pastors are negatively associated with racial diversity in mainline churches, but show positive association in evangelical churches. "For evangelical congregations, the presence of a clergy member from a nondominant race positively relates to membership diversity as compared to mainline Protestant congregations … . Racial diversity is actually lower in mainline congregations where there is a mismatch between clergy and the majority of congregants" (p. 35).
5. The percentage of white churchgoers reporting interracial worship increased from 34 percent (year 1978) to 45.6 percent (1990−94) and 46 percent (2006), while blacks increased from 36 percent in 1978 to 46−49 percent in later periods. The percentage for whites is artificially depressed because many live in rural areas (e.g., Montana) or towns with few blacks. In large cities (population over 250,000), more than half of black (52 percent) and white churchgoers (58 percent) claim interracial worship (Yi, 2009; Yi & Graziul, 2012).
6. See Gorski's (2003) discussion of Calvinist institutions in northern Europe: "the technology of observation − self-observation, mutual-observation, hierarchical observation … made it possible to unleash the energies of the human soul" (p. xvi).

7. Tocqueville (1969, p. 450).
8. The term "frame" denotes "schemas of interpretation" or cognitive structures that shape how individuals define reality (Goffman, 1974, p. 21).

REFERENCES

Biggart, N. W. (1989). *Charismatic capitalism: Direct selling organizations in America.* Chicago, IL: University of Chicago Press.
Dougherty, K. D., & Huyser, K. R. (2008). Racially diverse congregations: Organizational identity and the accommodation of differences. *Journal for the Scientific Study of Religion, 47*(1), 23–44.
Emerson, M. (2006). *People of the dream.* Princeton, NJ: Princeton University Press.
Emerson, M. O., & Smith, C. (2000). *Divided by faith: Evangelical religion and the problem of race in America.* New York, NY: Oxford University Press.
Goffman, E. (1974). *Frame analysis: An essay on the organization of experience.* Cambridge, MA: Harvard University Press.
Gorski, P. S. (2003). *The disciplinary revolution: Calvinism, confessionalism and the growth of state power in early modern Europe.* Chicago, IL: University of Chicago Press.
Guthrie, S. R. (1995). Liberating the Amazon: Feminism and the martial arts. *Women & Therapy, 16*(2–3), 107–119.
Hansen, S. B. (2011). *Religion and reaction: The secular political challenge to the religious right.* Lanham, MD: Rowman & Littlefield.
Heelas, P., & Woodhead, L. (2005). *The spiritual revolution. Why religion is giving way to spirituality.* Oxford: Blackwell Publishing.
Hunter, J. D. (1991). *Culture wars: The struggle to define America.* New York, NY: Basic Books.
Kim, R. Y. (2006). *God's new whiz kids?: Korean American evangelicals on campus.* New York, NY: New York University Press.
Krucoff, C. (1999, November 15). Marshaling the forces: Martial arts enjoys a healthy boom – Thanks to the masses who want to learn self-defense, get in shape and spend time with the family. *Los Angeles Times,* 1(S).
Lew, S., Chang, M., & Kim, T. (2003). Affective networks and modernity: The case of Korea. In D. A. Bell & H. Chaibong (Eds.), *Confucianism for the modern world.* New York, NY: Cambridge University Press.
Marti, G. (2009). Affinity, identity, and transcendence: The experience of religious racial integration in diverse congregations. *Journal for the Scientific Study of Religion, 48*(1), 53–68.
Moskos, C. C., & Butler, J. S. (1996). *All that we can be: Black leadership and racial integration the army way.* New York, NY: Basic Books.
Putnam, R. D. (2007). E pluribus unum: Diversity and community in the twenty-first century the 2006 Johan Skytte prize lecture. *Scandinavian Political Studies, 30,* 137–174. doi:10.1111/j.1467-9477.2007.00176.x.
Putnam, R. D., & Campbell, D. E. (2010). *American grace: How religion divides and unites us.* New York, NY: Simon & Schuster.

Rousseau, J. (1978). On the social contract. In R. D. Masters (Ed.). New York, NY: St. Martins.

Stark, R., & Iannaccone, L. (1997). Why Jehovah's Witnesses grow so rapidly: A theoretical application. *Journal of Contemporary Religion, 12*(2), 133–157.

Taylor, C. (1998). The dynamics of democratic exclusion. *The Journal of Democracy, 9*(4), 143–156.

Tocqueville, A. D. (1899). Democracy in America. In H. Reeve (Trans.), *Of the principal source of belief among democratic nations* (Vol. 2). Retrieved from http://xroads.virginia. edu/~HYPER/DETOC/colophon.html. Accessed on July 1, 2012.

Tocqueville, A. D. (1969). Democracy in America. G. Lawrence (Trans.) & J. P. Mayer (Ed.). New York, NY: Anchor Books.

Turner, F. J. (1893/1935). *The frontier in American history.* New York, NY: Henry Holt and Company.

Weisinger, J. Y., & Salipante, P. F. (2005). A grounded theory for building ethnically bridging social capital in voluntary organizations. *Nonprofit and Voluntary Sector Quarterly, 34,* 29–55.

Wilson, J. Q. (2006). How divided are we? Commentary, February. Retrieved from http://www.commentarymagazine.com/article/how-divided-are-we/

Yi, J. (2009). *God and karate on the southside: Bridging differences, building American communities.* Lanham, MD: Lexington Books.

Yi, J. (2013a). Tiger moms and liberal elephants of Southern California: Private, supplemental education among Korean-Americans. *Society, 50*(2)(April), 190–195.

Yi, J. (2013b). Atomized terror and democratic citizenship. *Political Quarterly, 84*(3) (September), 388–394.

Yi, J. & Graziul, C. (2012). Religious conservatives, outsiders, and pluralist virtues. Paper presented at the Annual American Sociology Association, Denver.

CIVIC AND ARTS ACTIVITIES CAN ENERGIZE POLITICS, FRANCE AND EUROPE

Daniel J. DellaPosta and Terry Nichols Clark
with Stephen Sawyer and Arkaida Dini

ABSTRACT

This chapter is one of the first to analyze how local culture − especially voluntary associations and public arts activities − can mobilize citizens and increase voter turnout. This general hypothesis is contextualized by contrasting types of elections (French presidential vs. European Union) and types of art (contemporary, patrimonial, folkloric). We test these contextualized hypotheses by analyzing demographic, cultural, and political data from 263 French communes using linear regression methods. Civic associations and some arts activities seem to increase turnout in European but not presidential elections. Further, arts types vary in their association with voting for different parties. These findings suggest the importance of civic and arts activities for future analyses of voting turnout and party voting.

Keywords: Culture; politics; arts; participation; Europe associations; voting

Can Tocqueville Karaoke? Global Contrasts of Citizen Participation, the Arts and Development
Research in Urban Policy, Volume 11, 91−113
Copyright © 2014 by Emerald Group Publishing Limited
All rights of reproduction in any form reserved
ISSN: 1479-3520/doi:10.1108/S1479-352020140000011019

The rise of the European Union (EU) as a globalizing force, and a new interest in arts and culture, led us to explore these changes for their political impacts in France. Why France? France is the leading country in the world to use arts and culture to enhance diplomatic and political policies. The Louvre Museum, a global cultural icon, was the king's residence, until the king moved to Versailles. Versailles and other kingly castles across France housed elegant people, personal and political intrigue, and captured the imagination of many European political leaders. Concerts and theater were sponsored by the king from Molière onward. Foreign aristocrats visited and emulated the French model. French became the language of international diplomacy. Local French aristocrats spent long months in Paris, weakening their local contacts, and facilitating consolidation of the French national state by quiet national administrators. This nation building via cultural politics was a new policy that S.N. Eisenstadt identified as distinctly French in his global historical analysis of *The Political Systems of Empires*. The French thus led in building a strong national state, enhancing cultural activities, while suppressing civic groups. Tocqueville featured American civic groups and churches, especially contrasting these with his native France, where most civic meetings were illegal through much of the nineteenth century. Since World War II, civic groups in France have grown vigorously, as have cultural activities – yet distinctly unevenly. Some places like Avignon and Aix have months of grand and very expensive theater and concerts, but other communes nearby have virtually none. These are local decisions, largely: in recent years more than 50 percent of local arts and culture was paid for by French local councils. The Ministry of Culture only pays about 15 percent. Socialist parties dominated communal politics for most years after 1945, far more than in national elections. Many local councils also sponsor a wide range of sports, neighborhood, and civic associations, illustrating *le socialism municipal*.

Does investment in these civic and arts associations impact citizens and voting? Many French political leaders, national and local, have hoped or assumed that they would. But there is precious little actual analysis testing this hypothesis. This is one of the first chapters that we have found to do so.

The rise of the EU creates a new context that provides a natural experiment to compare with French presidential and local politics. That is, voters in the same communes vote for French and EU candidates. We thus designed the study to compare presidential and EU elections, hypothesizing that the newer EU elections could engage new issues and parties more successfully than the more traditional class-based party politics that was salient in French elections for much of the twentieth century. Local civic groups and arts activities should matter more if local elections are less intense and party dominated, and turnout is lower. When new issues enter the political arena – especially consumption concerns like the environment, lifestyle, parks, sports, and entertainment – traditional parties and class politics should explain less. These have been central themes in broader studies of the decline of class politics and rise of new political issues featured in labels like the Third Way, Bobo, and New Political Culture (Clark and Hoffmann-Martinot (1998) and Clark and Lipset (2001) review these debates). These new political themes have spread with the rise of globalization, especially the EU in Europe.

Turnout in EU elections has been consistently lower than nearly all other elections for virtually every EU nation. In France, approximately 57.5 percent of the total electorate voted in the first round of European elections in 1979 (Curtice, 1989). In presidential elections just 2 years later, 80 percent of the same electorate voted. Then 70 percent voted in the 1981 French general elections (Charlot & Charlot, 1984). This trend has only intensified in more recent years, as European elections continue to draw considerably fewer voters than all other national elections. Besides featuring low turnout, European elections have become notable as stages for small parties, particularly the French Greens and other European ecology parties (Curtice, 1989).

This chapter seeks to add a fresh perspective by posing two related questions:

Given that turnout in EU elections is so radically different from turnout in other national elections, how are traditional predictors of turnout reshaped or transformed within this (relatively) new electoral form?

As the traditional causal pathways leading to voter turnout or abstention are transformed, how are different classes of political parties impacted?

We analyze these questions by introducing the arts and local civic associations into analysis of local voting, although these have generally been two separate domains in past research. Namely, we consider how associational and arts activity at the local level can have the effect of maintaining an active electorate, even in cases where general public interest in an election is relatively low. (Some) leaders from Singapore to Finland also recognize new and previously unexplored pathways for engaging potential voters through civic participation and public arts, and are investing huge sums. So results from the French case have distinct global importance.

LITERATURE REVIEW

Traditional Understandings of Voter Turnout

Most previous literature on voter turnout has focused on three classes of predictors: socioeconomic, campaign-specific, and institutional. With regard to socioeconomic factors, cross-national studies have shown that turnout is higher in economically advanced countries and lower in poorer, less developed countries (Blais, 2006, p. 117; Blais & Dobrzynska, 1998). Other research has pointed to the robust effects of population size, concentration, and stability in explaining variance in turnout levels (Geys, 2006, p. 642). Similar analyses of socioeconomic effects on turnout for individuals, rather than ecological units, have produced mixed results. In some studies, individual propensities to vote have been tied to several socioeconomic measures, especially an individual's level of education (Blais, 2000).

Other work has found little or no connection between socioeconomic differences and differences in individual-level turnout, pointing out that higher socioeconomic status is much more robustly related to individual propensities to engage in other forms of political participation, such as campaigning and association activity (Verba, Nie, & Kim, 1978). Based on these mixed findings, we remain agnostic in terms of predicting how socioeconomic differences will broadly impact voter turnout in our models. However, we do predict − based on the findings of Verba, Nie, and Kim (1978) − that the impact of socioeconomic factors should be higher in elections where turnout is generally lower, and other forms of civic participation (for them mostly unions, for us associations and arts activity) play a larger role in mobilizing voters (see Hypotheses 1A and 1B).

While the importance of institutional predictors of voter turnout may at times be overstated (Blais, 2006, p. 116), they have nevertheless formed the primary foundation for most scholarly literature on the subject. Compulsory voting, concurrent elections, proportional representation, and ease of voter registration have all been tied to higher levels of voter turnout (Blais, 2006, p. 116; Geys, 2006, p. 651). In addition to these permanent institutional fixtures, several campaign-specific predictors of voter turnout have been shown to have robust impacts on voter turnout. These effects have been most powerfully shown with regard to closeness of elections and campaign expenditures by political parties, both of which consistently predict higher turnout (Geys, 2006, p. 646). With regard to European elections, then, we may surmise that lower turnout in European elections is in part due to the political parties' own perception of the election's unimportance and their consequent tendency not to spend as much money in these elections. However, as campaign expenditures are a consequence of European election turnout – in addition to being a predictor of turnout in future elections – they are not included in our models.

Are EU Elections Different?

Having discussed the broad traditional understandings of voter turnout, we next must understand the ways in which the dynamics of European election turnout differ from those of other national elections. Of course, we acknowledge the potential here for finding evidence of a null hypothesis: That the predictors of European election turnout do *not* differ significantly from predictors of turnout in other national elections. To this end, several studies have found that voters in European elections are largely driven by national – rather than European – political issues (Charlot & Charlot, 1984; Curtice, 1989; Kousser, 2004). Governing parties have generally fared miserably in elections for the EU parliament, while their major opponents have made consistent gains. This trend suggests that voters have used these elections to express their opinions of the national governing party and its domestic performance, rather than basing their votes on these parties' statements on issues of broader European importance (Curtice, 1989; Kousser, 2004). Of course, even if we accept this part of the null hypothesis, we still must deal with another major characteristic of European elections: The major success of small parties. However, even this difference between European elections and other national elections can be explained in fairly simple rational choice terms. Where small parties have achieved success in European elections, we may simply point to the use of proportional representation, which makes voting for a smaller party more rational than doing so in a national parliamentary election under majoritarian rule (Kousser, 2004).

Other research has found that some of the variation in European election turnout can be explained by the presence of electoral structures that exhibit similar effects on turnout in other election types. Compulsory voting laws, weekend elections, and the staging of simultaneous elections all contribute to higher levels of voter turnout in both European and other national elections (Mattila, 2003). Based on this evidence, we may suppose that European turnout has the same demographic, ideological, and structural predictors as turnout in more traditional election types (our null hypothesis), with the only major difference being that fewer voters see the

European elections as sufficiently important to actually get out and vote. Rather than seeing low European turnout as evidence of a new paradigm for the study of voting, should we instead simply see the problem as one borne out of low individual calculations of the real-world consequences of EU elections?

Our answer to the above question is an emphatic "No," and our findings will provide evidence to support this answer. First, though, we may point to considerable preexisting evidence suggesting that European election turnout *does* seem to vary a bit differently from turnout in other national elections. For example, European election turnout tends to be higher in nations with higher levels of public support for the EU as a political institution (Mattila, 2003; Niedermayer, 1990). Turnout is also stronger in countries that receive financial subsidies from the EU, such as Objective One structural readjustment funds (Jesuit, 2003), and weaker in the countries that are forced to pay for these subsidies (Mattila, 2003). Based on this evidence, we may justly question the validity of the null hypothesis previously put forward, and hypothesize that variation in European election turnout can sometimes vary in ways that cannot be completely explained by the same predictors that would explain such variation in other national elections.

Where Does Culture Fit?

In this study, we focus on two particular elements of local culture – voluntary associations and arts activity – and their potential as predictors of voter turnout in European elections. A brief justification for our focus on these two elements of culture is required here. In France, voluntary associations have traditionally been much weaker than in other Western democracies, owing to a long history of governmental repression (Gallagher, 1957; Saurugger, 2007). Due to this historical weakness, it has been difficult to perceive any major impacts that associations have had on French political culture and, more specifically, levels of voter turnout. In more recent years, associations have been more broadly accepted as legitimate elements of French political participation, even being used by local state entities for functions previously carried out by the national republican government (Nicholls, 2006). With this modern-day shift in French attitudes toward voluntary associations, we predict that association participation in France has now at least moved closer to filling some of the same integrative functions that these associations have long played in the United States and other Western democracies (see Putnam, 2000).

Like voluntary associations, culture and the public arts are now increasingly understood as fruitful venues for studying how individuals relate to their communities in postindustrial societies (Silver, Clark, & Navarro, 2010). As popular demand for public art has risen, especially in urban contexts, this and other elements of local aesthetic culture have become central to individuals' sense of "belonging" to their city or community (Lloyd & Clark, 2001). There is likewise a small but distinguished history of scholarship positing artistic creation as an example of collective activity, only made possible by the cooperative work that rises out of deep and complex social networks (Becker, 1974). Combining these two theoretical perspectives, we suggest that public art should today be studied more frequently alongside voluntary associations as expressions of active participation and social integration within a community. Following this line of thought, we incorporate measures of arts activity in our analysis in order to investigate whether and how these activities fit as potential sites of production for political engagement, especially in postindustrial societies and newer electoral forms (such as European elections).

HYPOTHESES

To test our theory of voluntary associations and arts activity as important drivers of voter turnout in European elections, we offer several hypotheses that we will test using ecological data drawn from 263 French communes.

First, we hypothesize that (1A) income and (1B) unemployment will act as more significant predictors of voter turnout in EU elections than in presidential elections. This hypothesis comes out of past research on the tendencies for members of higher socioeconomic strata to represent disproportionately large segments of voluntary associations (Verba, Nie, & Kim, 1978) and arts audiences (DiMaggio & Useem, 1989). Where associations and arts activity more strongly predict voter turnout (see Hypothesis 2A), we expect that socioeconomic status will also more strongly predict turnout.

Second, we hypothesize that (2A) voluntary associations and (2B) arts activity will act as significant predictors of voter turnout in European elections, but not in presidential elections. Whereas turnout is generally high in presidential and other national elections, we believe that the higher levels of political engagement enjoyed by those who vote in European elections will specifically be found among those who also engage actively with culture and the arts.

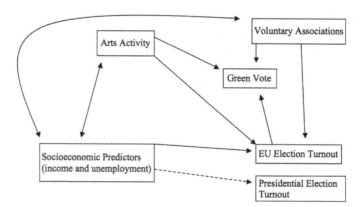

Fig. 1. Visual Representation of the Hypotheses Tested in Our Study. *Note*: Dotted line indicates a weaker predicted association; full lines indicate a stronger predicted association.

Third, we hypothesize that the particular impact of associations and arts activity on European election turnout should disproportionately benefit the Greens over parties of (3A) the right and (3B) the traditional left. Here, we propose the impact of associations and arts activity on European elections (Hypotheses 2A and 2B) as a potential explanation for the success enjoyed by the Greens in these elections. We see this as likely due to the particular history of European ecologist parties as emerging out of environmental associations and other loose networks of activists (Muller-Rommel, 1985) (Fig. 1).

DATA AND METHODS

Data Set

The data used to test these hypotheses come from several distinct sources. Demographic measures were collected from INSEE, the French census bureau. Meanwhile, counts of voluntary associations were drawn from the French *Pages Jaunes* and arts activity data come from the Ministry of Culture's *Bureau de l'observation du spectacle vivant*. Finally, data on electoral turnout and partisan voting were collected from publicly available sources kept by the Center for Socio-Political Data (CDSP), based at the *Institut d'Études Politiques de Paris*. Data from INSEE, *Pages Jaunes*, and the Ministry of Culture were collected for every commune in France. However, the CDSP's data on commune-level voting were limited to a selected sample of 263 large communes, accounting for approximately 30 percent of the total population of France. The mean population for the communes in our sample of 263 was approximately 72,541. By comparison, the mean population for the excluded communes was 1,265. Thus, our sample clearly skews toward highly populated and urban communes, and our findings should be understood as applying most directly to urban and high-population suburban environments. The communes in our sample also tended to be wealthier and more highly educated than excluded communes, although these differences were far less drastic than the aforementioned differences in population size.[1] Our sample included at least one commune drawn from each of France's 94 continental departments. The additional noncontinental departments of Corsica (2A and 2B), Guadeloupe (971), Martinique (972), Guyana (973), and La Reunion (974) were excluded from analysis.

Variables: Demographic

Our first set of independent variables measures different aspects of the demographic makeup of each commune. First, we include total commune population as determined in 2006 by INSEE. Our variable for mean income comes from INSEE's 2005 measurements and represents department-level data on the *"revenu annuel net/euros lieu residence."* Using these department-level data, each commune was simply assigned the corresponding mean income for its department. While commune-level income measures would be preferable, the department-level measures provide the best income measure generally available.

The percent of unemployed people in each commune was computed using the aforementioned commune population variable and INSEE's 2008 measure of the total number of unemployed residents of each commune. Our two broad occupational measures are based on INSEE's 2008 measures of the total number of people in each commune who worked as *"agriculteurs exploitants"* (Percent Agricultural Sector) and *"artisans, commercants, chefs entreprise"* (Percent Artisanale). Two higher-income occupational categories – *"cadres et professions intellectuelles superieures"* and *"professions intermediares"* – were also measured. However, these two categories were eventually excluded from analysis due to high levels of multicollinearity with other variables of interest, particularly mean income and percent unemployed. Our age variable was computed using INSEE's 2006 measure of the total number of commune residents aged 18–24. Finally, we computed a variable for the percent of nonnative French residents using INSEE's 2006 count of the total number of *"personnes etrangeres"* in each commune.

Variables: Voluntary Associations

To create our measures of voluntary associations in each commune, we used a relatively novel source for social science research, the downloaded *Pages Jaunes* from 2009 (thanks to Maxime Jaffre and other Scenes project staff). Using this source, we were able to find total counts of voluntary associations within 10 distinct categories for each commune.[2] First, we employ a simple per capita measure that gives the number of total voluntary associations per each 100 residents in a commune. Beyond this broad measure of associational activity, we also wanted to distinguish between different types of voluntary associations. For this purpose, we calculated the presence of associations within each of the 10 categories as a percentage of the total associations within a commune. For example, if a commune had five total associations, and two of these associations were sports clubs, then the corresponding variable for "Percent Sports Associations" would simply tell us that sports clubs made up 40 percent of the total associations in the commune. Some communes did not have any voluntary associations; as a consequence, the "Percent Sports Association" variable (and the variable for every other category) would be categorized as missing for this commune. We performed a principal components analysis on the resulting eleven variables (one for each association category, and eleventh variable for the total number of associations per capita). The four principal components derived from this analysis are shown in Table 1.

The four principal components extracted from this analysis represent four likely natural groupings of voluntary associations within a given commune. Component 1 distinctly reflects high numbers of trade unions and professional associations, as well as social associations. Communes that correlate heavily with Component 2 have more total voluntary associations per capita. Further, these associations contain higher than normal numbers of consumer associations, environmental groups, and humanitarian associations. Component 3 indicates a relative diversity of association types: including more total voluntary associations than the average commune, and virtually all types, with the notable exception of humanitarian groups

Table 1. Principal Component Matrix for Total Voluntary Associations Per Capita and Individual Percentage Measures for Each Category of Associations.

Input Variables	Extracted Principal Components			
	Component 1	Component 2	Component 3	Component 4
Total Associations Per Capita	0.161	0.708	0.348	−0.009
Cultural	−0.827	0.072	0.130	−0.278
Environmental	−0.100	0.473	0.245	0.148
Social	0.559	−0.158	0.266	0.069
Sport	−0.178	−0.375	0.376	0.565
Humanitarian	0.155	0.348	−0.881	0.219
Religious	−0.515	−0.097	0.170	−0.196
Consumers	0.031	0.623	0.349	0.138
Clubs	0.368	−0.328	0.244	0.297
Trade Unions	0.497	0.179	0.126	−0.218
Professional	0.411	−0.188	0.133	−0.710

(−0.881). Finally, communes that correlate positively with Component 4 have a lower-than-average number of total associations per capita. Those that are more present are sports associations. But cultural associations, trade unions, and professional associations are rare.

Variables: Arts Activity

In addition to demographic and association variables, we computed several measures of arts activity within each commune. These data are normally not reported by the Ministry of Culture for individual communes for data analysis, but Scenes Project staff assembled a list of events and activities from the Ministry of Culture – which also included specific categorizations of each event listed and the total number of recorded arts events and activities within each commune. These events cover a broad range of artistically inclined collective action, ranging from dance troupes to communal festivals to street performance. In the same manner as with previous variables, we used this total count to compute a per capita measure of arts activity per 100 residents. Next, we employed a unique coding approach that involved the creation of three distinct conceptual categories of arts activity – Contemporary Arts, Patrimonial Arts, and Traditional or Folkloric Arts – and the counts of total events within each category for each commune. These three categories were mutually exclusive, but did not cover every recorded class of arts activity.

The category of Contemporary Arts broadly covers activities that the Ministry of Culture has labeled as "*actuelles*" or "*contemporaine*," and prominently includes choreography, contemporary music festivals, and theater festivals.[3] Patrimonial Arts broadly cover activities that emerge from the French republican tradition and promote a sense of civic pride in the rich cultural history of the nation. This includes traditional opera, orchestra performances, and national theaters.[4] The third and final conceptual category was that of the Traditional or Folkloric Arts. This grouping was considerably smaller than the others, with circuses, traditional dance or music, and street performance festivals.[5] The number and percent of events in each of these three categories was computed for every commune. For example, if a commune had five total cultural events, and one Patrimonial Arts, Patrimonial Arts scored 20 percent of that commune's arts activities.

Variables: Voter Turnout and Partisanship

Voting measures are used as the dependent variables in each of our models. First, we employ measures of voter turnout from two distinct elections to test our primary hypotheses concerning differences in voter turnout between presidential and EU elections. Our measure of presidential election turnout was the percentage of registered voters who actually voted in the first round of the 2007 French presidential elections, measured at the level of the commune. Similarly, our measure of EU election turnout was the percentage of registered voters who actually voted in the first round of the 2009 EU parliamentary elections. There are several ways to measure voter turnout, but this method has generally been recognized as the least problematic due to the fact that it does not rely on potentially imprecise estimates of total population (Blais & Dobrzynska, 1998, p. 241), and has been used in much previous research (see Blais & Carty, 1990; Crewe, 1981; Franklin, 1996).

Unlike the measure of presidential turnout, our variable for EU election turnout uses mostly department-level measures, as commune-level turnout measures were only available for a subset of 74 communes in Paris and several surrounding departments. While we viewed this discrepancy as potentially problematic, the percent of variance explained in the models using department-level turnout was strikingly similar to equivalent models that used commune-level turnout as the dependent variable, suggesting that this difference was not likely to distort our results in any significant way. We also recorded the percentage of votes cast for each of four political parties in these two elections: *Les Verts* (Greens), *Parti Socialiste* (PS), *Union pour un Movement Populaire* (UMP), and *Front National* (FRN).[6] Our partisanship measures for each of these parties are comprised of the mean percentage of votes earned by the party between the 2007 presidential elections and the 2009 EU elections.

Analytic Methods

Table 2 provides descriptive measures for all variables. These were analyzed using ordinary least squares, linear regression with the SPSS statistical

Table 2. Descriptive Measures for Variables in the Analysis.

Variable		Mean	Standard Deviation	Valid Cases (N)
Demographic	Commune Population	72,540.77	77,553.40	263
	Mean income	18,595.53	3,654.63	263[a]
	% Unemployed	6.48	1.50	263
	% Agricultural	0.07	0.10	263
	% Artisanale	2.19	0.67	263
	% 18–24 Years Old	11.23	3.31	263
	% Nonnative French	9.72	6.32	263
Voluntary Associations	Total Associations Per 100 Residents	0.13	0.11	263
	Component 1	0.01	1.00	241
	Component 2	0.05	0.99	241
	Component 3	0.03	1.00	241
	Component 4	−0.001	1.00	241
Artistic Activity	Total Cultural Events Per 100 Residents	5.71	17.69	263
	% Modern	23.04	18.25	262
	% Patrimonial	8.86	24.15	262
	% Folkloric	0.67	3.96	262
Voter Turnout	European Turnout	41.36	4.44	263
	Presidential Turnout	83.38	3.41	263
Partisanship	Green Vote	9.38	2.55	263
	UMP Vote	29.34	6.62	263
	PS Vote	22.46	4.20	263
	FRN Vote	7.56	2.97	263

[a]Income is for the 94 departments of metropolitan France, whose means are assigned to each commune within that department. See note 1.

package. Cases were eliminated pairwise. One major concern – given a relatively low N of 263 – was the potential confounding effect of multicollinearity in our models. We controlled for this possibility by not including any two independent variables that correlated with one another at a level higher than 0.5 (calculated as Pearson r's). The simple method of linear regression can test if associational participation and arts activity matter. Further, by substituting partisanship measures for voter turnout in later models, we tested our hypothesis that this "cultural effect" in EU elections favors Greens over the more traditional parties (UMP, FRN, and PS). As in most social science analyses, we look for causal processes, but these associations and regressions can only show associations. One of the few over-time analyses we have seen of the impact of arts policy on attracting talented citizens in later decades is Falck, Fritsch, and Heblich (2011).

FINDINGS

Demographic Effects on Voter Turnout

Table 3 presents the results of regression models using EU election turnout as the dependent variable, while Table 4 presents the results for presidential election turnout. In both tables, Model 1 represents the initial test of the direct impact of major demographic factors on voter turnout. From these, it is apparent that the average income of a commune has at least as strong an effect – and likely even stronger – on turnout in EU elections as it does on presidential elections. Income acts as a powerful and positive predictor of higher turnout in both presidential and European elections in all of the tested models. Indeed, none of the other tested variables seem to have any effect of lessening the predictive power of mean income. Thus, Hypothesis 1A is supported and we find that mean income appears to predict voter turnout more powerfully in European elections than in presidential elections.

By contrast, we see significant differences in the effect of unemployment on voter turnout when comparing the two distinct election types. For EU elections (Table 3), unemployment is a significant positive predictor of voter turnout with other demographic measures controlled (Model 1). Yet when any other variables are added to the model (Models 2 through 6), unemployment lacks statistical significance. However, for turnout in the presidential election (Table 4), we see that unemployment is a significant

Table 3. Effects of Demographic Variables, Voluntary Associations, and Arts Activity on Voter Turnout in 2009 EU Election.

Independent Variables		Model 1 β	Model 2 β	Model 3 β	Model 4 β	Model 5 β	Model 6 β
Demographic Variables	Commune Population	-0.041	-0.041	-0.029	-0.035	-0.032	-0.031
	Median Income	0.793***	0.782***	0.741***	0.755***	0.702***	0.800***
	% Unemployed	0.111*	0.082	0.090	0.073	-0.016	0.089
	% Agricultural Sector	0.192***	0.190***	0.200***	0.194***	0.152***	0.179***
	% Artisanale Sector	0.240***	0.169***	0.185***	0.145**	0.154**	0.152***
	% 18–24 Years Old	0.251***	0.167***	0.220***	0.156***	0.130**	0.157***
	% Nonnative French	-0.477***	-0.422***	-0.465***	-0.419***	-0.346***	-0.419***
Voluntary Associations	Total Associations Per Capita		0.205***		0.191***		0.169***
	Component 1					0.103**	
	Component 2					0.233***	
	Component 3					-0.040	
	Component 4					-0.082*	
Cultural Activities	Total Events Per Capita			0.113**	0.060	0.056	0.055
	% Modern						-0.043
	% Patrimonial						0.168***
	% Traditional						0.003
	Adjusted R-squared	0.508	0.540	0.515	0.541	0.558	0.563
	N	263	263	263	263	241	262

Note: Multicollinearity is controlled by not including variables with bivariate Pearson correlations above 0.500. Numbers presented represent Beta coefficients from linear regressions.
$*p < 0.1$, $**p < 0.05$, $***p < 0.01$.

Table 4. Effects of Demographic Variables, Voluntary Associations, and Arts Activity on Voter Turnout in 2007 French Presidential Election.

Independent Variables		Model 1 β	Model 2 β	Model 3 β	Model 4 β	Model 5 β	Model 6 β
Demographic Variables	Commune Population	0.023	0.023	0.024	0.022	0.025	0.018
	Mean income	0.379***	0.376***	0.374***	0.378***	0.373***	0.379***
	% Unemployed	−0.499***	−0.507***	−0.501***	−0.506***	−0.506***	−0.494***
	% Agricultural Sector	0.116**	0.115**	0.117**	0.115**	0.110*	0.116**
	% Artisanale Sector	0.115**	0.095*	0.109*	0.097	0.130**	0.106*
	% 18–24 Years Old	0.121**	0.097*	0.118**	0.098*	0.112*	0.096*
	% Nonnative French	0.133**	0.149**	0.134**	0.149**	0.166**	0.145**
Voluntary Associations	Total Associations Per Capita		0.059		0.060		0.048
	Component 1					0.044	
	Component 2					0.022	
	Component 3					−0.035	
	Component 4					0.081*	
Cultural Activities	Total Events Per Capita			0.012	−0.005	0.018	0.007
	% Modern						0.053
	% Patrimonial						0.018
	% Traditional						0.021
	Adjusted R-Squared	0.506	0.507	0.504	0.505	0.503	0.502
	N	263	263	263	263	241	262

Note: Multicollinearity is controlled by not including variables with bivariate Pearson correlations above 0.500. Numbers presented represent Beta coefficients from linear regressions.
*$p < 0.1$, **$p < 0.05$, ***$p < 0.01$.

negative predictor of voter turnout when other demographic factors are controlled (Model 1), and this effect stays the same or even grows slightly stronger when other variables are added to the model (Models 2 through 6). Based on these results, it appears that communes with low levels of unemployment are significantly more likely to have high voter turnout in presidential elections than communes with high levels of unemployment but otherwise similar demographic profiles. However, differences in unemployment do not seem to be nearly as consequential in explaining inter-commune differences in EU election turnout. Therefore, Hypothesis 1B is rejected and it seems that unemployment actually impacts presidential turnout more than it impacts EU election turnout.

Two measures of occupational distribution are included: the percent of commune residents who work in the agricultural sector, and the percent in the *artisanale* sector. For EU election turnout (Table 3), both increase voter turnout in all six models. For presidential election turnout (Table 4), the agricultural sector is a positive predictor in all six models, but the beta coefficient and significance level is lower than in EU elections. The same is generally true of the *artisanale* sector, which loses significance for one of the six models of presidential elections (Model 4). Other measures of occupational distribution (namely, *cadres* and *professions intermediares*) were excluded from the final results due to strong association with other variables.

Voluntary Associations and Voter Turnout

Model 2 in Tables 3 and 4 adds a count of total voluntary associations per capita to the slate of demographic variables controlled in Model 1. For the EU elections (Table 3), total associations per capita are a strongly positive and significant predictor of voter turnout (Model 2). Furthermore, the addition of associations suppresses unemployment to insignificance and considerably decreases beta coefficients for age (Percent 18–24 Years Old) and *artisanale* (Percent Artisanale Sector). The increase in R-squared values from Model 1 to Model 2 indicates that total voluntary associations per capita explain about 3.2 percent of the total variance in EU election voter turnout. By contrast, for the presidential election (Table 4), associations do not significantly predict voter turnout in either direction, and adding associations to the model only increases the total variance explained by 0.1 percent. These findings provide strong support for Hypothesis 2A that local

voluntary associations raise turnout in EU elections but seemingly have little or no effect in presidential elections.

The explanatory power of our EU turnout model (Table 3) becomes
even stronger when we remove the total associations per capita variable
and replace it with our four principal component measures for voluntary
associations (Model 5). Here, Component 1 and Component 2 both emerge
as strong positive predictors. We can thus identify which *types* of voluntary
associations contribute most significantly to turnout in EU elections. We
find two particular ecologies of associations that heighten turnout.
Component 1 includes trade unions, professional associations, social associations, and clubs for leisure activity. Component 2 – which most strongly
predicts higher turnout – disproportionately favors consumer groups,
environmental associations, and humanitarian activist groups, while also
including much higher than average numbers of total associations per
capita.

In addition to the two component variables that positively predict EU
election voter turnout, we also see one component that surprisingly emerges
as a significant negative predictor of turnout (Table 3, Model 5).
Component 4 features slightly fewer total associations per capita than average, but many sports clubs. Interestingly, none of the other association
types have a component score here of 0.3 or above (Component 4 is the
only one of the four components that features only one association type
with a component score above 0.3). This suggests that sports clubs are relatively isolated from other types of voluntary associations, and can have
impact on turnout even where other voluntary associations generally do
not. Past research has identified sports associations as being relatively isolated from other association types (Paxton, 2007), although this past work
similarly classified trade unions and religious associations as "isolated," a
finding that is not necessarily supported by our study. Similarly, these
sports associations (Component 4) *positively* predict voter turnout in the
presidential election (Table 4, Model 5).

Arts Activity and Voter Turnout

As with voluntary associations, arts activities show different impacts in EU
and presidential elections. EU election turnout is higher in locations with
more total arts activities per capita (Table 3, Model 3). However, arts activities are suppressed when voluntary associations per capita are added to
the model (Model 4). Meanwhile, in presidential elections (Table 4), arts

activity has no significant effect with or without voluntary associations in the model (Models 3 and 4).

When we go beyond this total count of arts activities and analyze the three categories of arts activity (Model 6), however, Patrimonial Arts appears as a strong predictor of voter turnout, with a beta coefficient nearly matching that of voluntary associations (Table 3, Model 6). Thus, while the totality of arts activities does not appear as a consistent predictor of voter turnout, the "republican" and nation-glorifying arts of the French *patrimoine* are robust in their connection to turnout. These findings support Hypothesis 2B, but with the qualification that the Patrimonial Arts in particular – rather than arts activity in general – help explain voter turnout in EU elections.

Where Do the Parties Fit?

Table 5 presents three regression models for four parties, the mean vote percentage over two elections (2007 presidential and 2009 European) for the Greens, the UMP, the PS, and the FRN. In models for the Greens and the FRN, the Socialist vote (PS vote) was additionally controlled to avoid potential confounding effects.

In the Green vote analysis (Table 5A), voluntary associations are not significant (Model 2), but the total count of arts activities per capita is positive and significant (Model 3). For the UMP (Table 5B), voluntary associations are again insignificant, while arts activities are significant and negative (Model 3). This is particularly interesting considering that the UMP and Greens communes appear to have quite similar demographic profiles. Both voluntary associations and arts activities are strong positive predictors of higher vote percentages for the PS (Table 5C, Models 2 and 3). Lastly, voluntary associations negatively predict FRN voting, while arts activities appear to be insignificant (Table 5D, Models 2 and 3). These findings support Hypothesis 3A and suggest that, where turnout is tied to arts activities (as in the European elections), the Greens will generally benefit more than parties of the right (namely, the UMP and the FRN). However, we do not find support for Hypothesis 3B, and instead find that the PS seems to benefit at least as much (if not more) than the Greens in such cases. Of course, this examination of partisanship is admittedly brief, but demonstrates the need for further study of the associations, arts activities, and partisanship in France.

Table 5. Effects of Demographic Variables, Voluntary Associations, and Arts Activity on Major Party Votes (Measured as Mean Percent in 2007 Presidential and 2010 EU Elections).

Independent Variables	Dependent Variables											
	A. Green Vote			B. UMP Vote			C. PS Vote			D. FRN Vote		
	Model 1	Model 2	Model 3	Model 1	Model 2	Model 3	Model 1	Model 2	Model 3	Model 1	Model 2	Model 3
Commune Population	0.104**	0.103**	0.118**	0.074	0.074	0.062	−0.061	−0.061	−0.044	0.006	0.008	0.009
Mean Income	0.561***	0.557***	0.489***	0.234***	0.235***	0.285***	−0.074	−0.080	−0.144**	−0.372***	−0.363***	−0.384***
% Unemployed	−0.211***	−0.217***	−0.233***	−0.267***	−0.262***	−0.246***	0.259***	0.242***	0.231***	0.558***	0.573***	0.555***
% Agricultural Sector	−0.025	−0.025	−0.013	−0.036	−0.036	−0.044	0.037	0.036	0.049	0.094**	0.095**	0.096**
% Artisanale Sector	0.288***	0.265***	0.206***	0.430***	0.441***	0.485***	−0.310***	−0.352***	−0.384***	−0.226***	−0.170***	−0.240***
% 18–24 Years Old	−0.023	−0.045	−0.060	−0.029	−0.015	0.003	0.240***	0.191***	0.197***	−0.145***	−0.092*	−0.152***
% Nonnative French	0.071	0.088	0.092	−0.204***	−0.213***	−0.217***	0.183***	0.214***	0.199***	−0.140***	−0.182***	−0.136**
PS Vote	0.385***	0.376***	0.360***							−0.568***	−0.546***	−0.572***
Total Associations Per Capita		0.059			−0.033			0.119**			−0.142***	
Total Arts Events Per Capita			0.151***			−0.111**			0.150**			0.026
Adjusted R-Squared	0.528	0.529	0.542	0.475	0.473	0.481	0.382	0.399	0.395	0.637	0.651	0.636
N	263	263	263	263	263	263	263	263	263	263	263	263

Note: Multicollinearity is controlled by not including variables with bivariate Pearson correlations above 0.500.
Numbers presented represent Beta coefficients from linear regressions. $*p < 0.1$, $**p < 0.05$, $***p < 0.01$.

CONCLUSION

This chapter is one of the first we know of which explores the impact of local associations and arts and culture groups on elections in France; such studies also seem minimal in other countries. We thus assess a previously unexplored potential driver of politics, especially of voter turnout and party choices, in French presidential and EU parliamentary elections. The results suggest that promotion of voluntary associations and the public arts may engage citizens, distinctly so in EU elections. Besides this broad hypothesis, we tested several narrower propositions with original important findings for voting.

First, we wanted to test how socioeconomic variables differentially impact voter turnout in presidential and EU elections. Income is a stronger predictor in EU elections, while unemployment is a much stronger predictor in presidential elections. Second, as hypothesized, voluntary associations and arts activity seem to increase voter turnout in EU elections, but not in presidential elections. We indeed found this case. Voluntary associations strongly predicted European election turnout. While total arts activity per capita was insignificant in most models, the particular category of Patrimonial Arts robustly increased turnout. These findings support our general hypothesis and suggest that associations and arts activity can act as important incubators of political engagement, in some contexts. These local activities should have greater impact where public interest in politics is lower. Future research might investigate the critical questions of how specific voluntary associations and arts groups create the impacts captured here. What are the mechanisms through which the Patrimonial Arts, in particular, may politically engage citizens? One idea is that citizens develop more social contacts with one another through the collective and networked nature of arts (Becker, 1974). A second is that the nation and patriotic themes that may be featured by associations and art spectacles are distinctly important in countries where Kings, Presidents, and the Roman Catholic Church have long sponsored patriotic art, and sometimes suppressed dissenting groups. Third, new themes have entered the political arena as immigration has risen as a political issue. One can see these themes tangibly creating a new political context as posters appear before elections inviting citizens to vote for Esperanto and against English as an official EU language and to oppose immigrants. Still the most important issue is environmentalism in both domestic and EU politics. These types of impacts are explored in the last chapter of this volume. If Tocqueville sings La Marseillaise, it raises EU turnout.

NOTES

1. Mean income and education came from the level of the department rather than the commune. Thus, each commune was assigned approximate measures of income and education based on its department. This method, of course, assumes that each commune in a department is equivalent in income and education, obviously not the case. However, using department-level measures still represents the best use of available data for these key variables. Using these department-level data, we estimate that the average income in our 263 sample communes was approximately 18,596 net Euros per year, while the average for excluded communes was approximately 16,360 net Euros per year. In our selected communes, the average proportion of residents without any educational diploma was 18.73 percent; in excluded communes, this proportion was 20.74 percent.

2. These categories were: "associations culturelles, éducatives, de loisirs"; "associations de défense de l'environnement"; "associations diverses, amicales"; "associations et clubs de sport"; "associations humanitaires, d'entraide, sociales"; "associations religieuses ou philosophiques"; "associations de consommateurs et d'usagers"; "clubs, associations de loisirs"; "syndicats de salariés"; and "syndicats et ordres professionnels."

3. The following categories of artistic activity were included as measures of Contemporary Arts: CCM, CNAR, scènes conventionnée, autres lieux de musiques actuelles, SMAC, centre de développement choréographique, EMA, PRMA, festivals de musiques actuelles, and festivals de théâtre.

4. The following categories of artistic activity were categorized as pertaining to the Patrimonial Arts: CDN, CCN, opéra national, opéra/théâtre lyrique, orchestre, EP, théâtre national, scène nationale, ENM, CEFEDEM, autre institution de formation, EP de formation, ADDM, centre de ressources, and festival de musique.

5. The official category names that went into our grouping of Traditional or Folkloric Arts are as follows: pôle cirque, musique et danse traditionnelles, and festival: arts de la rue.

6. A vote for the Greens was defined as a vote for Dominique Voynet in the presidential elections or a vote for Europe Écologie in the EU elections. A vote for the PS was defined as a vote for Ségolène Royal in the presidential elections or a vote for Changer L'Europe Maintenant Avec Les Socialistes in the EU elections. A vote for the UMP was defined as a vote for Nicolas Sarkozy in the presidential elections or a vote for the Majorité Présidentielle in the EU elections. A vote for the FRN was defined as a vote for Jean-Marie Le Pen in the presidential elections or a vote for the Liste Front National Présentée Par Jean-Marie Le Pen in the EU elections.

REFERENCES

Becker, H. S. (1974). Art as collective action. *American Sociological Review, 39*, 767–776.

Blais, A. (2000). *To vote or not to vote? The merits and limits of rational choice.* Pittsburgh, PA: University of Pittsburgh Press.

Blais, A. (2006). What affects voter turnout? *Annual Review of Political Science, 9*, 111–125.

Blais, A., & Carty, R. K. (1990). Does proportional representation foster voter turnout? *European Journal of Political Research, 18,* 167–181.

Blais, A., & Dobrzynska, A. (1998). Turnout in electoral democracies. *European Journal of Political Research, 33,* 239–261.

Charlot, J., & Charlot, M. (1984). France. *Electoral Studies, 3,* 274–277.

Clark, T. N., & Hoffmann-Martinot, V. (Eds.). (1998). *The new political culture.* Boulder, CO: Westview.

Clark, T. N., & Lipset, S. M. (Eds.). (2001). *The breakdown of class politics: A debate on post-industrial stratification.* Baltimore, MD: Johns Hopkins University Press.

Crewe, I. (1981). Electoral participation. In D. Butler, H. R. Penniman, & A. Ranney (Eds.), *Democracy at the polls: A comparative study of competitive national elections.* Washington, DC: American Enterprise Institute.

Curtice, J. (1989). The 1989 European election: Protest or green tide? *Electoral Studies, 8,* 217–230.

DiMaggio, P., & Useem, M. (1989). Cultural democracy in a period of cultural expansion: The social composition of arts audiences in the United States. In A. W. Foster & J. R. Blau (Eds.), *Art and society: Readings in the sociology of the arts.* Albany, NY: SUNY Press.

Falck, O., Fritsch, M., & Heblich, S. (2011). The phantom of the opera: Cultural amenities, human capital and regional economic growth. *Labour Economics, 18,* 755–766.

Franklin, M. N. (1996). Electoral participation. In L. LeDuc, R. Niemi, & P. Norris (Eds.), *Comparing democracies: Elections and voting in global perspective.* Thousand Oaks, CA: Sage.

Gallagher, O. R. (1957). Voluntary associations in France. *Social Forces, 36,* 153–160.

Geys, B. (2006). Explaining voter turnout: A review of aggregate-level research. *Electoral Studies, 25,* 637–663.

Jesuit, D. (2003). The regional dynamics of European electoral politics: Participation in national and European contests in the 1990s. *European Union Politics, 4,* 139–163.

Kousser, T. (2004). Restrospective voting and strategic behavior in European parliament elections. *Electoral Studies, 23,* 1–21.

Lloyd, R., & Clark, T. N. (2001). The city as an entertainment machine. In K. F. Gotham (Ed.), *Critical perspectives on urban redevelopment (research in urban sociology)* (Vol. 6). New York, NY: JAI Press.

Mattila, M. (2003). Why bother? Determinants of turnout in the European elections. *Electoral Studies, 22,* 449–468.

Muller-Rommel, F. (1985). The greens in Western Europe: Similar but different. *International Political Science Review, 6,* 483–499.

Nicholls, W. J. (2006). Associationalism from above: Explaining failure through France's Politique de la Ville. *Urban Studies, 43,* 1779–1802.

Niedermayer, O. (1990). Turnout in the European elections. *Electoral Studies, 9,* 45–50.

Paxton, P. (2007). Association memberships and generalized trust: A multilevel model across 31 countries. *Social Forces, 86,* 47–76.

Putnam, R. D. (2000). *Bowling alone.* New York, NY: Simon & Schuster.

Saurugger, S. (2007). Democratic "misfit"? Conceptions of civil society participation in France and the European Union. *Political Studies, 55,* 384–404.

Silver, D., Clark, T. N., & Navarro, C. J. (2010). Scenes: Social context in an age of contingency. *Social Forces, 88,* 2293–2324.

Verba, S., Nie, N. H., & Kim, J. (1978). *Participation and political equality.* Chicago, IL: University of Chicago Press.

SECTION II
CREATIVITY AND DEVELOPMENT: CONTEXTUALIZING THE LINK BETWEEN BOHEMIA, THE "CREATIVE CLASS," AND ECONOMIC GROWTH

INTRODUCTION TO SECTION II

What does the urbane city add to the Tocquevillian civic group dynamic? Cities and neighborhoods provide distinct contexts where the meaning of civic engagement varies. Here, we engage theories that have linked bohemia and the so-called "creative class" with economic development and innovation. The elements of these ideas are ancient, in noting that cities are distinctive locales fostering freedom, tolerance, and new ideas. Trade and cosmopolitanism, travelers moving in and out with unusual products are classic. Marx and Weber pursued these themes, while Georg Simmel stressed that cities fostered more diverse types of groups, which permitted individuals to combine their memberships in more complex ways, generating more unusual forms of individuality. Joseph Schumpeter extended this idea by stressing how innovation drove economic growth. Jane Jacobs played up the bohemian lifestyle, the neighborhood social ties, as contextual frames fostering more individuality.

Edward Glaeser and Richard Florida have pursued testing these ideas with their collaborators, and reported general support in the United States, although Glaeser et al. have stressed more education and urban density while Florida reports more on bohemian items like gays and tattoo parlors as new drivers of development. Since local differences and competition among local areas for jobs and migrants were seen as key intermediary links, some Europeans initially resisted these theories, considering European cities as more closed and stable. This changed with such studies as those of Michael Frisch, which showed for Germany in detail, and in cities in many European countries, that locations with more artists and arts-related activities enjoyed more creative industries and growth. European critics have then held up Catholic southern Europe as distinctly inhospitable to such dynamics. They are challenged by the new studies of Navarro and his colleagues, in two chapters in this volume, two further books on citizen politics and scenes in Spanish cities, plus papers that have compared Spanish cities to others across Europe. They show systematically, using large samples of cities and mayors, how the arts and culture are a new public policy, distinct from normal left-right politics, and often having important impacts on politics and the economy. To report these results from southern Spain, where they should be least likely to hold per the critics, makes them all the more innovative and compelling.

In "Cultural Strategies, Creativity, and Local Development in Spain," Rodríguez, Mora, and Navarro extend these ideas. They explore the impact of local cultural policy on the link between the creative classes and local economic development. They identify two categories of cultural policy: (1) instrumental – which pursues cultural amenities that have economic development as their direct goal (e.g., sports arenas, amusement parks) and (2) planning – focused on education and integration of the local population (e.g., libraries, museums, local businesses, and restaurants). They find that more creative populations are indeed positively linked with economic development, innovation, and local income. But these effects rise where local cultural policies are more instrumental. In other words, the context of distinct public policies significantly shifts the link between the creative class and local economic development. Context is captured in an index these authors develop to measure specific cultural amenities. Using scores on subdimensions, they provide an overall measure of a municipality's tendency more toward instrumental cultural development or planning cultural development. This innovative methodology joins the logic of scenes theory.

There is much discussion of the creative class and bohemia, but how can we give these labels more coherence and identify their impacts? Utilizing scenes theory, Jang, Clark and Byun explore multiple ways to codify the cultural category of bohemia. Their work is driven by the complexities raised in opposition to the creative class model in Asian contexts. While the theories were broadly global, empirical research has supported this more slowly, first in the United States, then northern Europe, and slowly in southern Europe – by linking bohemia with economic development, technological innovation, new patents, and the like. But while Asia excels in many of these outputs, there have been fewer and less obvious elements of bohemia in Asia, at least using standard definitions of bohemia. The solution proposed by Byun, Jang, and Clark is to detail 10 distinct subtypes of bohemia, making it a more varied category than is usual. This broader definition is more critical in Seoul and Tokyo where results show that some aspects of the bohemian category hold, but others not, often related to the influence of local culture and family social structures. Many countries outside Europe and the United States also have less zoning defining distinct neighborhoods, which weakens neighborhood cultural impacts. In other words, there are different sorts of bohemia based on the different local contexts in which it exists. These findings not only shed light on Asia, but can also help in understanding variations in local creative populations within

Western countries (such as between neighborhoods or ethnic and cultural subgroups). For instance, concepts like neighborhood turf, political clout, and cultural solidarity enhanced resistance to yuppies (Young Urban Professionals) in Chicago more than in other cities where neighborhoods are less culturally coherent.

CULTURAL STRATEGIES, CREATIVITY, AND LOCAL DEVELOPMENT IN SPAIN

María Jesús Rodríguez-García,
Cristina Mateos Mora and
Clemente J. Navarro Yáñez

ABSTRACT

City governments know well that culture is a powerful tool they can use to promote local development. Those governors also know that there are different ways to pursue that process. Two main strategies considered here are: instructional strategies, which promote cultural services among local inhabitants, and instrumental strategies to promote economic development creating big cultural spaces and large events. This chapter shows the impact of cultural strategies on the attraction of creative residents (creative class), as well as on income differences among Spanish municipalities.

Our main hypothesis is: in comparison with instructional strategies, instrumental strategies have a positive impact on local creativity and economic development. Using secondary data from the Spanish census, cultural strategies in a local area are analyzed, and are included in multiple regression models to test this idea.

Can Tocqueville Karaoke? Global Contrasts of Citizen Participation, the Arts and Development
Research in Urban Policy, Volume 11, 121–134
Copyright © 2014 by Emerald Group Publishing Limited
ISSN: 1479-3520/doi:10.1108/S1479-352020140000011021

These analyses show that, first, instrumental strategies have a positive impact on creative class localization; second, these strategies have a positive impact on local income regardless of the presence of a creative class, and moreover, the impact of a creative class on local income depends on the orientation of cultural strategies. This implies that the impact of creativity on local development is contextual according to the nature of local cultural strategies.

Keywords: Creativity; cultural strategies; creative class; economic development; Spanish municipalities

CULTURE AS LOCAL DEVELOPMENT POLICY: INSTRUMENTAL VERSUS INSTRUCTIONAL STRATEGY

An essential part of the change from industrial to postindustrial societies is the growing importance of culture as a driving force in social, political, and economic transformation. Furthermore, just like the past transition from traditional to industrial societies, it is primarily in cities that these contemporary shifts take their most dramatic expression. Therefore, they are privileged spaces for analyzing the role of culture in postindustrial societies.

Culture is considered, by both the academic sphere and public agencies, as a resource which local development strategies and policies should utilize in pursuit of their program goals. Over time, two orientations or strategies have evolved. Until the 1960s, culture-related policy in cities was dedicated to promoting the "fine arts." However, toward the end of that decade and into the 1970s, within the framework of a postmaterialistic cultural shift, culture was progressively integrated into council agendas with the aim of making it more broadly available to its city residents, thereby engaging the State as a partner in the production of a "popular" culture. Since the 1990s, culture has been explicitly conceived as a tool for the city's development as a new economy was cultivated through links to creativity, information technology, and the rise of tourism and entertainment (Bassett, 1993; Bianchini, 1993; Kong, 2000).

In light of this diversity of approaches, city councils often find themselves in a dilemma over which of these cultural strategies to pursue. Some councils take an "instrumental approach," which views culture as a tool to promote economic development – think big cultural events and spaces associated with the diffusion of artistic and sport activities (theaters, museums, stadiums, etc.) meant to attract creative people and/or visitors to a place. Other councils choose an "instructional approach," aimed at promoting cultural services and events for their residents based on a belief that the proliferation of such programming will help to attract or develop the "creative types" so clearly needed for economic growth (Bassett, 1993; Hesmondhalgh & Pratt, 2005; Navarro & Clark, 2009) (Table 1).

To a large extent, these two strategies are closely related to the literature on culture's role in the city and its potential effects. The instrumental strategy relates to the "creative city" approach and its effect on economic development. The main objective here is to generate or attract cultural and creative industries as well as the "creative class" that is associated with them (Judd & Fainstein, 1999; Landry, 2000; Landry & Bianchini, 1995; Scott, 1997, 2007).

If the presence of the "creative class" generates economic development with a certain independence from other conventional factors, such as human capital and the presence of technological industries (Florida, 2002; Florida, Mellander, & Stolarick, 2008), attracting this group is an important objective for city councils. According to this approach, the creative class is attracted (or maintained) by a social climate characterized by tolerance, cultural diversity, and the existence of cultural consumption opportunities (Florida, 2002). This would include local contexts where cultural innovation is promoted as an economic sector and where it can be enjoyed from the perspective of cultural consumption. A vibrant cultural life revolving around cultural services and unconventional lifestyles increases the pull on the "creative class," neo-bohemians, and visitors (Florida, 2002; Lloyd, 2006).

Table 1. Local Cultural Policy: Two Approaches.

Main Characteristics	Instrumental Strategy "Creative City"	Instructional Strategy "Educational City"
Objectives	Economic development	Civic or community development
Facilities such as ...	Creative or cultural industries	Cultural services
Main activity	Cultural production and distribution	Access to culture
People such as ...	Creative class or visitors	Citizens (inhabitants)
Model sites	Cultural districts as spaces for cultural and creative industries (museums, theaters, opera, concerts, etc.)	Neighborhood as a space for civic development (civic and cultural centers, libraries, etc.)

Source: Navarro and Clark (2012).

In contrast, the instructional strategy and its "educational city" focuses on educational and cultural services designed to encourage the cultural life of its citizens. In this case, the main objective is to promote equal and effective access to culture, leisure, and education as one of the principal components of citizenship (in addition to the traditional social welfare policies). It involves facilities and public services such as libraries, schools, rehearsal halls, and neighborhood cultural events. The goal of this strategy is less geared toward direct economic development and more toward community integration and citizen participation (Semm, 2011).

Up to this point we have dealt with these two strategies from an analytical perspective; their actualization depends on the environmental context and the specific initiatives that are developed in each city. Without a doubt, this complicates the policy-making process for local authorities. Instrumental strategy has a greater orientation toward economic development than instructional strategy. Thus, according to the literature, whether by directly cultivating, or through the attraction of the creative class, instrumental strategies should have a positive effect on local development. From these assumptions, it is possible to propose at least three hypotheses:

H1: Orientation toward a more instrumental cultural strategy positively influences the attraction of the creative class, notwithstanding other factors related to the social climate (such as tolerance or diversity).

H2: Orientation toward a more instrumental strategy positively influences local economic development, regardless of other conventional factors (human capital, technological industries) or the presence of the creative class.

H3: Those cities that combine an instrumental strategy with the presence of a creative class will have greater development, because the former not only influences the attraction or location of the latter, but also presumes a favorable cultural climate for the development of that creativity. (This is a contextual hypothesis, given how the effect of the creative class on development will differ according to the strategy adopted by cultural policy.)

CULTURE AND LOCAL DEVELOPMENT STRATEGIES: HOW CAN THEY BE MEASURED?

In order to characterize the cultural development strategy used in each city we could inquire about initiatives, services, and policies implemented by public authorities and private agents. However, we could also gauge this strategy indirectly by researching existing cultural facilities in the city, as argued by the perspective of cultural scenes with respect to lifestyles (Silver, Clark, & Navarro, 2010). The idea is that a city's existing cultural facilities would show, at least in part, the orientation of their cultural development initiatives; or at least, the existing facilities would capture the existing opportunities (resources) that orient cultural policy toward one strategy or another.

Thus, our approach does not limit itself to counting and classifying the existing cultural facilities in a city, but also includes an analytical reading of these using the dimensions and subdimensions we have developed to explore the dynamic relationship between instrumental and instructional strategies. Specifically, we propose that the orientation of a city's cultural development opportunities can be described according to three main dimensions and seven subdimensions, as shown in Table 2 (Navarro, Clark, & Silver, 2012).

The first dimension refers to the main objective of the amenity, cultural service, or facility. We have defined three subdimensions (or objectives), which are not necessarily incompatible: economic development, because its specific prevailing objective is the creation of jobs and wealth (gastronomy, restoration, hotels, casinos, etc.); the dissemination of cultural production (museums, theaters, scenic areas, exhibition halls, concerts, etc.); and lastly, cultural education for transmitting values and learning (libraries, archives, etc.). For the second main dimension – the target population or

Table 2.   Culture and Territorial Development Opportunities.

Dimensions	Subdimensions	Definition
Objective	Economic development	To generate economic activity and/or employment
	Cultural dissemination	To raise awareness about culture/make it more available
	Cultural education	To educate, train ...
Public	Visitors	To attract activities and/or people
	Inhabitants	For the city's inhabitants to enjoy
Type of resources	Collectivization	Probability of the use of a resource or service is not reduced due to its use by other people
	Targeting	Whether a group of users exists (or not): there are rules for its use or it is specifically targeted (even if not formally)

Source: Navarro et al. (2012).

"public" – two subdimensions have been specified: facilities that are mainly aimed toward cultural consumption by visitors (theme parks, casinos, large museums, specialized shopping, etc.) and those aimed toward the city's inhabitants (small business, bars, pubs, etc.). The last main dimension – the type of resource produced – includes two subdimensions: targeting and collectivization. Targeting implies that facilities are aimed toward a specific target audience designed for their preferences and/or the existence of formal or informal rules that define its use (casinos, the opera, gyms, etc.). Collectivization means that the use of a resource provided at a facility is not reduced by previous use (a historical monument, a park, a civic center, etc.).

The central idea here is that each facility can be characterized using these seven subdimensions. For example, a theme park is aimed more toward economic development than cultural education or dissemination, intending to attract visitors over the city's inhabitants, selecting a specific group of people, but with a low level of collectivization. Compare this to a library, which is not targeted at any population in particular, aimed toward use by the city's inhabitants, with the objective of disseminating culture or developing educational activities. The former is a clear example of instrumental strategy, while the latter demonstrates instructional strategy.

Stated another way, instructional strategy represents the combination of cultural dissemination and education in the dimensions' objective, and orientation toward city inhabitants, and a high degree of collectivization. In contrast, instrumental strategy focuses its efforts on the objective of economic development, visitor attraction, and effective targeting. These examples provide a descriptive picture of the analytical perspectives; we understand that the orientation of cultural development strategies can lean more toward instructional strategy or instrumental strategy without being entirely exclusive (Table 3).

To measure these strategies, different types of facilities common to other analyses on the role of the creative class in economic development (Florida et al., 2008) were chosen from categories in the National Classification of

Table 3.　Culture and Territorial Development Strategies – Ideal Types.

Dimensions	Instrumental Strategy (Subdimensions)	Instructional Strategy (Subdimensions)
Objective	Economic development	Cultural dissemination and education
Public	Visitors	Inhabitants
Resource	Targeting	Collectivization

Source: Navarro et al. (2012).

Economic Activities. Each facility type was then rated in each of the seven subdimensions on a Likert scale of five points. A minimum value (1) means that the activity has no relation whatsoever with the subdimension and a maximum value (5) means that it is closely associated with it. Subsequently, the value assigned was multiplied by the number of amenities which promote this type of activity in each locality. This value was divided by the total number of amenities in the locality, which we will call the performance indicator. This indicator represents the specialization of a locality in each subdimension.[1] Then, we combined these scores, so a locale's orientation for both the instrumental and instructional strategy is the total of the performance indicators of their respective subdimensions. Finally, we subtract the instrumental strategy indicator score from the instructional indicator score. The result is our development strategy indicator, or the measure of a city's predominant strategy. A positive value indicates a more instrumental strategy while a negative value indicates an emphasis on instructional strategy. These scores, as well as strategies, should be understood as continuous; public policy is not a zero-sum game. Extreme values, therefore, denote more exclusivity in strategy approach.

DATA AND METHOD

From the hypotheses above, the key questions of this study focus on discovering whether development opportunities − derived from existing cultural facilities in terms of instrumental and instructional strategy − affect the presence of the creative class in cities. Further, we explore how this is reflected in economic development rates of localities, all else being equal. Finally, we investigate whether the effect of the creative class is reinforced by the orientation of the cultural strategy.

Given the high degree of municipal fragmentation that exists in Spain, the 806 local work systems as defined by Boix and Galleto (2006) have been chosen as a unit. These represent aggregations of municipalities in correlation to the relations of home-work mobility, accounting for territorial units that are larger than the municipalities and defined by productivity criteria. This does not eliminate the existing route between reduced territorial areas and the big cities, but more adequately reflects the location of workspaces where economic activity occurs in Spain. Therefore, the indicators represent the aggregation of the municipalities' values, integrated in each local work system, which we will refer to exclusively as localities.

Almost all of the variables used are derived from the Housing and Population Census of 2001, the most recent one in Spain. To measure local economic development, the average municipal per capita income from 2002 was taken.[2] The social climate of each locality was measured using a diversity indicator (% of foreigners) and another for tolerance (total of the percentage of homosexual couples and unmarried couples), both basic and common indicators in the literature on the creative class. To measure the creative class, we have grouped occupations according to the proposal of Florida (2002), and McGranahan & Wojan's (2007) correction, in light of its adaptation to the Spanish Classification of Occupations (Navarro & Mateos, 2010). With regard to a city's entrepreneurial climate, the presence of technological industries has been considered following Hansen's (2007) specifications. In order to measure human capital, the percentage of the active population with university education has been taken. Lastly, the orientation of the development strategy was measured by subtracting the difference between the instrumental strategy performance indicator values from the instructional strategy performance indicator values. Except in this last case, given the distribution of all the variables, the logarithms of their respective localization indices have been used.

In order to test the proposed hypotheses, various multiple regression models were performed. First, we took the creative class as a dependent variable, including social climate (tolerance and diversity) as independent variables (Table 4), in addition to locality size and development strategy orientation. Then, we took income as a dependent variable, including as independent variables factors that are derived from the creative class theory (their presence, tolerance, and diversity), as well as other conventional explanatory factors (human capital or the technological orientation of the entrepreneurial climate), in addition to the orientation of development strategies. Lastly, we investigated whether or not the cultural development strategy has a reinforcing effect on the presence of the creative class in the explanation of differences in inter-municipal income, including in the model of an "interactive effect" between these two variables.

ANALYSIS AND DISCUSSION

A bivariate analysis of the presence of the creative class and the orientation of development strategies shows that the former tends to be localized where instrumental strategy dominates (Fig. 1). But does this relationship

Table 4.   Variables Used in the Analyses.

Concept	Dimension	Index	Mean	Standard Deviation
Economic development	Income	Average income (2002)	4.28	2.01
Size	Population	Number of inhabitants	51,489.57	238,435.81
Social climate	Diversity	Foreigners (%)	2.95	4.35
	Tolerance	Homosexual and unmarried couples (%)	7.28	7.31
Talent	Creative class	According to profession (%)	14.98	4.42
Entrepreneurial climate	Technology	Industrial technology (%)	2.22	2.09
Territorial development opportunities	Strategy: orientation	Instructional vs. Instrumental	−0.59	0.13

Source: Housing and Population Census, 2001 (INE: National Institute of Statistics). *N* = 806 local work systems.

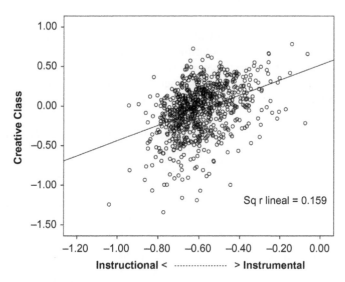

Fig. 1.   The Presence of the Creative Class Is Greater in Localities Geared Toward an Instrumental Strategy.

disappear when other factors are included, those which are linked to the creative class' location? The results show that instrumental orientation explains the variations in the creative class' presence, independent from the size of the local labor market or its levels of tolerance and diversity. We consider this as confirmation of the first of our proposed hypotheses (Table 5).

The above also confirms previous analyses performed in Spain: the creative class normally settles in larger, more diverse and tolerant areas, as well as localities where cultural facilities promote unconventional cultural scenes (Navarro, Mateos, & Rodríguez-García, 2012). Our analyses show that the creative class is also localized in localities that are more oriented toward the instrumental strategy. This implies that with size and social climate being equal, the nature of the city's existing facilities affects the presence of the creative class.

Given the literature, we also expect that the presence of technological industries accounts for greater levels of local development, observed through the per capita income of a locality's inhabitants. To what extent does this relationship also depend on the development strategy of a locality? According to our second hypothesis, instrumental orientation should have a positive effect on income (H2) in addition to reinforcing the creative class' effect on the latter (H3).

The results show, as is common in other analyses, that income is lower in localities of greater size, but increases with human capital, the presence of the technological sector, tolerance, diversity, and the presence of the creative class. The latter accounts for the difference in inter-municipal income, as held by the creative class theory, and as shown by other analyses for the Spanish case (Navarro, Mateos et al., 2012; Rodríguez-García,

Table 5.   Location of the Creative Class: Social Climate and Development Strategies.

| | OLS Regression | | |
	Coefficient	Error	Significance
Size	0.101	0.008	0.000
Tolerance	0.148	0.020	0.000
Diversity	−0.020	0.009	0.023
Strategy: Instructional versus instrumental	0.720	0.077	0.000
Constant	−0.579	0.079	0.000
R^2 (corrected)		0.439	

Dependent variable: Creative class.

Table 6. Differences in Inter-Municipal Income: Creative Class and Development Strategy.

	OLS Regression					
	Model 1			Model 2		
	Coefficient	Error	Significance	Coefficient	Error	Significance
Size	−0.418	0.045	0.000	−0.376	0.045	0.060
Human capital	0.395	0.184	0.032	0.344	0.183	0.000
Creative class	0.583	0.222	0.009	2.783	0.577	0.000
Technology	0.994	0.070	0.000	1.009	0.069	0.000
Tolerance	0.726	0.098	0.000	0.598	0.102	0.000
Diversity	0.345	0.044	0.000	0.380	0.044	0.000
Strategy: instructional versus instrumental	4.247	0.399	0.000	4.381	0.397	0.000
Strategy: instrumental creative class				3.559	0.863	0.000
Constant	11.595	0.419	0.000	11.211	0.425	
R^2 (corrected)		0.683			0.690	

Dependent variable: Income per capita (2002).

Mateos, & Navarro, 2012). These results further indicate that development strategy derived from cultural facilities also explains variations in levels of municipal income. As we expected, levels of income are higher when strategies are oriented toward the instrumental model (model 1, Table 6).

Our analysis shows that the development strategy positively reinforces the effect of the creative class on the levels of local income (model 2, Table 6). The interactive effect is positive and adds, albeit modestly, an explanatory capacity to the models. This implies that those localities that achieve a greater concentration of the creative class and possess cultural facilities oriented toward an instrumental strategy present higher levels of income, especially when both factors occur together, as is apparent in Fig. 2.

LOCAL DEVELOPMENT AND CREATIVITY: THE IMPORTANCE OF CULTURAL CONTEXT

The objective of this study was to analyze the relationship between development strategies based on cultural facilities and local economic development

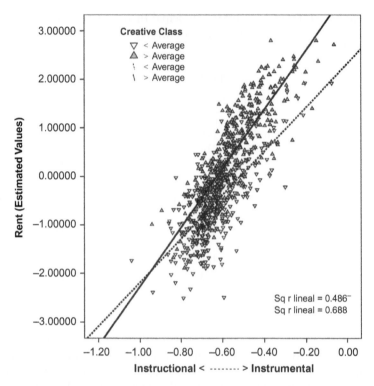

Fig. 2. Cultural Strategy, Creative Class, and Local Income: Income Is Higher When the Creative Class Lives in a Locality with an Instrumental Orientation.

on a level defined by spatialized localities. The analysis confirms, with a certain degree of independence (from the conventional factors identified above), that the cultural strategy pursued by policymakers in a locality affects the attraction of the creative class (H1), the growth of local income (H2), but furthermore, that the effects of the creative class differ in response to the interaction of environmental (and social) context and the policy strategies implemented in a locality (H3).

An orientation toward a "creative city" implies competitive advantages in relation to local economic development, which we observed as a difference in inter-municipal income. Not only because it attracts, for example, the creative class or visitors, but also because it indicates an environment which reinforces the effects of the creative class' presence in localities. Clearly, the development strategy based on cultural facilities is not the simple direct cause of development (or of the attraction of the creative class), but our analyses show that the strategies do have a distinct role in explaining these phenomena.

Above all, we observe that creativity has a contextual influence. Cultural amenities within a municipality, whose aggregate effect is observable through scoring and analysis, both depend upon and support the implementation of cultural policy programs. Likewise, the particular character of a locality will dictate the orientation of strategy therein – and whether that orientation is one that emphasizes more of an instructional, or an instrumental focus.

NOTES

1. For more details on the methodology, as well as the validity and reliability of the subdimensions, please consult Navarro (2012) or www.upo.es/cspl/scenes/.
2. This indicator is the one used by the Socioeconomic Report of La Caixa. This index is an interval scale from 1 to 10.

ACKNOWLEDGMENT

This study has been developed within the framework of the project "The cultural dynamic cities" (CSO2008-04288) founded by the Spanish National Research Programme (Department of Science and Innovation, Government of Spain). More details in www.upo.es/cspl/scenes.

REFERENCES

Bassett, K. (1993). Urban cultural strategies and urban cultural regeneration: A case study and critique. *Environment and Planning A*, *25*, 1773–1788.
Bianchini, F. (1993). Remaking European cities: The role of cultural politics. In F. Bianchini & M. Parkinson (Eds.), *Cultural policy and urban regeneration: The West European experience* (pp. 1–20). Manchester: Manchester University Press.
Boix, R., & Galleto, V. (2006). Sistemas industriales de trabajo y distritos industriales marshallianos en España. *Economía Industrial*, *359*, 165–184.
Florida, R. (2002). *The rise of the creative class*. New York, NY: Basic Books.

Florida, R., Mellander, C., & Stolarick, K. (2008). Inside the black box of regional development – Human capital, the creative class and tolerance. *Journal of Economic Geography, 2*, 1–35.

Hansen, H. K. (2007). *Technology, talent and tolerance – The geography of the creative class in Sweden*. Rapporter och Notiser 169. Department of Social and Economic Geography, Lund University, Lund, Sweden.

Hesmondhalgh, D., & Pratt, A. C. (2005). Cultural industries and cultural policy. *International Journal of Cultural Policy, 11*(1), 1–13.

Housing and Population Census. (2001). Madrid: National Institute of Statistics.

Judd, D. R., & Fainstein, S. S. (1999). *The tourist city*. New Haven, CT: Yale University Press.

Kong, L. (2000). Culture, economy, policy: Trends and developments. *Geoforum, 31*, 385–390.

Landry, C. (2000). *The creative city. A toolkit for urban innovators*. London: Earthscan.

Landry, C., & Bianchini, F. (1995). *The creative city*. London: Demos.

Lloyd, R. (2006). *Neo-bohemia: Art and commerce in the postindustrial city*. New York, NY: Routledge.

McGranahan, D., & Wojan, T. R. (2007). Recasting the creative class to examine growth in rural and urban counties. *Regional Studies, 41*(2), 197–216.

Navarro, C. J., & Clark, T. N. (2009). *La nueva cultura política. Tendencias globales y casos Iberoamericanos*. Buenos Aires: Miño y Dávila.

Navarro, C. J. (Ed.). (2012). *Las dimensiones culturales de la ciudad*. Madrid: Catarata.

Navarro, C. J., & Clark, T. N. (2012). Cultural policies in European cities. *European Societies, 14*(5), 636–659.

Navarro, C. J., Clark, T. N., & Silver, D. (2012). Las dimensiones y el carácter cultural de las ciudades. In C. J. Navarro (Ed.), *Las dimensiones culturales de la ciudad* (pp. 13–45). Madrid: Catarata.

Navarro, C. J., & Mateos, C. (2010). *La clase creativa en los municipios españoles. propuesta de medición y análisis descriptivo*. Working Paper Series, DT_0410 CSPL.

Navarro, C. J., Mateos, C., & Rodríguez-García, M. J. (2012). Cultural scenes, the creative class and development in Spanish municipalities. *European Urban and Regional Studies*. doi:10.1177/0969776412448188.

Rodríguez-García, M. J., Mateos, C., & Navarro, C. J. (2012). Dinámicas culturales, clase creativa y desarrollo urbano. In C. J. Navarro (Ed.), *Las dimensiones culturales de la ciudad* (pp. 158–173). Madrid: Catarata.

Scott, A. (1997). The cultural economy of cities. *International Journal of Urban and Regional Research, 21*(2), 323–339.

Scott, A. (2007). Capitalism and urbanization in a new key? The cognitive-cultural dimension. *Social Forces, 85*(4), 1465–1482.

Semm, K. (2011). Neigborhood milieu in the cultural economy of city development: Berlin's Helmholtzplatz and Soldiner in the German "social city" program. *Cities, 28*, 95–106.

Silver, D., Clark, T. N., & Navarro, C. J. (2010). Scenes: Social context in an age of contingency. *Social Forces, 88*(5), 2293–2324.

(RE)DEFINING BOHEMIA IN SEOUL, TOKYO, AND CHICAGO

Wonho Jang, Terry Nichols Clark and Miree Byun

ABSTRACT

As noted in this volume's introduction, Bohemia is considered a core component driving innovation and urban development in the West. From Balzac through Richard Florida, Bohemians are creative. Artists are the quintessence in the sense that breaking the eggs of tradition is a prerequisite to cooking a new omelet. The core idea seems broadly accepted by many readers and commentators in the United States and Western Europe. However, many Korean intellectuals react with puzzlement when asked what or where is the local Bohemia. Many imply that there are none in most Asian countries. There is evidence for this argument. Korean university students seem to dress more elegantly than Westerners. Many female students often wear skirts or dresses and high-heeled shoes and make up to class. Regarding tolerance of homosexuals, there is a famous story about a television star who "came out" with his gay identity and was fired from his job. Dressing inelegantly and tolerating gays are two possible indicators of Bohemia that Richard Florida has stressed, but a critical point to reassess is whether the idea of Bohemia should be revised or whether a new concept should be considered as Asian variations are more specifically incorporated into international theory.

Can Tocqueville Karaoke? Global Contrasts of Citizen Participation, the Arts and Development
Research in Urban Policy, Volume 11, 135–147
Copyright © 2014 by Emerald Group Publishing Limited
ISSN: 1479-3520/doi:10.1108/S1479-352020140000011022

*This chapter will examine whether or not Bohemia is absent using scene
data. The results will also be compared with those from Chicago to lead
to incorporate Asian variations more specifically.*

Keywords: Culture; arts; politics; economic development; Asia;
participation

WHAT IS BOHEMIA?

Bohemia is multidimensional and joins several interrelated concepts, some
of which are present in Asia. It may be possible to specify a sharper way of
analyzing Bohemia's sources and impacts if the separate dimensions are
considered in more detail. Thus, the subcomponents of Bohemia are listed
and the degree of Bohemia is compared between the West and Korea/
Japan.

1. Dressing in a nonconformist manner such as long hair, choosing casual
   clothes like dungarees and T-shirts, and wearing these in surroundings
   where others are more formally attired. This is widespread in the West,
   but minimal in Korea and Japan.
2. Reacting against people nearby – parents, friends, relatives – who
   may articulate a moral or broader sense of lifestyle. Or this may be
   simply, "Do it my way because I'm your father" and the son does the
   opposite just because "He's my father and he told me to do it his way
   so I rebel." In this second dimension the rebellion is narrowly interpersonal and limited. A decade or so back, Koreans scored very high on
   "deference to parents" as a desirable trait among children, in citizen
   responses to the World Values Survey. The gap with the West seems to
   have narrowed over time.
3. Reacting against the more general economic, social, and political establishment that is often seen as oppressive, hierarchical, and authoritarian. The establishment was relatively clear in cases like Czarist Russia
   in the 19th century or military dictatorships in 20th century Latin
   America or Korea.
4. Ideological opposition to a distinctive lifestyle. The normal target is
   considered bourgeoisie or middle class. The opposition to the bourgeoisie or the middle class is seen as more ideological in the sense that the
   principles of capitalism or accumulation or carrying tradition are seen

as wrong or immoral. Here, this takes on a moralistic perspective and critique. This moralistic perspective has grown more salient across the world with the spread of a Calvinist biblical style, albeit often secular perspective, often and one that relates to the lifestyle of the average person in a more egalitarian manner. Broad categories of action and ideas have become classed as politically incorrect or worse. In the Marxist version, the rules of history are working for progressive forces and following these principles of scientific socialism there is no choice but to step onto the train that is moving history forward. The bourgeoisie is condemned to death. Join the rising proletariat and be a political progressive even if it is a smallish minority in terms of voting or political activities.

5. Anarchy – revolt against all. From the 19th century Russians and French and Italian anarchists to the intellectual postmodernists of the late 20th century, all rules are wrong. Break them all, ignore them, challenge them, declare a pox on all your houses, be angry. This may be openly political and potentially linked to a program, but the frequent pattern of the past is fairly loose and open in terms of any ideology. Its main program is antiprogrammatic. The anarchists were initially a political movement.

6. Artistic anarchy. Many arts movements have sought to break all past rules or at least those presently dominant in any period. From Dada to Surrealism, to abstract painting rather than portrait or realistic painting, to atonal music rather than tonal music to writers who ignore many grammatical traditions like capital letters. Artistic movements may become a movement in a middle or later phase, but often begin with what feels like total opposition to a tradition surrounding them.

7. Juvenile delinquency, gangs, warlords. From a neo-Hobbesian war of all against all may emerge a sense that we tried to form a gang or follow a warlord, but adhere to almost no laws or flaunt the established laws that may be there for others. This may be narrowly self-serving and materially focused such as for the thieves and bandits who were common in medieval Europe, or for people who lived in forests and robbed travelers, highway bandits, outside the law.

8. A lifestyle that challenges the establishment and is conducted in a geographic area like the Latin Quarter/Greenwich Village. This is the classic meaning of the term from Balzac and others who were able to explore the lifestyle independence that became possible after the decline of patronage to an individual and the rise of markets or abstract ways of raising funds to live, such as for a novelist to sell books to people he did not know.

9. The intellectual independence and freedom of the artist. The intellectual freethinker may be concentrated in the geographic neighborhood and may share an outlook symbolized to others who dress and act in similar manner. Or, independence may be highly individualized: it may be a so-called inner migration as the Germans discussed in the early 19th century; it may be a reaction against the surroundings on an individualized level, like that of Thomas Mann who wrote that his ability to dress like a proper bourgeois gave him greater intellectual freedom to think and write and act than if he dressed in a manner which made him noticeably different from the people surrounding him (he lived in a small German town, not Paris or Berlin).

10. The artist. Many artists support several above dimensions of Bohemia to the degree that some writers on these themes identify empirically artists as the most obvious carriers of the Bohemian ethos. Richard Florida's Bohemian Index is no more or less than a sum of census categories of artists, used in several of his books such as *The Rise of The Creative Class* and later. However, if one looks a little bit, it is clear that there are many corporate wives who paint flowers and quietly vote for conservatives. They are not earning money or reporting to the census that they are artists. But neither do most taxi drivers, waitresses, and bartenders who become hopeful artists after 5 p.m.. Most national censuses thus omit many (less than full time working) artists (Germany is an exception).

Bohemia, in sum, can potentially include from #1 to #10 of these dimensions in various combinations and weights depending on who is thinking and talking. This is true of many concepts of the layman and scientific experts. One need not hope for or wait for a general consensus to reformulate a particular concept or label in ways that help advance science, which is a more general set of propositions about how in life processes work that can build on and extend the implicit or explicit meaning such as is deconstructed above.

MEASURING BOHEMIA IN SEOUL, TOKYO, AND CHICAGO

In this section, we produce a quantitative concept of Bohemia using our scene subdimensions. Based on past and recent discussions of the nature of Bohemia, an ideal-typical Bohemian scene is developed as shown in Table 1.

Table 1.   Bohemia Defined by Weights on 15 Scenes Dimensions.

Subdimension (Legitimacy)	Score	Subdimension (Theatricality)	Score	Subdimension (Authenticity)	Score
Traditionalistic	2	Neighborly	2	Local	4
Self-expressive	5	Formal	3	Ethnic	4
Utilitarian	1	Glamorous	3	State	2
Charismatic	4	Exhibitionistic	4	Corporate	1
Egalitarian	2	Transgressive	5	Rational	2

Note: 1 and 2 are negative; 3 is neutral; 4 and 5 are positive; 1 and 5 are just stronger than 2 and 4.

Defined thusly, a scene is more Bohemian if it exhibits resistance to traditional legitimacy, affirms individual self-expression, eschews utilitarianism, values charisma, promotes a form of elitism (Baudelaire's "aristocracy of dandies"), encourages members to keep their distance, promotes transforming oneself into an exhibition, values fighting the mainstream, affirms attending to the local (Balzac's intense interest in Parisian neighborhoods), promotes ethnicity as a source of authenticity (Lloyd, 2006, p. 76), attacks the distant, abstract state, discourages corporate culture, and attacks the authenticity of reason (Rimbaud's "systematic derangement of all the senses"). Scenes whose amenities generate profiles that are closer to this ideal-type receive a higher score on our Bohemian Index (measured as the value distance from the "bliss point" defined in Table 1). This measurement from a bliss point is analogous to policy distance analyses in voting (Riker & Ordeshook, 1973). Operationally, we subtract the distance of each zip code on each of the 15 dimensions from the Bohemian "bliss point" defined in Table 1. We then aggregate these 15 distances and take the reciprocal score and multiply by 10. More detail on Scenes and scoring is in the works listed at the end of Chapter 2.

BOHEMIAN SCENES IN SEOUL, TOKYO, AND CHICAGO

Using the method in the above section, Bohemian scene scores were calculated for Seoul, Tokyo, and Chicago. Fig. 1 shows boxplots of the Bohemian scores of the three cities.

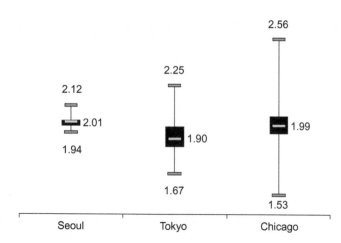

Fig. 1.   Mean Bohemian Scores and Deviations. *Note*: The three cities have similar means, but Chicago has the most varied neighborhoods, indicated by the larger range.

What is interesting from the boxplots is that the mean Bohemian scene score of Seoul is higher than that of Tokyo and even Chicago. Does this mean that Seoul is more Bohemian than Chicago? We don't think so. The reason why the mean Bohemian score in Chicago is lower than Seoul is the difference in residential areas. In Chicago, the Bohemian-like scenes of self-expression and transgression are (often strongly) negatively correlated with neighborliness, tradition, and localism. People pursuing these distinctive activities are in different neighborhoods. By contrast, in Seoul all of these are more often together geographically; many scenes dimensions are positively or at least not negatively related. This comes from the lack of Western-style specialization stressed in much of the land use in Seoul and perhaps also in Tokyo. That is, on one street you can find a Christian church, a traditional grocery store, a high-rise apartment building, a tattoo parlor, and bars. This is more culturally diverse than in a Western planned and zoned city where this would be illegal. In most U.S. cities, residential neighborhoods are separate from commercial neighborhoods. Areas with churches and schools cannot have liquor stores or bars nearby.

This is why the variance in scene performance score is low (shown in the ranges of the boxplots) in Seoul and Tokyo. On the contrary, those areas in Chicago with highest Bohemian scene scores can be considered as geographically concentrated authentic/genuine Bohemian places. Wicker Park is one of the classic Chicago Bohemian neighborhoods, detailed in Richard Lloyd's book *Neo-Bohemia*.

We found Bohemian culture in Seoul and Tokyo as well, but it is distributed around all areas of the city. Thus, to Westerners, it is hard to pinpoint the Bohemian place and the phenomena of Bohemia. On the contrary, the Bohemian places in Chicago are very different from other areas and have deep impacts on people living and visiting the places.

In the next section, Bohemian scenes maps of Seoul, Tokyo, and Chicago are drawn.

Bohemian Scenes in Seoul

Hongdae is an area in Seogang-dong near Hongik University, which is well known for its architecture, strong design, and arts scenes. Yeonsei University, Seogang University, and Ehwa Woman's University are also located near Hongdae. The area is famous as a center of youth arts in Korea as well as the heart of indie culture and for its clubs. It features ateliers, galleries, cafes, clubs, and performance halls. This area is a popular area among young foreigners due to the numerous elegant dance clubs located there. Therefore, it could be said this area has a strong Bohemian character. Shinchon, near Hongdae, also shows a Bohemian character because of several small performance halls located in Seogang-dong and Shinchon-dong (Fig. 2).

Jongno-gu also has some Bohemian areas, including Samcheong-dong, Jongno 1·2·3·4-dong, and Ihwa-dong. Samcheong-dong is known for traditional Korean tea houses, high-class restaurants, cafés, art museums, and private art galleries. Jongno 1·2·3·4-dong has a variety of cultural, educational, and entertainment facilities. This area features a jewelry store street, bars, karaoke, night clubs, language institutes, and sport centers. Ihwa-dong is known as Daehangno, which means "university street." Many drama and music theaters are located in this area.

Itaewon also has a Bohemian character. This area is well known as an area for foreigners. It features famous clubs and bars. Citizens from many different nations gravitate to Itaewon.

Apkujeong-dong and Cheongdam-dong are famous as the fashion meccas of Seoul. Many brand boutiques and fashion shops are located here. The entertainment industry is also developed around this area. Bangbaebondong and Banpo 4-dong are known as a small French enclave. Famous cafés and restaurants are located in this area.

Those areas mentioned above have high Self-Expression, Exhibitionism, and Glamour scores. In addition, Namkajwa 1-dong has a high Transgression score and a Bohemian character.

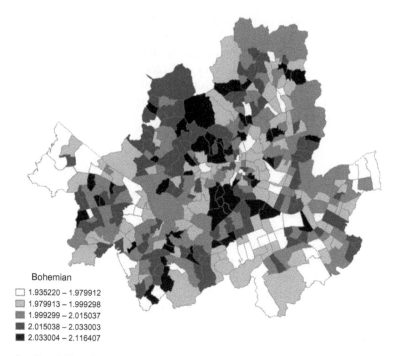

Bohemian
☐ 1.935220 – 1.979912
▒ 1.979913 – 1.999298
■ 1.999299 – 2.015037
■ 2.015038 – 2.033003
■ 2.033004 – 2.116407

Fig. 2. Seoul Has Several Bohemian Neighborhoods, and More Clustering Than Tokyo.

Bohemian Scenes in Tokyo

Shibuya-ku and Minato-ku have a strong Bohemian character. There are galleries, museums, shopping malls along Yoyogi Park and the Meiji Shrine in Shibuya-ku. The area has high Self-Expression, Glamour, Exhibitionism, and Charisma scores. Yoyogi Park is known as a good resting place as well as an area for live street performances. Many big and small performances play in and near the park. The Yoyogi flea market is famous. Shibuya Station is famous for its shopping street. The area features department stores and shopping malls. Haraju-ku is a center of teenage fashion and culture. Minato-ku also has high Bohemian scores with Self-Expression, Exhibitionism, Glamour, and Ethnic scores. Minato-ku is famous for its night culture as many clubs, bars, and iza-kayas are located in this area. The area is a tourist spot because of the night life (Fig. 3).

Bohemian
☐ 1.669451 – 1.848484
▨ 1.848485 – 1.930052
■ 1.930053 – 1.972693
■ 1.972694 – 2.013489
■ 2.013490 – 2.253742

Fig. 3. Tokyo Has Many Bohemian Neighborhoods Scattered across Its Entire Area.

Shinjuku-ku and Shinagawa-ku also have Bohemian characters as well. They have high Glamour and Transgression scores since they are entertainment areas. Kabukicho, in Shinjuku-ku, is full of department stores, shopping malls, restaurants, and izakayas so that the area has a high Transgression score. Shinokubo also has a Bohemian character because the area has a high Ethnic score. The areas have Bohemian characters with high Expressivism, Exhibitionism, and Glamour scores, much like Seoul.

Bohemian Scenes in Chicago

Lake View and Boystown have strong Bohemian character. These areas have high Transgression scores. They are close to the home of the Chicago Cubs and are famous for the local gay community (Fig. 4).

Wicker Park and Humboldt Park are Bohemian in character. Wicker Park and Humboldt Park are famous for a variety of events and facilities for leisure sports. Bucktown has a café street and is similar to Garosugil or Hongdae.

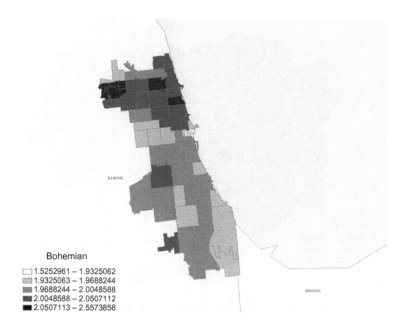

Fig. 4. Chicago Has the Most Concentrated and Fewest Bohemian Neighborhoods
of the Three Cities.

The areas have high Expressivism, Exhibitionism, and Glamour scores
much like Tokyo and Seoul's Bohemian scenes.

NO BOHEMIANS IN ASIA?

Asian societies include a Confucian and Buddhist background. This provides the theological justification for deference to authority, tradition, and
specifically to the family and older family members. It undermines revolts
and challenges the tradition of potential insurgents or critics. On the other
hand, it tends to be fairly delimited and family-specific rather than generalized in the form of political ideology. This provides a solution for Korean
children who live with their parents, attend a good university, even if they
also go to political meetings where they can become politically active, challenging, critical, even anarchist or more. They may deeply disagree with
their parents intellectually and politically, but they (at least classically) still
live with their parents or see their parents for weekend dinners, religious

and cultural services, and simple socializing. It is expected that they are close to them for life and that they will make space for their parents and grandparents to live in the same physical home – the classic tradition. Hence, it is not thoughtful to be in open political debate and confrontation with one's nearby family. This sort of straddling encourages one might even say a two-faced theory of communication – the deferential traditional child when sitting at dinner with parents, but the challenging antiestablishment protester when away from the home and parents, away from authority figures in the street or in a protest context. The challenge may be loud or silent. The silent version can be a candlelight ceremony where persons walk silently carrying candles in protest against a recent political action, to lament the tragic death, to blame, or to grieve. These are emotionally powerful and potentially seriously reconstruct a new political and moralistic base that challenges the surroundings.

This challenge is not recognized perhaps by the Westerner as Bohemian, because it is not associated with dressing differently from one's parents. Indeed, to the contrary, young Koreans in particular are noted for their glamour, for their style that could be termed pre-1968 to the Western eye. Young women wear dresses and heels to university lectures in Korea whereas in the West the more common attire is made up of dungarees, T-shirts, and running shoes. However, there have been visible protests in Korea, in the past against military dictators, then more recently in the beef protests, which suggest more continual turmoil among Koreans. The stylish young Koreans have also participated in candlelight protests. That is, it is more politically incorrect to dress differently, to think or act as an anarchist and to engage in any behavior that can be visibly seen by a grandmother at dinner looking across the table at her 23-year-old granddaughter. On the other hand, the 23-year-old granddaughter may be highly creative in finding ways where she can join a candlelight ceremony or a miniskirt brigade (which was one of the official organizations that participated in the Seoul beef protests in 2008).

Therefore, just because there is minimal distinctive dressing and less tolerance of homosexuals, it cannot be said that there is no Bohemia in Asia, especially in Korea. Indeed the age divide between young and old Korean voters is visible and major, more so than in most Western countries, especially Northern Europe and the United States, leading to labels like the "386 generation." To understand the different grammar of Bohemia East and West, all of the multidimensional structures that Bohemia was deconstructed into above should be examined and an attempt should be made to classify where and how they would be present, at least in a very broad manner. The units of comparison could then be countries or other units like Korea or Paris or the Paris Latin Quarter or the zip code 60637. These columns are historical combinations of chance, great warriors, lost wars, heroic terrorists and quiet resolution of persons whose names never figure in history books. They have a distinct arbitrariness that troubles social scientists, which is why one can try to aim for the abstract categories (like the 10 subcomponents above) and nevertheless note that they can be conceptually recombined in many different ways. This illustrates the principle of deconstruction and reconstruction as in the grammar of scenes. We lack data to do this completely. But our scenes data indicate some of the many important dimensions of socio-political cleavages that can be used to contrast neighborhoods, cities, and nations.

To pursue a particular context like Korea might build on these above ideas to ask: "in what way should the Western idea that the Bohemian is the source of innovation be transformed?" Searching for an answer might suggest a new perspective on the West. It becomes clear that these deconstructed elements are not by any means uniformly joined in the West if the above points are more closely examined. This suggests for instance that the post-1968 youthful "counterculture," well known from American campuses to the crowds around the Paris Sorbonne, is only one of a family of combinations of elements that may lead toward individuality and creative independence. That they do not hold together as a "counterculture" in some locations like Seoul does not mean that all deconstructed components are absent. This is not just true for the Seoulite. The Caltech engineer who emulates and elaborates aspects of themes from a Disney film aimed at 8-year-old girls (this is a noted story from the *New York Times*) may be engaging in his own version of antiestablishment action, or at least intellectually challenging, thinking in ways analogous to the post-1968 counterculture. However, the Caltech engineer may dress or look like his parents or neighbors. Just like the Caltech engineer, Seoul Bohemians are driving innovation and changing the political horizon in their own ways.

It is illuminating to see how these patterns join in distinct historical periods and local contexts. For instance, in Japan, China, and Korea, student demonstrations with speeches and political protests against the government were classic in the early 20th century. These often continued in post–World War II years, especially against authoritarian leaders and military dictators. Then for a few years after the 1970s, some Japanese and Koreans added more socially challenging themes, in dress code (beards, brightly colored hair) and political violence (famous in Tokyo subways, blocking access to the Tokyo airport and threatening or actual explosions).

But by 2010 or so, most of this more visible confrontation had subsided, perhaps as the "opportunity structure" became more accessible, petitions replaced violence. We lack a systematic global mapping of these patterns by country and time period analogous to the Lipset and Rokkan mapping of the emergence of class and party politics in the West. We have, however, offered selected propositions about factors that seem especially salient, such as the stronger Asian family and living at home. Similar if moderated patterns are common in Catholic Southern Europe, where there was minimal counter culture in the 1970s, whereas the counter culture was strong in Protestant Northern Europe and North America. This fits the analysis in Chapter 14.

REFERENCES

Lloyd, R. (2006). *Neo-bohemia: Art and commerce in the postindustrial city*. New York, NY: Routledge.
Riker, W. H., & Ordeshook, P. C. (1973). *An introduction to positive political theory*. Englewood Cliffs, NJ: Prentice-Hall.

SECTION III
THE POWER OF BUZZ: HOW THE ARTS AND CULTURE CAN ENERGIZE PARTICIPATION AND DEVELOPMENT

INTRODUCTION TO SECTION III

In "Was Tocqueville Wrong?" Clark and Silva explore some strong cases that do not fit the Tocqueville/Putnam approach. Los Angeles (LA) is the major city in the United States where citizens trust other citizens and the government least. What did LA leaders do in seeking to build trust? They followed Tocqueville's theory and created some 95 neighborhood councils starting in 1999, assuming that citizens would participate more and that it would build confidence. It worked in some neighborhoods, but failed in many others, per evaluations. With large numbers of Mexican immigrants, many LA neighborhoods shared the low trust common in most of Latin America. What to do? We suggest not looking to WASPy New England which did not fit the Latin tradition, but south of the border, for success. One of the most dramatic in Latin America is Bogotá, Colombia, which was deeply transformed by strong mayors, not citizen groups. Mayors Mockus and Penalosa used entertainment and cultural activities to oppose corruption and criminal groups. They mobilized citizen support from above, by using cultural symbols and the media. In a drought, Mayor Mockus broadcast over TV from his bathroom, demonstrating how to take a shower and conserve water. Water consumption dropped dramatically. Corrupt cops were replaced by clown-like mimes, which made the streets look like a circus and cut traffic fatalities. They used the arts, popular culture, consumption, and entertainment activities as a powerful non-Tocquevillian path to build social cohesion and government legitimacy, which they evaluated with citizen surveys. While many cities have sought to encourage local culture and social trust, the dramatic success of Bogota is particularly instructive on how these dynamics can actually work. Adding nuance to these case studies, the authors show how scenes theory suggests alternative paths to legitimacy, expanding from Weber's three authority types to more. The takeaway is that the path to legitimacy and social trust is broader than just what is proposed by Tocqueville and Putnam. Arts, culture, and consumer amenities can play a critical role.

Silver and Clark's chapter "Buzz: A Theory, Illustrated in Toronto and Chicago" explores how the arts and culture have transformed city politics. They use "buzz" to theorize this link. "Buzz" here refers to the aesthetic and symbolic feel of a cultural scene that in turn signifies that participants may enjoy certain experiences and lifestyles there. Buzz enlivens the experience of participants *within* the scene, but builds on broader cultural and political activities. It shows how artists, entertainers, and museum staff — low on traditional forms of political influence, like money or holding political office — can succeed in engaging the political process. The New York Guggenheim Museum spread globally to create affiliates from Moscow to Venice, Bilbao, and Berlin by building on buzz, combined with creative leadership, which in turn generated sponsorships. That is, buzz brought money, more than vice versa. As city policy makers increasingly seek to capitalize on the buzz created by local cultural scenes, local participants can help build policies that further their cultural activities, or mobilize loud buzzing opposition if they fail. Toronto is detailed, as a major powerful example of success, where local bohemian artists organized by local neighborhoods to preserve the character of local arts scenes against commercial development. Chicago, on the other hand, built on its traditional hierarchies of corporate leadership, a strong mayor, and coherent Democratic Party to create a more top-down set of new arts and entertainment activities, *without* the sort of overt citizen and arts group activism in Toronto. Buzz played a key role in both cities, as they moved toward becoming leaders in cultural activities. The chapter helps codify buzz as a concept to use both to interpret and influence cultural policy. Others use buzz more broadly, but we restrict it to arts-related activities.

The global importance of arts and culture is systematically documented in the chapter by Clark and Achterberg. Using the World Values Surveys (some 78,000 citizens surveyed in 22–34 nations since 1981), the authors start with the Tocqueville/Putnam/Verba et al. approach, but differ in not summing all forms of civic group participation. Rather, Clark and Achterberg pursue issue specificity and analyze arts and culture, unions, churches, and other groups separately. While many types of groups are in decline, their original contribution is to demonstrate a broad and emphatic rise in arts and culture participation and activities in many countries globally. Why has this trend been essentially ignored in social science scholarship and public policy to date? The first reason is that many cultural activities have been omitted or not recorded in standard surveys or census-like sources, especially the many new media, like watching web videos that are not sold, or belonging to an "underground" band, or performing in small, volatile improv theater groups. Related is the second reason for omission: "arts and culture" has often been construed, and reported on by the U.S. National Endowment for the Arts, for instance, primarily for their "benchmark," institutions, generally large and established like museums and opera. These are stable and sometimes in decline, like the Lions Clubs surveyed by Putnam. Yet when one asks all citizens about any arts and culture they pursue, a very different pattern appears: broad, deep, and expanding support emerges for such activities as indie rock bands, book clubs, digital art, and culture sometimes mixed with social media. People sing in church choirs, record videos of their own rap songs, and post them on YouTube and other web-based options, which provides a global audience, for instance, to Brazilian favela rappers. The arts and culture audience was growing faster among lower than higher educated persons around the year 2000, showing that this was not an elite movement. But cultural activists were very disproportionally young. Other studies by the French Ministry of Culture and more targeted surveys have added detail about specific niches, but the main result is the opposite of *Bowling Alone*; culture is on the rise.

In "How Context Transforms Citizen Participation: Propositions," Clark and Silva present eight propositions about citizens and cultural dynamics, related to the broader discussion of the rise (or decline) of culture. But they seek to move outside the Northwest European Protestant cultural area, and contrast experiences from other locations. Some propositions thus introduce factors less often discussed, such as (1) *as the welfare state retreats, civil society organizations become more important sources of legitimacy and trust.* This is a major issue in China, for instance, as the government has been dramatically supporting cultural activities, but is debating how to continue such efforts. Similar issues were widely debated in France in the early twenty-first century, as the classic "patrimonial" (national) institutions were challenged by the new (generally global) media. Or (2) the *"Democracy is more than trust" proposition: The higher the religious, ethnic, class homogeneity, the higher the levels of generalizable trust. Corollary: Trust covers only a small part of the democratic experience.* The chapter distills a wide range of ideas about how culture works, clearly stated, to help debate or empirical testing.

Navarro and Rodríguez explore the impact of local cultural amenities on the development of lifestyle practices in Spanish cities. Their main contribution is to assess and contrast individual and contextual effects involving cultural policy and citizen lifestyle. They start with a widely used status/class-based analysis of individual citizen characteristics like income and education, stressed by Bourdieu and others as driving much cultural policy. These factors, especially education and income, do have some impact on one's lifestyle choice. But they are limited. Navarro and Rodriguez include not only the social background characteristics of Bourdieu, DiMaggio, and most class analysts, they also add the social surroundings, as discussed by Jane Jacobs and others. They introduce then the local context, in terms of the mix of consumer choices on offer, and find that it too is highly signifi- cant. Think, for instance, of Seville with its grand tradition of bull fights and flamenco dancing, contrasting with the modern art galleries and contemporary music in nontraditional Barcelona. But various subgroups of the population do not react uniformly to these contextual influences. For instance, a nontraditional lifestyle seems enhanced by (at least positively associated with) the presence of nontraditional amenities, but more tradi- tional groups may reject such influences or, alternatively, may gradually assimilate to them. One takeaway is that local amenities seem to affect significantly the development of certain types of local lifestyle and, further- more, that cultural policy makers can leverage local amenities toward citizen involvement with creativity and urban development. But they also report that *less* educated citizens seem to adapt *more* to their surrounding contexts than the more educated; this might be read as consistent with Yi's findings about authoritarian leadership having more impact, even when the new policies conflict with citizen's traditional views. Navarro and Rodriguez offer an innovative approach to cultural policy theorizing. They show how adults may shift cultural consumption as they move to new locations, or as new events are presented. This is a different view of culture than the strong class perspective that treats persons whose parents were lower-status as also likely to follow "lower-status" art and culture. Their original thrust is to ask how strong are the effects of social background variation in explaining lifestyle and culture, as measured by clothes, music, and cinema? Answer, about half of the variation comes from social background. By contrast, the other half comes from the social context. This is big news. That is half the variation in reported lifestyles is not explained by the "classic" social characteristics. Life is thus less "deterministic" than these iron laws have posited.

Rather this local cultural policy focus parallels work by Laurent Fleury, for instance, in documenting the role of specific local institutions and poli- cies that can shift how citizens engage in unusual cultural activities. Distinctive arts activities, supported by corresponding arts policies, they sug- gest, can drive urban development and broaden citizens' cultural horizons.

The final chapter "Global Contexts of Politics and Arts Participation," by Clark, Silva, and Cabaço contrasts how arts and culture participation operates in three political cultures (clientelist, class politics, and the new political culture) and four cultural traditions (Eastern religions, Orthodox

Christianity, Catholicism, and Protestantism). These shifting relations are explored with the World Values Surveys and ISSP citizen surveys for hundreds of thousands of citizens globally. Democratic impacts of several sorts were analyzed, including voting, protest, trust, and support for various norms about democracy, such as duty. These multiple dimensions and contexts were used since the patterns were complex, and varied across cultural areas. For instance, arts groups and participants lean toward the bohemian or at least challenge the establishment with citizen protests, only within the new political culture and Protestant contexts, but no other contexts. Arts participation and voting are positively linked in only one context, that of class politics. But trust is unrelated to arts participation in class politics and heavily Catholic contexts, where Church support is key to trust. Clientelist contexts differ again: this is the only context where arts participation is positively related to a duty-based conception of democracy, and consistent with this ethos of duty, a citizen who belongs to an arts organization in a clientelist context is not more but less likely to participate in marches or protest activities or to support a rights-claiming conception of citizenship. Think here of the traditions of art patronized by the Roman Catholic Church, generating paintings of Christian tradition in Southern Italy or Portugal. By contrast in Orthodox Christian contexts, arts participation is minimally related to all democratic participation measures; this suggests a more passive or quiescent role for the arts, not surprising for areas with centuries of authoritarian leadership (Czarist then communist). Finally, in areas with strong Buddhist-, Taoist-, and Confucian-based civilizations, arts participation is positively related with supporting norms of citizen engagement, especially among the well-educated. But arts participation is unrelated to trust, reaffirming the Kim finding with which we began the book.

One simple lesson then is that arts participation is highly varied in its meaning and associations with different forms of citizen democratic engagement as one moves around the world. Only a handful of arts participants lean toward the more bohemian, even though many Westerner theorists, and artists, see this as standard. The chapter offers one of the first global overviews of arts participation with substantial supporting evidence. But it is best read and interpreted along with more detailed, focused studies, like the other chapters. Tocqueville changes songs as he travels globally, and his impacts range from cheers to rejection.

WAS TOCQUEVILLE WRONG? BUZZ AS CHARISMA, CREATIVITY, AND GLAMOUR; NEW SOURCES OF POLITICAL LEGITIMACY SUPPLEMENTING VOTING, AND CIVIC PARTICIPATION

Terry Nichols Clark and Filipe Carreira da Silva

ABSTRACT

This chapter explores the idea that democratic political legitimacy can emerge by other means than voting or citizen participation. Beyond these conventional methods of building legitimacy, we contend that alternative modes are emerging all over the world. Among these emergent forms are a wide range of policies, from China's economic growth to Bogotá's use of pantomime street crossing guards, replacing corrupt traffic police. Matched to their context, these policies may enhance political legitimacy. Particularly in locations with weak traditions of citizen participation, exploring alternatives to classic Tocquevillian participation may have more impact. Examining some major successes can illuminate alternative

Can Tocqueville Karaoke? Global Contrasts of Citizen Participation, the Arts and Development
Research in Urban Policy, Volume 11, 157–173
ISSN: 1479-3520/doi:10.1108/S1479-352020140000011024

dynamics. We thus feature some specific non-Tocquevillian policies to open consideration of options.

Keywords: Legitimacy; participation; comparative politics; government; public policy

GENERAL SOCIAL AND CULTURAL BACKGROUND: THE RISE OF THE NEW POLITICAL CULTURE

For centuries, leaders and their counselors have used nonparticipatory activities to seek to build legitimacy. The Roman circuses and cooptation policies were theorized by Machiavelli. Military parades on national holidays are classic around the world. But in recent decades, consciousness and discussion of political differences have increased, helped by more direct comparisons via television, travel, and new media. World courts are punishing national leaders who violate global justice standards.

But what is justice? Globalization can enhance recognition of and expansion of local differences. The League of Women Voters thought that it was a moral duty to vote, but many Chinese do not. All this can raise our consciousness about alternative ways of governing, some more and others less democratically. How can we codify these developments? Since 1982, the Fiscal Austerity and Urban Innovation (FAUI) project has surveyed over 10,000 local governments in some 35 countries. It has documented major political transformations across the world, including value shifts away from class politics and clientelism. These classic political rules have been challenged by a New Political Culture (NPC). Its new style of politics is the cumulative combination of many previous social changes, some mutually contradictory in terms of the traditional class political model: e.g., the last decades have seen moves (1) toward social liberalism (captured by Ronald Inglehart's indexes and other items) and (2) toward fiscal conservatism or, at least, resistance to taxes. How these two apparently contradictory policies have been joined is a critical issue that the NPC analysis has been detailing. What drives the shift toward the NPC? Clark and Ronald Inglehart identify 22 specific propositions, which fall under three general ideas: hierarchy, empowerment, and structural conditions (Clark & Hoffmann-Martinot, 1998: 36 ff.). Clark and Inglehart suggest seven general elements to distinguish this NPC from traditional class politics: (1) the classic left-right dimension has been transformed; (2) social and fiscal/economic issues are explicitly distinguished; (3) social issues have risen in salience relative to fiscal/economic issues; (4) market individualism and social individualism grow; (5) questioning the welfare state (national governments seem to be losing much of their legitimacy as federalism and regionalism claim new converts); (6) the rise of issue politics and broader citizen participation, alongside the decline of hierarchical political organizations; (7) these NPC views are more pervasive among younger, more educated and affluent individuals, and societies (Clark & Hoffmann-Martinot, 1998, pp. 10–13).

Two of these defining elements of NPC are particularly connected to the new forms of legitimacy discussed here. We refer to (1) "social issues have risen in salience relative to fiscal/economic issues" and (2) the "rise of issue politics and broader citizen participation." As we will show, if one takes a global view on these general changes in political culture and combines these with detailed local analyses of change, a compelling case emerges for one to discard, or seriously qualify, the power of the orthodox Tocqueville/Putnam model which holds that political participation through formal associations builds legitimacy. The alternative points rather to new forms of leadership and legitimacy that are not only more globally widespread than the New England Tocqueville/Putnam political model, but are also more in tune with the emergent forms of political culture in the past few decades. To sum up, on the one hand, one finds more individualism, consumerism, entertainment, and amenities as globalization, the Internet, and market capitalism reach more and more people around the world; on the other hand, one watches the decline of clientelism, hierarchy, and class politics. At the same time, new models of political leadership and legitimacy are needed that overcome the Anglo-Saxon bias of the prevalent Tocqueville/Putnam proposal.

UPDATING WEBER: THEORIZING LEGITIMACY THROUGH THE "THEORY OF SCENES"

Music, art, and theater critics have long invoked "scenes," but social scientists have barely addressed the concept (Blum began). Silver, Clark, and Rothfield suggested a "theory of scenes" as elements of urban/ neighborhood life; scenes have since grown into an international approach to studying contexts more coherently. Scenes have risen in salience as analysts recognize that jobs and distance explain less, and amenities and lifestyle are critical elements driving economic development and migration.

This theory of scenes is more than (1) neighborhood, (2) physical structures, (3) persons labeled by race, class, gender, education, etc. Scenes include these but stress (4) the specific combinations of these and activities (like attending a concert) which join them. These four components are in turn defined by (5) the values people pursue in a scene. General values are legitimacy, defining a right or wrong way to live; theatricality, a way of seeing and being seen by others; and authenticity, as a meaningful sense of identity. These three in turn add subdimensions, like egalitarianism, traditionalism, exhibitionism, localism, ethnicity, transgression, corporateness, and more. All the dimensions combine in specific ideal-types of scenes like Disney Heaven, Baudelaire's River Styx, and Bobo's Paradise.

Researchers have long recognized that the organization of life's necessities into meaningful social formations (neighborhoods) and that the organization of labor into larger formations (firms, industrial districts, classes) can produce significant consequences that go beyond the sum of these formations' parts (Putnam, Marx, and many others). Our proposal is that scenes organize consumption into a meaningful social activity and that these social formations can and must be studied in their own terms as modes of association.

There are three broad dimensions of experience that define what it is to approach the world as a consumer out to experience the world (rather than to reside in it or to make new products). Being a consumer means being oriented toward (1) the pleasures of appearances, the way we display ourselves to others and see their images in turn. This is theatricality. Determinate scenes give determinate meaning to the theatricality of consumers' lives. Being a consumer also means (2) being oriented toward the pleasures of having an identity, who we are and what it means to be genuine and real rather than fake and phony. This is authenticity. Determinate scenes give determinate meaning to the authenticity of consumers' lives. And finally, being a consumer means (3) orienting oneself toward the pleasures of holding moral beliefs and intentions, the authorities on which we take our judgments to be right or wrong. This is legitimacy. Determinate scenes give determinate meaning to the legitimacy of consumers' lives.

This third legitimacy dimension is most central for this chapter. Let us now see exactly how. To enter into a space of shared consumer activity is, as we have seen, to open oneself up to a world of seeing and being seen as if playing a scene, as if one were a work of art to be enjoyed and taken in. Scenes give specific meaning to this part of the consuming self through the ways they determine what counts as successful theatrical behavior. But the activity of consuming is not exhausted by its theatricality; scenes are more than human showcases. The activity of consuming is an intentional activity in which one makes decisions about what to consume, what to enjoy, what to appreciate. Intentions imply reasons; and reasons rest on authoritative standards of judgment.

Legitimacy thus defines for consumers a goal (right belief), an activity (submission/rejection of imperatives and prohibitions), and a set of substances to be worked on (the will, the intention to act). But these goals and activities can give determinate meanings to consumer life in different ways, and determinate scenes will provide different sorts of symbolic legitimations to the activity of consuming: legitimacy may be rooted in ancestral heritage and the wisdom of generations, in the exceptional personality of charismatic individuals, in the notion of equal respect for all, in the efficient and productive pursuit of individuals' material self-interest, in the expression of each person's unique creative imagination. These are five types of legitimacy that assume different rules of the game in their respective contexts or scenes. Specific scenes become the scenes they are in part by making this aspect of the consuming self-determinately meaningful in these various ways. Because the goals, activities, and standards that legitimate consumption must always be determinately specified, we focus on five specifications, or, again, subdimensions, that allow us to recognize specific forms of scenes in terms of the specific ways in which they promote different senses of the legitimacy of the consumption: traditionalistic legitimacy, egalitarian legitimacy, charismatic legitimacy, utilitarian-individualistic legitimacy, and self-expressively individualistic legitimacy.

These five types of legitimacy are certainly not exhaustive, but they do capture, to a large extent, the most common legitimation practices which groups of amenities help to cultivate. This list is an adaptation from the work of Max Weber, Robert Bellah, and Daniel Elazar. Weber, of course, famously identified three types of legitimate authority: traditional, legal-rational, and charismatic (Weber, 1978). These describe different ways in which subjects can experience exercises of power as appropriate and right rather than as arbitrary force. For our purposes, these types of legitimacy describe standards by which members of a scene experience their cultural participation as a valuable and appropriate use of their time and energy rather than wasteful, radical, sinful, or boring.

We have supplemented Weber's categories on two fronts. First, we replaced his legal-rational category (where legitimate authority is based on the formal structure of laws) with two categories: utilitarianism and expressivity. We do so, following Robert Bellah, because modern American individualism is more complicated than Weber's typology can capture. Many individuals make their judgments based on standards of efficiency and rationality, but many others seek opportunities for creative expression (Bellah, Madsen, Sullivan, Swidler, & Tipton, 1996). Secondly, following Daniel Elazar, we include egalitarianism to capture the power of the strands of New England moralism running through some parts of American and global political culture (Elazar, 1975). A moral approach to culture fits cultural activity into the larger goal of creating a "city on a hill" where all humans are treated equally regardless of origins or heritage, the pursuit of private interests is viewed as corrupting, and creative expression is a dangerous luxury. There may, of course, be important gaps in this typology, but it does describe the dominant terms in which cultural life matters to many twenty-first century citizens: as an expression of their heritage, their creativity, their charismatic heroes, their righteousness, or their industriousness. Analyzing how these vary is what makes local and national comparisons take on power through global analysis. Bogotá and Seoul must be joined with Paris and Los Angeles (LA) to bring out distinctive variations, as pursued in other chapters.

Consider the following examples of nontraditional policies that worked. These come from our FAUI project, which for over 20 years has identified creative policy innovations and helped bring them to other locations. Naples had hundreds of shrines and small parks that were closed for decades. A new administration engaged local groups to mobilize citizens and classroom students to reclaim the small shrines and parks and keep them open, in an explicit effort to broaden civic engagement, starting from neighborhood amenities. Crime is salient everywhere. Chicago's Alternative Policing Strategy created regular meetings of police and local neighbors to review strategies and collaborate on improving safety. Crime has dropped substantially. Chicago has created Tax Increment Financing districts that sponsor neighborhood development initiatives. They obtain funding from property value growth in the neighborhood area. Funds are used to improve the district, thereby channeling funds that are not reviewed in the normal ways by the city government.

These examples seem to suggest that democracy does not require voting and citizen participation, i.e., political legitimacy can be attained through channels other than those suggested by Tocqueville.

CONCRETE CHALLENGES TO THE NEW ENGLAND TOCQUEVILLE/PUTNAM POLITICAL MODEL: THE LA CASE

A New Political Culture (NPC) as the FAUI project has abundantly shown since the 1980s (in numerous publications, see www.faui.org), is emerging as class politics and clientelism decline, especially among the most urban, affluent strata of societies. The proposed "theory of scenes" comprehends several dimensions, including legitimacy. In the remainder of the chapter, we show how the emerging forms of legitimacy, leadership, and citizenship in Latin America, southern Europe, and Chicago are expressions of the NPC, and in particular, how the theory of scenes is a distinctly useful analytical tool to make sense of contextual variations.

An alternative to the Tocqueville/Putnam analytical model is that a more sensitive cultural palette might help us repaint some of the traditional (New England-inspired) institutions to make them more palatable to persons who find their intricacies off-putting. Or altogether different institutions may be crafted or ridden to capture the energies and passions of persons whose cultural backgrounds are closer to the matador than the civics teacher. One source of inspiration one can draw upon is concrete, successful cases of new modes of securing democratic political legitimacy other than voting or citizen participation.

With those categories in mind, let us now turn briefly to a specific example: LA. National studies show that LA citizens are among the most alienated from their government, and least trusting of other citizens as well as political leaders (in studies by Putnam, DeLeon, and Baldassare). Much of the "crisis" of governance in LA today concerns legitimacy. What rules should be followed in local governance? The secession effort of Hollywood and the San Fernando Valley, the referenda limiting rights of immigrants, the termination of affirmative action in the University of California system, the recall of one governor and election of another in mid-term, and choosing Terminator Schwarzenegger as governor — these all testify to deeper and broader challenges over legitimacy and competing rules of the game.

One solution adopted in LA was inspired by Tocqueville: create nearly 100 Neighborhood Councils where citizens could participate more actively. How does this compare to other policy options?

These problems are not unique to LA or California. A classic theme in our FAUI project is the conflict between clientelism/patronage and democratic reform. This is the deepest single issue facing governments the world over in the early twenty-first century. With the majority of LA ethnic groups (45% of LA residents) from Latin America, others from Asia, and earlier the American South and Southern-border states (African-Americans and whites), these citizens come from political systems and cultural traditions with deeply different conceptions of rules than Tocqueville's New England, and very different definitions of legitimacy and morality. The day to day conflicts over personality and smaller issues are often surface manifestations of divisions over what are the appropriate rules of the game to follow in government/citizen relations.

The classic clientelist pattern was that the Padrone/patron would care for his followers in paternalistic manner – in jobs, favors, and contracts. Followers in turn would support his leadership, via voting, political work, or cash. This approach to politics and civic life is still dominant in most of the world today, and was long strong in areas like the American South (the old boys' network) and cities like Chicago and Boston. But California was created when Progressives were dominant nationally, the mood was one of democratic reform and the state constitution even required nonpartisan elections for local government. California had the strongest tradition in the USA of the efficient city managers, who governed in nonpartisan, low-keyed manner, with civic groups and elected officials in the background. The style was quietly consensual. This long dominated California state and especially local politics, as shown in repeated studies over the twentieth century, such as Eulau and Prewitt, *Labyrinths of Democracy*, and a series of works by Eugene Lee and others from the Institute of Local Government at the University of California, Berkeley.

But in the late 1960s, this political culture was openly challenged as "WASPy, nonresponsive, unprogressive" and worse – by activists including women's groups, Hispanics, African-Americans, and others. Dale Marshall, Browning, and Tabb probed this transition with specific case details in a volume, then repeatedly updated. Originally, they focused on 10 cities in the Bay Area, but as they updated, they added LA, which they characterized as distinctly "uncivil" and fraught with ethnic tensions. Robert Putnam led national surveys of citizen participation in some 60 U.S. metro areas about 2000, including San Francisco and LA. Richard DeLeon analyzed these Putnam-collected data and showed LA citizens to be on many measures the most alienated, individualist, nonparticipatory, fearful, and untrusting set of persons surveyed in any major U.S. city. Distilled versions of this angst fill the books on LA by Mike Davis, Michael Moore, and Michael Dear.

Most of these studies are based on comparing contemporary California with its past or with other U.S. regions, and identifying the cleavage as ethnic, associated with the rise in numbers and political visibility of Hispanics especially. But one distinctive contribution of our FAUI project is to help show that California for much of the twentieth century was the outlier, if one took a global perspective. Since 2000, California is being forced to confront many of the same deep problems that citizens and leaders are fighting over in Taipei, Mexico City, Cairo, and Bogotá. Clientelism versus democratic participation continues globally.

Hispanic citizens in LA are thus torn between (1) the political tradition that they knew, with like or dislike, in Mexico, essentially for most, a strong party-led clientelism; (2) political reform in Mexico, with leaders like Vincente Fox focusing on morality, corruption, and symbolic issues, dramatically challenging traditional Mexican party clientelism, (3) white protestant style politics and Tocquevillian civic activity. The pattern across Latin America is alienation, distrust, cynicism, and low participation. This is seen as bordering on crisis by many observers, in books from Alejandro Moreno, John Sudarsky and others, who have done careful surveys of citizen participation in civic groups across Latin America and contrasted these patterns with those in Europe and North America. The same patterns that Putnam/DeLeon report for LA are thus even more intense and conflictual in Latin America (and many other countries around the world).

This is complex to interpret as there are thus many competing sub-cultures and political candidates among Hispanics in LA (and the rest of the USA). The traditional patronage leaders are being challenged, but the new alternative forms of leadership are not clear or broadly accepted. It is a period of fundamental transition and thus inevitable conflict over whose rules are legitimate or corrupt. Confrontation over the basic rules of the game are thus to be expected as much of the policy content is far from New England Tocquevillian style politics, which only began to challenge for instance Chicago traditions in the late twentieth century.

Most of the world is closer to the American South, to Latin America, than it is New England. Seen globally, LA's "glamour" can be reframed in ways that fit better with indigenous themes in Taipei or Dakar than do many aspects of civic life in Salem, Massachusetts.

The voyage of discovery is not seeking new landscapes but in having new eyes.

Marcel Proust

OTHER CONCRETE EXAMPLES: LATIN AMERICA, SOUTHERN EUROPE, CHICAGO

Bogotá, Naples, and Chicago are the sources of a new style of leadership and citizenship, new modes for engaging citizens that often are in conflict with the Tocqueville/Putnam tradition which focuses on participating in the formally organized group, like the Kiwanis Club or League of Women Voters or the new LA Neighborhood Councils.

Rather, mayors in Naples, Chicago, and especially Bogotá have developed highly popular, symbolic forms of leadership, joined in specific actions, as alternative modes of governance that work (instead of the classic civic group). We have worked with Eleonora Pasotti, whose *Political Branding in Cities* details policies in these three cities. Many patterns are broadly shared by many other locations in Southern and Eastern Europe, Latin American, and other parts of the world, including Chicago. Chicago's residents in the twentieth century were predominantly Roman Catholic. The neighborhood parishes and Democratic Party precinct captains, with leaders from Ireland, Poland, Italy and others who came up through the Church and Party built a political culture drastically different from Tocqueville's New England (see Chapter 10). The traditional patterns were founded on distrust, alienation, and cynicism felt by many outside the Church and Party that makes the Tocqueville model distinctly more difficult to construct. It is much harder for groups and citizens to negotiate and compromise if they barely trust the others. These examples seem to suggest that democracy does not require voting and citizen participation, i.e., political legitimacy can be attained through channels other than those suggested by the Tocqueville/Putnam model. But how to transcend the classic distrust and alienation resurfaced in the Eurozone fiscal crisis about 2010, dividing the Southern from Northern Europeans. The Chinese leadership is similarly exploring ways to gradually involve more citizens, for instance by using "social organizations," and other nongovernmental voluntary-type associations. (Meghan Kallman, Terry Clark, and Jianzhong Xia completed a volume on these issues, published in Mandarin by the Chinese Ministry of Civil Affairs, termed *The Third Sector in English*: https://dl. dropboxusercontent.com/u/5559963/China%20Report.Version.35.2.Feb. 2011.PLUS. Appendix.doc.zip). The lessons in the present volume should feed into these policy debates as well as more general theorizing.

As the world area with the lowest trust scores recorded in standard surveys, Latin America is the first place we looked for some sort of success.

How could one negotiate around distrust and offer policy solutions that built on a political culture very different from New England's Calvinism? Most writers offer despair, revolution, or a loose version of Tocqueville. There is more. Packaged together, they might be termed buzz, with a Spanish accent. Take the example of Colombia's capital, Bogotá. During the 1980s and 1990s, Bogotá was known mostly for being murder capital of the world, one of the most violent cities globally, with a peak rate of approximately six times the US murder rate. Bogotá was a clear reflection of Colombia's critical situation of continuing civil war, drug-related crime, and rampant political corruption. But in 1995, after an unusual political campaign, former university professor of math and philosophy, Antanas Mockus, was elected mayor. This highly charismatic mayor introduced a new style of political leadership that contradicted most of the assumptions of the Tocqueville/Putnam model. Yet his "Civic Culture Program" was a resounding success, creatively empowering citizens to solve many of the common problems that affect urban life.

In fact, Mockus turned Putnam's Tocquevillian logic on its head. Instead of conceiving of good government as the product of civicness, Mockus's innovative "Civic Culture Program" demonstrated that civicness could actually be a product of good government. Bogotá's administration under Mockus made extensive use of every sort of pedagogical device, communication strategies, and symbolic language to engage citizens in the transformation of the everyday use of urban contexts. In short, city government became a catalyst for collective action and cooperation. Mockus said the city was his classroom. How did Mockus' Civic Culture Program promote an increased sense of belonging and responsibility among Bogotá's residents? What kinds of policies were developed in his two 3-year terms as mayor? He featured these when he ran for President of Colombia, and had some 40% support in the polls. Consult the brilliant set of YouTube videos with English subtitles. Some of these new, creative policies are listed here (Fig. 1).

1. Policy: Traffic-directing mimes
   The original introduction of nearly 500 mimes to remind citizens of traffic rules. Dressed in outrageous costumes, with white faces, and using grand, exaggerated movements, they created a circus-like atmosphere. People laughed. By "interrupting" bad old habits, the traffic-directing mimes achieved in a few months what decades of conventional law enforcement had failed to achieve: it reintroduced citizens to traffic rules by confronting them with an unexpected, artistic event. Interruption in order to

Fig. 1.   Mayor Mockus as "Super Citizen."

reframe usual procedures was the rationale behind the usage of mimes: dressed like clowns and monks, the mimes discouraged bad habits like honking.

2. Policy: Use of referee-like cards

   Almost 350,000 referee-like cards were distributed to the Bogotá's motorists to express their approval or disapproval with "thumbs up" or "thumbs down" cards. The adoption of the cards by motorists was so successful that they soon became part of social interactions in everyday life of Bogotá.

   Result: 50% decrease in traffic accidents in less than 10 years.

3. Policy: Antigun campaign

   Mockus' administration launched an antigun campaign calling for the voluntary handing over of guns. Even though only 1% of weapons were collected (some 1,500), the fact that they were melted and made into sculptures of Gerber baby spoons had a significant symbolic impact.

   Result: In the month of the voluntary decommissioning, the homicide rate dropped by 26%.

4. Policy: "Women's Night Out"
This government-decreed voluntary curfew for men was meant to articulate the gender biases underlying violent criminality. It basically encouraged women to go out at night, and discouraged men from doing so in those particular nights (Pérez, 2006).
Result: Police statistics show no homicides during those "Women's Night Out."

5. Policy: Vaccination against violence
This symbolic vaccination against violence involved some 45,000 children and adults, in a city-wide performance therapy against the "epidemic" of rampant violence that had become a cliché in Colombia.
Result: The combined effect of this and other initiatives such as reconciliation between antagonistic groups and peaceful conflict resolution was a dramatic decrease of the homicide rate from 81 per 100,000 in 1993 to 35 per 100,000 on 2000, a rate lower than many cities in the USA.

6. Policy: Water consumption reduction campaign
In 1997, due to a tunnel malfunction, Bogotá faced substantial water shortages, which called for investment in a new water reservoir. Mockus' innovative solution was to show up on TV with very practical consumption saving tips, including showing himself showering, frugally. This showed citizens that saving water began in your shower, and could work. Moreover, the population was kept informed of the water consumption levels through widely publicized weekly reports.
Result: Water consumption dropped so much that the need for investment was deferred 15 years, and savings reallocated to help the disadvantaged.

7. Policy: Participatory budget
Mayor Mockus introduced a consultation form of participatory budgeting. His approach, however, was much more symbolic (and funny) than most similar experiences in South America and Europe. Each citizen attending the meeting in their local mayoralty was given coins and a card. On the card, they were supposed to write what they considered the most pressing need for their locality, and they were then supposed to deposit the coins in a ballot box with six transparent tubes, one for each policy area of the development plan.
Result: The results were immediately quantifiable and made public, itself a lesson of (quite literally) transparency.

8. Policy: Solving urban traffic congestion through Transmilenio SA

Transmilenio SA is a government agency, created by the successor of Mockus, Peñalosa, to coordinate the city's transportation through a partnership with the 62 private bus companies operating in Bogotá. This setup allowed the city government to lower pressure from trade unions, compared to cities where bus drivers remain city employees. The Transmilenio model was a high-capacity arterial network of buses very much like a subway system: it travels in exclusive lanes, passengers buy their tickets on the platforms, and within a few seconds 160 passengers mount and dismount the bus. Additionally, car usage was discouraged and bicycle paths were built on a massive scale (42% of Bogotá residents used these systems).

Result: In just 3 years, the Peñalosa administration revolutionized transportation in Bogotá: average speed during traffic hour improved from 5 to 18 km/h; number of cars during rush hour decreased by a third; delegations from cities as different as Lima, Jakarta, and Teheran flocked to Bogotá to learn from this new experience, boosting citizen's pride (on its website, Transmilenio is subtitled "Capital Pride").

In sum, as the examples above show, improvements in security, finances, transportation, and public space suggest that Bogotá generated more successful collective actions and boosted citizen cooperation. Contrary to the Tocqueville/Putnam model, membership in voluntary associations actually decreased by 40% in that city between 1997 and 2001 (Sudarsky, 2003).

In addition, participation in community action boards and local action boards dropped between 1980 and 1997, with no other form of association taking their place (Gutiérrez, 1998, pp. 39–41). Other institutional innovations, such as citizen overseeing organizations (Veedurías Ciudadanas), also declined despite the initial enthusiasm with which the promoters of participatory democracy defended them. This already hints at one of the distinctive traits of Bogotá's transformation. In contrast to a society-centered perspective such as that of Putnam, the city government played a crucial role in creating the conditions for cooperation and collective action. Bogotá's innovations thus illustrate a paradigmatic shift toward an NPC based on citizen empowerment and issue politics. Irony, humor, the arts, and theatricality were introduced into the streets by the mayor and street mimes to save lives, money, and water, and transform citizen's feeling about their city and its leadership.

The lesson to draw from Bogotá, Naples, and LA, is that new problems and new publics require new solutions. In other words, old forms of political legitimacy are weakened and undermined: citizens, especially in locations with weak traditions of citizen participatory democracy, are nowadays more alienated, individualistic, and sophisticated than in the past. Mayors in such locations thus often consider other ways to engage citizens than the participation prescribed by the Tocqueville/Putnam tradi-tion. Some, like Mockus in Bogotá, took recourse to a mixture of charis-matic legitimacy and self-expressively individualistic legitimacy to attain his goals, with considerable success. Even though traditionalistic, egalitarian- and utilitarian-individualistic forms of legitimacy might still retain some of their appeal and power, his success illustrated support for more individua-listic, charismatic, and creative forms of legitimacy. These may not work everywhere, but Bogota is not a college town in Northern Europe.

Innovations, i.e., exceptions to the Tocqueville/Putnam model, abound. We need to look further across the world, and incorporate more diverse approaches to enrich our understanding of democratic options and pat-terns. In Brazil, for instance, a growing number of congressmen were elected for religious reasons; ethnic voting is often as strong as it ever was; new electronic media (blogs, talk-shows, chat-groups, social media) are changing the political landscape. (Putnam openly derides their potential for building trust since electronic media lack face-to-face personal interaction.) The New England-inspired rule of civic participation seems, from this perspective, more an anomaly than the normal global pattern. Yet, political legitimacy can be enhanced by means other than voting: India's strong economic performance, with over 150 million lifted out of poverty since 2000 (Rao, 2013), is an eloquent example of actions connecting to citizens' values that make electoral participation and civic engagement through formal associations superfluous from the standpoint of political legitimacy. Many roads lead to political legitimacy, and the Tocqueville/Putnam one is no more than that – one among others. When these different political cultures clash, as say in LA, it may be vain to attempt to impose one normative model on citizens unfamiliar with one specific political tradition. Alienation will, and has, followed.

CONCLUSION

Discussion of building legitimacy via citizen participation, by many civic leaders and by social scientists, has been dominated by the Tocqueville/ Putnam approach. It is not wrong, but incomplete, especially in areas of the world with weak exposure to the Northwest European Protestant tradi-tions of individualistic democracy. We need more.

This chapter proposes a set of concepts and some core propositions about alternative mechanisms that may successfully engage citizens with their political systems, in addition to voting and civic participation, as stressed by the Tocqueville/Putnam tradition. Charisma and individualistic self-expression are two resources, as well as two dimensions of legitimacy, which political leaders around the world have employed with considerable success to attain their political goals, including legitimating themselves and building trust among citizens. Take the example of the arts and entertainment as new major areas of especially local policy making. The joining of dozens of individual amenities (food, drink, music, crowds, youthful excitement) in festivals and mega-cultural events, etc., can powerfully engage citizens, as an alternative to participation in the local neighbors association. To value more the latter than the former, as suggested by most of literature (that portion influenced by Tocqueville/Putnam), is to miss what is perhaps the fundamental social change in the late twentieth century – the shift from a class-based style of politics to an issue-based, more individualistic and consumption-oriented mode of citizenship and political legitimacy. There is a new kid in town and he is not joining the local Kiwanis Club or Boy Scouts. He seldom votes. But he goes to large concerts, enjoys certain sports events as participant and spectator, hangs out at locations he finds attractive in his leisure time, and has a distinctive set of friends. Sensitive civic and political organizers, those who work in the streets with new social movements and new forms of activism, do not waste time lamenting the past but seek to engage these participants via building new scenes. In the years to come, as the media and more fluid arrangements like scenes grow more visible and more thoroughly documented, even social scientists may come to accept that race, class, and gender are not sufficient drivers to join and to vote, and that joining and voting are not the only mechanism that build legitimacy and trust, and a workable political system.

ACKNOWLEDGMENT

Revised from presentations to European Conference on Political Research, Pisa, Italy, 6–8 September 2007 and International Social Survey Programme, Chicago, 2008.

REFERENCES

Bellah, R., Madsen, R., Sullivan, W. M., Swidler, A., & Tipton, S. M. (1996). *Habits of the heart*. Berkeley, CA: University of California Press.
Clark, T. N., & Hoffmann-Martinot, V. (Eds.). (1998). *The new political culture*. Boulder, CO: Westview Press.

Elazar, D. (1975). The American cultural matrix. In D. J. Elazar & J. Zikmund II (Eds.), *The ecology of American political culture* (pp. 13–42). New York, NY: Thomas Y. Crowell.

Gutiérrez, F. (1998). *La ciudad representada: Political y conflicto en Bogotá.* Bogotá: Tercer Mundo Editores.

Pérez, F. (2006). *Unsettling civil society and democratization: Cultural practices and politics in Bogotá.* M.A. thesis. University of Chicago.

Rao, K. (2013, July 24). Poverty level in India drops to 22%: PlanComm. Retrieved from http://www.hindustantimes.com/business-news/poverty-level-in-india-drops-to-22-plan comm/article1-1097415.aspx

Sudarsky, J. (2003). Densidad y articulación de la sociedad civil de Bogotá:localidades y sectores. Alcaldia Mayor de Bogotá.

Weber, M. (1978). *Economy and society: An outline of interpretive sociology.* In G. Roth & C. Wittich (Eds.). Berkeley, CA: University of California Press.

BUZZ: A THEORY, ILLUSTRATED IN TORONTO AND CHICAGO

Daniel Silver and Terry Nichols Clark

ABSTRACT

The rise of arts and culture is transforming citizen politics. Though new to many social scientists, this is a commonplace for many policy makers. We seek to overcome this divide by joining culture and the arts with classic concepts of political analysis. We offer an analytical framework incorporating the politics of cultural policy alongside the typical political and economic concerns. Our framework synthesizes several research streams that combine in global factors driving the articulation of culture into political/economic processes. The contexts of Toronto and Chicago are explored as both enhanced the arts dramatically, but Toronto engaged artists qua citizens, while Chicago did not.

Keywords: Art; culture; policy; urban; politics; economic growth

How can the arts be joined with citizen participation? This chapter proposes reorganizing past concepts to illuminate the arts. Ideas like resources, context, framing, and political culture are adapted to incorporate arts and

Can Tocqueville Karaoke? Global Contrasts of Citizen Participation, the Arts and Development
Research in Urban Policy, Volume 11, 175–220
Copyright © 2014 by Emerald Group Publishing Limited
All rights of reproduction in any form reserved
ISSN: 1479-3520/doi:10.1108/S1479-352020140000011025

culture through the concept of buzz. Buzz adds more coherent dynamics to the "soft power" idea from international relations.

In the concluding paragraphs of *The Economy of Cities*, Jane Jacobs left her readers with a fanciful piece on what she considered "one of the most pressing and least regarded" problems facing cities.

> I'm not one who believes that flying saucers carry creatures from other solar systems who poke curiously into our earthly affairs. But if such beings were to arrive, with their marvelously advanced contrivances, we may be sure we would be agog to learn how their technology worked. The important question, however, would be something quite different: What kinds of governments had they invented which had succeeded in keeping open the opportunities for economic and technological development instead of closing them off? Without helpful advice from outer space, this remains one of the most pressing and least regarded problems. (Jacobs, 1969, p. 235)

Jacobs' book barely touches on politics. Instead, she focuses on urban economics, arguing that (1) development in general is driven by cities more than the countryside and (2) urban development is driven by innovation more than efficiency. She elaborates these points in rich and detailed ways that have been popularized and expanded by her followers such as Edward Glaeser and Richard Florida. But she could not even begin to imagine the potential forms of urban politics that would foster what would later be called "creative cities." Such governments in her mind could only be the stuff of science fiction.

Writing in 1968, Jacobs can be excused for this failure of imagination but contemporary urban theorists – followers of Jacobs, but not only those – cannot. The social world has changed since 1968. Citizens participate more in the arts, culture, and creative activities of all sorts in recent years. Increases are higher for middle and low status persons, especially in the United States, Canada, and Northern Europe, detailed later. "The Creative City" features high on political agendas of cities worldwide. Political leaders and styles of urban government have in some cities dramatically changed, adding culture and innovation to their past repertoires. How can we analyze and interpret these new developments? What kinds of governments and forms of political power do they involve?

We suggest some theoretical tools to add arts and culture to broader social science concepts. Our primary contributions in this chapter are conceptual, synthetic, and analytical. Many of our points are not new per se. We bring them together into a single picture and seek to join them with traditional models where the arts and culture barely register.

We first outline key global factors driving the "rise of arts culture" and discuss how these are mediated by local context. The global factors we identify synthesize research in parts of sociology, politics, and economics.

The local processes we discuss highlight the "bearers" of these global factors. We then develop a theoretical framework for interpreting these changes. We build on classic approaches (e.g., Dahl, Peterson) stressing the plurality of resources that can be brought to bear on political decisions in different ways depending on the issue area. Drawing on the notion of "symbolic media of exchange" from Talcott Parsons and Jeffrey Alexander, we propose treating "buzz" as a valuable symbolic resource generated by cultural scenes. This is a resource, we suggest, that can be wielded, in certain situations and issue areas, to influence political decisions. "Cultural power" is increasingly a real factor; it is part of the soft power that international relations analysts have used to extend work on military and economic factors. We illustrate this power at work with a compressed summary of our studies of political controversies over cultural policy in Toronto and Chicago. Both actively used culture to transform their images and economies since the late 20th century, but Toronto illustrates a rather Tocquevillian dynamic, driven by neighborhood arts groups, while Chicago does not.

THE ARTICULATION OF CULTURE AND CREATIVITY INTO POLITICS

Cultural and creative activity is growing more important worldwide. Particular cases must be situated in the context of these broader developments. We see three major trends driving this global process. Each heightens the others.

The Rise of Arts and Culture among Citizens

Though Putnam's *Bowling Alone* (2000) sparked discussion and controversy with the finding that American participation in civic associations has declined since the 1950s, he failed to detail changes in specific types of activities. There may be fewer bowling and Kiwanis clubs, but other types of belonging are gaining salience. Indeed, as given in Table 1, there is overall growth between 1981 and 2000 in cultural organization membership (like museums) by citizens in 27 out of 35 countries surveyed by the World Values Survey (only 35 include over time data by organizational type). Growth is strongest in the Netherlands, Scandinavia, the United States, and Canada, where membership in cultural organizations rose over 10 percent and was much higher among younger persons. Fig. 1 illustrates the dramatic

Table 1.   The Rise of Culture: Membership in Culture Related
Organizations, World Values Survey.

Country	1981	1990	2000	Delta
Netherlands	12.5	34.6	45.2	32.7
USA	13.9	19.7	36.9	23
Sweden	13.0	12.7	26.7	13.7
Finland	3.1	20.1	14.6	11.5
Canada	9.7	17.7	20.1	10.4
Denmark	6.2	12.5	16.6	10.4
Belgium	10.3	16.2	18.9	8.6
Iceland	7.6	13.8	15.5	7.9
Estonia		11.1	7.9	7.9
South Korea	3.2	11.0		7.8
Japan	3.8	6.0	11.0	7.2
Norway	6.6	13.5		6.9
Italy	3.9	4.9	9.9	6.0
West Germany	6.1	12.0		5.9
South Africa	8.2		13.5	5.3
Britain	6.1	9.3	10.4	4.3
Ireland	6.7	10.1	10.9	4.2
Argentina	5.3	5.9	9.0	3.7
Mexico	6.5	11.5	9.5	3.0
France	5.6	8.8	8.1	2.5
Spain	4.9	5.3	6.6	1.7
Northern Ireland	6.1	10.9	7.6	1.5
Hungary		2.5	3.6	1.1
Romania		1.6	2.6	1.0
Austria	13.0	8.0	13.2	0.2
Chile		9.3	9.3	0.0
Bulgaria		4.3	4.0	−0.3
Portugal		6.2	3.7	−2.5
Brazil		5.4	2.4	−3
Latvia		6.8	3.7	−3.1
Russia		4.9	1.2	−3.7
Lithuania		7.3	2.9	−4.4
China		7.3	2.2	−5.1

Data are from World Values Surveys of national samples of citizens in each country, about 1,500 per country, 3,525 in the United States. The three columns for each year show the percent of citizens who replied that they participated in cultural and related activities. "Delta" is the percentage change from the first to the last year. Question: A066. "Please look carefully at the following list of voluntary organizations and activities and say ... which if any do you belong to? Education, Arts, Music or Cultural Activities." To assess measurement error due to inclusion of education, we recomputed the results for parents and nonparents of school age children. There were minimal differences.

scale of this process in the particular case of Canada. Between 1999 and 2008, the number of bowling alleys, amusement and theme parks, and drinking establishments declined, while musical groups, dance companies, independent artists, and performing arts establishments increased, outpacing a total average growth rate of 14 percent for all businesses. Sports facilities and clubs also rose steeply. Many of these changes are even more dramatic in specific cities and regions, not only in Toronto and Vancouver which enjoyed large gains in many arts establishments, but also in smaller places like Peterborough, ON, and Penticton, BC, which saw significant increases, for example, in the number of interior design firms. This sort of

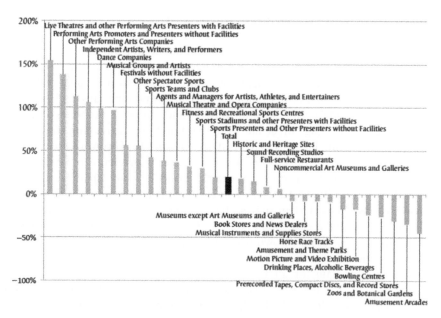

Fig. 1. Canadian Percent Change in Various Amenities, 1999–2008. The figure shows the percentage change in the total number of various arts, culture, and leisure business establishments across Canada between 1999 and 2008, according to Canadian Business Patterns. For example, dance companies and musical groups nearly doubled in this period. The black bar shows change in total businesses as a benchmark; everything to the left grew faster than total businesses did, everything to the right either grew more slowly or contracted during this period. These are six digit NAICS categories, descriptions of which are available at http://datalib.chass.utoronto.ca/codebooks/cstdli/naics.htm. *Source*: Statistics Canada, Canadian Business Patterns (1999–2008).

transformation, far beyond what population change or income growth alone could explain, suggests a potentially major breakthrough of expressive culture and personal creativity into the populace at large.

This rise is also evident in other arenas: household spending on culture, the size of cultural industries, the growth of cultural employment, and government spending. The movement is uneven across localities and not always linear within them, yet still large and cross-national. See Clark and da Silva (2009) for these cross-national trends, as well as more specifics on key countries like France and Korea.

Rediscovery of the Urbane

If the mid to late 20th century was an era of suburbanization, the early 21st century is rediscovering and reclaiming the urbanity of central cities. Internationally, there is a general rise since the 1980s in young, affluent college graduates, and retirees moving into cities and especially their down-town cores, raising urban cultural tourism and stressing day-to-day urban issues such as walking, street life, adaptive reuse, and gardening (from the Paris Plage to the Times Square pedestrian zone to Toronto's Evergreen Brickworks). These movements are supported by globally oriented city governments vying for creative people, tourists, and financial capital (e.g., CEOs for Cities) and seeking to cultivate urbanist sensibilities among local citizens.[1] Why? Urban analysts have mapped components of the change, yet not formulated a clear interpretation. Gyourko, Mayer, and Sinai (2006) show that the rise of downtown real-estate values and rent in the largest U.S. cities is much faster than the national average. Analogously, Cortwright (2005) presents data for all U.S. metro areas on the dramatic increase of young persons. But these authors do not explain why; they stay close to stan-dard census data. Richard Florida's interpretation stresses preferences of a creative class for tolerant cities. Edward Glaeser highlights increases in idea generation that arise from dense concentrations and thick networks of skilled persons. On his account, the rediscovery of the urbane is occurring because idea production has become more economically significant with the decline of manufacturing and the rise of knowledge work. Saskia Sassen suggests the importance of personal relations among global actors who prefer downtowns, and that producer services and globalization of capital are drivers. David Harvey stresses a shift from managerialism to entrepreneurialism in local gov-ernance caused by heightened interurban competition, leading cities to pursue intensive development strategies often oriented less toward local service provision and more toward cultural image and place making on the global stage (Harvey, 1989; see also Brenner & Theodore, 2005).

Rise of a New Political Culture

This is documented in Clark and Hoffmann-Martinot (1998), Clark (2003), and elsewhere. Forms of political activism and legitimation are changing. Lifestyle and social issues have been rising in salience relative to party loyalty, class, and material concerns. Fiscal conservatism is increasingly joined with social liberalism; new forms of participation and legitimacy have emerged, driven less by traditional class and primordial group characteristics and more by consumption and quality of life issues, like Starbucks, NASCAR, Wal-Mart, hunting, art galleries, and farmer's markets. Ramirez, Navarro, and Clark (2008) provide a detailed review of the literature and data for business and political salience in hundreds of North American and European local governments, documenting a striking increase in the weight given by citizens to social and lifestyle issues as well as new forms of political activism outside of traditional parties.

This process has been driven by a number of factors across multiple domains. Fig. 2 summarizes these, adding a specifically cultural pathway to the model initially presented in Clark and Hoffmann-Martinot (1998). Economic factors include rising general affluence and high-tech/ information services and declines in agriculture and manufacturing employments. Social factors include the slimming family, increasing individualism, and gains in general levels of education and media access. Cultural factors include the decline of absolutist and mechanistic styles of thought and the rise of relativism, from Einstein to Picasso. Governmental factors include the welfare state and other social programs.

Our present concern is not to detail and assess the causes or nature of these processes but rather to highlight their collective impacts, such as on city politics. Typically, these dynamics are treated in isolation, or only two out of three analyzed.[2] However, all three processes generate increasing salience for arts and cultural matters as key drivers of local politics, that is, neighborhood and city decisions, coalitions, and controversies. Fig. 3 illustrates their joint operation.

These three factors join to link culture to local politics through a number of mechanisms:

1. The rise of culture gives new importance to expressive concerns – what kind of person am I? How is this expressed in film, music, clothes, and

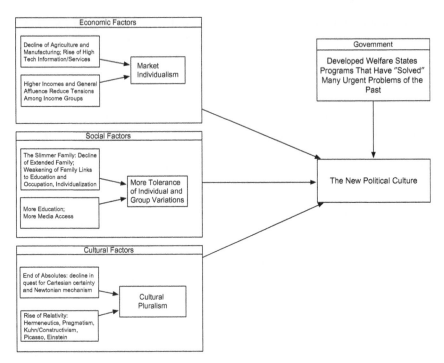

Fig. 2.   Factors Driving Toward a New Political Culture.

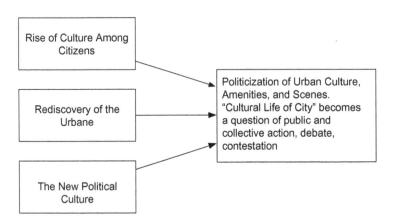

Fig. 3.   Global Factors Driving the Articulation of Culture into City Politics.

comportment? What sorts of social audiences are in a position to appreciate and share such expressive performances of self? The goals or functional purposes of products are complemented by their design, their appeal to the personality, and meanings valued by consumers – the iPod is a prototypical case. Talcott Parsons (1971) traced the emergence of this attitude in the 1960s counterculture to a reaction against utilitarian rationalism and bureaucracy. This, he argued, recombined and heightened, in a new context, the early Christian notion of Love, 19th century Romanticism, and Eastern practices of meditation and body work. He called it the "expressive revolution" and considered it to be as world historically important as the industrial, democratic, and educational revolutions. Noting a diffusion of what Harold Rosenberg called "the tradition of the new," where culture becomes more closely identified with modernist creativity and innovation, Daniel Bell (1973) and Charles Taylor (2007) have made similar statements, as have European authors such as Boltanski and Chiapello (2005). Dozens of case studies explore recent aspects of these trends, like those of Elizabeth Currid (2007) and Daniel Pink (2006), some of which have made their way into more popular literature, such as Postrel (2004).

2. The rediscovery of the urbane joins quality of life to quality of place concerns. This motivates considerations about what kind of place, neighborhood, or city enables one to pursue a life deemed worthy, interesting, beautiful, or authentic (on authenticity, see Grazian, 2003; Zukin, 2010). Cultural scenes, defined by the expressive meanings projected by cafes, restaurants, music venues, galleries, bakeries, farmers' markets, and the like, become fixtures in the urban landscape and more salient in decisions about where to live and work (Silver, Clark, & Navarro Yáñez, 2010). Even Logan and Molotch (1987) in the new introduction to *City Fortunes* stress these concerns. These expressive dynamics are enhanced by global processes including the Internet and wider competition, spurring deeper searches for meaning and identity which can be distinctly symbolic in addition to the more widely discussed economic (Harvey, 1989; Sassen, 1994). Thus, symbolic entrepreneurs can play critical roles in developing new cultural themes and products alongside financial entrepreneurs; and sometimes the two can overlap and even be identical.

3. The new political culture redefines these issues of quality, culture, and place in political terms: by emphasizing how nascent leaders and social movements champion specific lifestyle issues and consumption concerns. New questions gain political and policy traction, such as how to create attractive and vibrant scenes that offer amenities (parks, music venues,

bike paths, etc.) supportive of citizens' quality of life demands; how to use these amenities and scenes as levers for economic growth, community development, and social welfare concerns; and how, for elected officials and movement leaders, to mobilize citizens' emotional allegiance to particular types of cultural activities and scenes for electoral advantage and other policy goals.

These three factors have combined to make city political and civic leaders a new vanguard party reshaping cities in a more culturally expressive direction (cf., Lee, 2003; Pasotti, 2009; Smith, 2002). In 1975, Saul Bellow wrote, "there were beautiful and moving things in Chicago, but culture was not one of them" (Bellow, 1975, p. 69). Yet by 2009, the Director of the National Endowment of the Arts could say: "Mayor Daley should be the No. 1 hero to everyone in this country who cares about art" (in The Theater Loop, 2009).

THE ARTICULATION OF CULTURE INTO CITY POLITICS: LOCAL LOGICS

The bearers or agents of these new processes grew more active after the 1970s via "New Social Movements" (NSMs). They drove many cutting edge issues emerging in the closing decades of the 20th century. They extended both individualism and egalitarianism. They also joined consumption and lifestyle issues with the classic production and workplace concerns championed by unions and parties. These new civic groups pressed new agendas – ecology, feminism, peace, gay rights, etc. – that the older political parties ignored. Over time, other aesthetic and amenity concerns also arose, such as suburban sprawl, sports stadiums, flowers, museums, and walkability. In Europe, the national state and parties were the hierarchical "Establishment" opposed by the NSMs. In the United States, local business and political elites were more often the target. Many governments were often seen as closed to these citizen activists. For instance, in the 1970s in Italy, even communists and socialist parties rejected the new issues.

Opposition of this sort encouraged the more informal organization of the NSMs and their often confrontational tactics. But as some political parties and governments embraced the new social issues, the opportunity structure (Della Porta, Kriesi, & Rucht, 1999; McAdam, McCarthy, & Zald, 1996) drastically shifted. Movement leaders then broke from "urban guerilla warfare" and began participating in elections, lobbying, and advising governments. As their issues were incorporated into the political system, their demands moderated. Yet they added a heightened sensitivity to the emotional, musical, image-driven, and theatrical aspects of life (McDonald, 2006). Correlatively, developers and politicians grow more green and artistic, as they refashion concepts like loft living or boho into their rhetoric and policies. They add managerial know-how and political clout to the NSM concerns. "Creativity" emerges as a more general value, shared by entrepreneurs and artists.

This fairly abstract and general "moderating" process of linking the 1960s countercultural social movements with official city politics has varied by local context. Arts policies have often risen out of new social movements, with a marked bohemian past. Some arts groups oppose the transition into more established leadership roles; others support it. Yet once this "categorical" leap into a city politics with cultural concerns at its core has been made, conflict does not disappear. It is reframed over access to, control over, and utilization of the city's cultural and expressive spaces and resources. New issues become hotly contested: attracting tourists or new globetrotting "creative class" residents versus cultivating local artists and distinctive scenes; building downtown condominium developments for yuppies and "ruppies" (retired urban professionals) versus promoting creative industries and organic, more countercultural scenes; treating art and artists as public goods versus devoting municipal funds to public housing, welfare, or growth; stressing grants to individual artists or focusing on place-building initiatives; subsidizing major cultural institutions like the museum or opera to attract corporate investment or incubating grassroots and independent scenes for the purpose of community development in residential areas outside of downtown glamour districts; joining artistic and economic interests in a growing cultural economy versus sustaining solidarity between marginal artists, service workers, and the poor; defining "authenticity" as innovative independent activities versus long-term residence. In different settings even within the same city these sorts of issues are framed and interpreted differently, sometimes as dichotomous oppositions, other times as mutually supporting. But they all show a concern for arts, culture, and creativity as a part of a new urban agenda.

CULTURE AND POLITICS IN CITIES: REFRAMING A RESEARCH AGENDA

Artists, cultural industry representatives, and other cultural groups have in many places achieved an unprecedented centrality in policy discussions.

However, translating that centrality into a seat at the table with real capacity to influence events raises a new question. What *resources* have been rendered newly potent and valuable by the altered opportunity structure? How have various groups been able to wield these resources within urban political contestations and specific issue areas? Exerting influence requires controlling institutionally recognized but scarce resources that others wish to have.

The answer we elaborate here is *buzz*. "Buzz," we suggest, has become a valuable urban resource, one generated by vibrant urban cultural scenes and sought after by residents, businesses, and political actors. Buzz signals that significant aesthetic experiences are available to be consumed in a given place, that "something is happening" (Currid & Williams, 2009). Yet buzz is often produced and controlled by cultural actors such as artists and "bohemians," who are (relatively) low in other resources like money, political office, or local trust. Accordingly, as the value of buzz has generally increased, conflicts over controlling its production, distribution, and consumption are reshaping city politics, giving new groups access to power and creating potential coalitions between them and older institutional actors. How can we reformulate research agendas into the culture and politics of cities to include this political aspect of the rise of culture?

A NEW THEORETICAL FRAMEWORK

Most past work on urban culture and municipal cultural policy has not linked politics, political actors, and citizen activism of the sort discussed earlier to "culture-led" urban development. Research instead tends to focus on the economic impacts and drivers of cultural development or on policy mechanisms divorced from political culture. Despite this neglect, there have been some efforts to link cultural policy with city politics, such as Markusen (2006), Indergaard (2009), McGovern (2009), Barber (2008), Catungal and Leslie (2009), and Grodach (2012).

We applaud these recent efforts to join culture, politics, and development, and build on some of their insights to interpret these new processes. We go further by situating cultural policy disputes within a more systematic theory that includes "cultural power" among multiple bases of influence over urban politics, stressing interchanges across the variations within subgroups, contextual shifts in how various resources are weighted, and how these transform the content of key policy issues.[3] Substantively, this means that knowing a leader works in business does not explain much of her specific policy views. This is far more evident when one considers policy issues like improving public schools or building an art museum. These sorts of issues have no simple, direct relationship to any single business, in contrast, for instance, to a business that sells rock salt to the city. Consequently, if we look at engagement of political, business, and cultural leaders in specific issues, we find some on one side, and others opposing them. How do they divide? It may be useful to classify policy issues and participants with more general norms and values such as "maintain the stable middle class neighborhood," or "go bohemian," or "protect high art," or "grow commercial cultural industries."

These concerns are quite different from those of the regimes in most urban studies, which are more narrowly business oriented.[4] We introduce them here to convey the importance of conceptualizing and investigating the whole array of resources at stake in urban politics, beyond but still including money and power. Social movements researchers have similarly stressed the importance, for instance, of identity and solidarity in addition to money and power. Observers of Chicago have highlighted the relative autonomy of politics from business, where economic growth often serves as a vehicle for holding political power rather than the other way around. Yet neither group solidarity, nor money, nor political power seems sufficient to capture the distinctive resources through which arts and cultural movements and industries are at least sometimes able to exert influence over city policy and exploit the political opportunities opened up by the large-scale transformations discussed earlier. What the arts have, we suggest, is "buzz." And buzz is based not in a city's economic and business infrastructure, not in its residential communities, not in its political apparatus. It lies in its cultural scenes.

INDUSTRIAL CLUSTERS, RESIDENTIAL NEIGHBORHOODS, POLITICAL ARENAS, AND CULTURAL SCENES

By "scene" we refer to the aesthetic or ambient character of a place, the way a place offers experiences, dramas, and meanings to be enjoyed or rejected by potential consumers. A city's scenes are thus more than its physical spaces, occupational bases, political parties, and groups of persons labeled by demographic characteristics, although these all contribute to its scenes. Scenes also express the distinct aesthetic energy generated by numerous activities like dancing, sharing meals, listening to music, visiting galleries, sipping coffee, strolling plazas, attending street festivals, film openings, and the like. These join to paint an attractive and compelling urban scene: here is a place for glamour, there for transgression: here for tradition, there for self-expression (Silver et al., 2010).

Table 2 contrasts scenes with other ways of treating places, as industrial districts, residential neighborhoods, and political arenas. Each defines a specific issue area and resources for influencing urban affairs: for residents of neighborhoods, citizens of governments, producers of goods and services, and consumers of experiences and amenities. From the producer's standpoint, places are composed of workplaces and organized to facilitate the production, distribution, and exchange of goods and services. They are *industrial clusters* that, when successful, generate *money* for firms and workers. From the resident's standpoint, places are composed of residences – houses, apartments, condominiums, etc. – and organized to facilitate life's basic needs and services such as housing, safety, sustenance, childrearing, and sleep. They are residential *neighborhoods* that, when successful, generate *trust* among community members that communicates their solidarity. For politicians, parties, and citizen activists, places are typically power centers – party offices, polling places, organizational headquarters, city government offices, etc. – and are organized to support collective goal attainment, coalition formation, conflict resolution, and the exercise of authority. They are *political arenas* that, when successful, generate *power* communicating the capacity of actors to achieve and implement collective goals (e.g., through votes or leadership positions). From the cultural consumer's standpoint, places are collections of amenities to be aesthetically appreciated or rejected. They are cultural *scenes* that, when successful, generate *buzz* communicating the types of meaningful experiences one might find there: self-expression, transgression, and glamour; local authenticity, neighborliness, tradition, and more.

This multidimensional approach to urban places makes four new theoretical contributions to urban politics and policy studies. First, it identifies key dimensions for coding empirical variations across cities and neighborhoods. Some do all four of these; others just one or none. Second, it stresses that no one of these domains provides an adequate conceptualization of current urban policy, politics, culture, and economic development. Analysts need to pay more heed to all four components to avoid omitting critical processes. It thus extends the issue specifically of Dahl (1961) and arenas focus of Lowi (1964) and Peterson by adding cultural content via scenes. Third, it encourages new forms of research questions about the interchanges across

Table 2.   Contrasts Cultural Scenes with Residential Neighborhoods, Industrial Clusters, and Political Arenas.

Organization	Cultural Scene	Residential Neighborhood	Industrial Cluster	Political Arena
Goal	Expressing and communicating feelings, experiences, moods	Necessities, basic services, housing, schools, safety, sanitation, community development	Works, products	Collective action
Agent	Consumers	Residents	Producer	Citizen/leader/ officials/activist
Physical units	Amenities	Homes/apartments	Firms	Power centers
Basis of social bond	Lifestyles/sensibilities	Being born and raised nearby, long local residence, heritage	Work/production relations	Ideology, party, issues, citizenship
Symbolic resource	Buzz	Trust	Money	Power

the four domains: What sorts of productive activities support what type of scene, and vice versa? What sorts of residential communities support what types of scene, and vice versa? What types of scenes empower what sorts of governments and political movements, and vice versa? Fourth, it lists specific new types of symbolic resources – buzz – that play more central roles than identified in most past research on urban politics.

BUZZ AS A SYMBOLIC RESOURCE

The idea of symbolic resources in general and the notion of buzz as such a resource deserve elaboration. The central notion is that different forms of social activity are communicated through different symbols. For instance, money facilitates economic activity by providing producers and consumers with symbolic representations of valuable goods and services. Power facilitates collective action through communicating shared symbols of authority and efficacy, such as political office, elections, and official policy documents. Trust facilitates residential community through communicating shared symbols of mutual support and good faith, as in parent–teacher association membership stickers, neighborhood watch signs, well-groomed lawns, and the like. Parsons (1971), Alexander (1987), and Lidz (2001) provide useful accounts of this general approach to symbolic media as well as studies of particular media.

We suggest that participants in cultural scenes communicate the available experiences of scenes to one another through a symbolic resource we designate "buzz." The buzz around a scene signals the distinctive types of experiences participants can expect to enjoy in a scene. For instance, film festivals, high fashion, and movie stars might generate buzz that communicates the presence of a *glamorous* scene; tattoo parlors, punk music, body art, and piercing studios generate the buzz of a more *transgressive* scene; antique stores, farmers markets, and local arts festivals generate buzz communicating a *local* scene.[5] Such symbols signal the presence of the scene to a wider audience, potentially drawing in new participants and enabling persons from multiple backgrounds to share similar experiences.

THE TWO FACES OF BUZZ

Buzz, like all symbolic media, leads a kind of double existence (Alexander, 1987). It faces in two directions. On the one side, buzz enables participants in scenes to communicate and circulate the experiences of the scene for their own sake. This is the autonomous face of buzz. It indicates for participants the chance to, for instance, express original feelings rather than conform to pale imitations, stay true to rather than do violence to a tradition, shine glamorously rather than fade into anonymity, project warmth and intimacy rather than distance and aloofness, maintain an authentically real life rather than a phony existence. The autonomous face of the buzz around a scene communicates the "internal life in scenes" (Hitzler, Bucher, & Niederbacher, 2005), where success in the scene – being glamorous, self-expressive, transgressive, traditional, locally authentic, ethnically authentic, etc. – is its own reward.

In its other aspect, a scene's buzz faces outward, toward the economic, political, and residential environments with which scenes interact. This is the heteronomous face of buzz. On this level, the buzz of the scene makes functional contributions to the internal needs of these other domains. It creates the wealth, power, and trust through which the scene can potentially earn its keep in the broader system of which it is a part. Conversely, scenes can receive external support from business groups, political actors, and residential groups in the form of money, political assistance, and community trust. Where, for instance, the strong buzz around a more independent and self-expressive scene has drawn significant attention, investment, and personal emotion for the wider city, scene representatives are likely to be able to act more effectively to preserve and grow their scene relative to representatives of less buzzing scenes with similar sensibilities, elite support, and financing. The greater these interchanges, the more deeply these particular scenes are likely to become enmeshed into the social fabric of a city. The opportunity to connect with scenes would become a part of the day-to-day cultural needs of residents, business, and political officials just as scenes and scene supporters become more deeply concerned with their own contributions to neighborhood issues, economic development, and local governance. How can we describe in more detail these hypotheses about the dynamic interchanges between scenes and the other aspects of urban life?

POLITICS AS RESOURCE INTERCHANGE, BOUNDARY WORK, AND SYMBOLIC

The points of contact among the domains highlighted in Table 2 are where much of the conflict and creativity in politics occurs, where habits and sensibilities from one area enter into the other and are redefined, rejected, or assimilated. Consider a developer is in the business of extracting economic value from new buildings. This endeavor is not intrinsically aesthetic, but it can be (1) enhanced if the buzz of the surrounding scene attracts attention and investment, (2) authorized or stymied by the power of political regulations, and (3) legitimated or delegitimized by the influence of local residents. Buzz, political power, and community influence are inputs into the economic process. At the same time, from the perspective of scene enthusiasts, the developer's cash and the politician's authority might in some circumstances enable the scene to continue to express and share the experiences that it cultivates. Similarly, to the extent that political support for city politicians depends on meeting citizens' quality of life demands and lively scenes are key providers of what makes for quality urban living, then buzzing scenes will provide key inputs useful for the exercise and maintenance of political power; politicians would be more likely to express solidarity with local scenes and scene makers. If active scenes enhance community and neighborhood trust, then local neighborhood leaders, who depend on that trust to wield their influence, will be increasingly dependent on cultivating the artists, cultural groups, and amenities that generate vibrant local scenes. At the same time, support from influential neighborhood leaders can earn scenes solidarity with residents who are in turn more likely to treat the scene as a neighborhood asset rather than a source of deviance and instability.

Interchange does not mean agreement. At every point, there is opportunity for political struggle, coalition, and for creative reinterpretation of business, aesthetic, neighborhood, and political practice. For instance, a community leader who seeks to build trust among neighbors through growing a local cultural scene stakes her influence on the scene engaging rather than enraging local residents' sensibilities. Aesthetic disagreements about art and artists become intertwined with disagreements about the nature of the community. Political leaders who seek to win elections and mobilize citizen action through cultural policies stake their political power on the scene enriching citizens' lives. They would have to deliver the cultural goods, and failure to do so could be politically damaging. Scene enthusiasts who grow their scenes by using its buzz to attract money, political clout, and residential community support may make the ongoing vitality of the scene more dependent on generating wealth, power, and local trust. They may face charges of co-optation, selling out, and domestication. And conversely, often amidst rising rents, increasing property values, and new condominium developments, scenes may need to deliver backing, and residential solidarity that keeps the scene solvent political backing, and residential solidarity that keeps the scene solvent and anchored in terms of *its* characteristic experiences and practices.

Cultural scenes may create other forms of policy debates. Their buzz may become "inflated," decreasing its power to provide reliable signs about what experiences a scene offers. That is, as buzz expands, more people may come to possess the external symbols of the scene. This can reach a point that possessing such symbols (wearing T-shirts, owning music tracks, reading certain magazines, preferring certain interior décor) is not a clear indication of a person's readiness to engage fully in the emotions and practices that "back" the scene's buzz, diluting its symbolic potency and expressive energy. Similarly, buzz "interest rates" may vary, with some pursuing expansionary policies to lend buzz with few strings attached (as in pop music or a club district) and with others placing high costs on borrowing their buzz (as in Goth music or perhaps the classic local Chicago pub). Low interest rates in buzz may attract considerable investment in a scene (in monetary and other forms), if many people decide to give it a try. This can lead to rapid growth but also to unsustainable inflation. High interest rates in buzz may drive up the price of participation, making the scene more exclusive (and the rent higher), as in scenes that place limits on expansion to preserve their authenticity. Zukin's (2010) discussion about political-economic dilemmas around the desire to preserve authenticity of places like New York City's lower east side is one recent case in point.

More generally, many public officials have responded by crafting policies designed to build up their cultural assets and scenes to bring tourists, new businesses, and residents; retain and energize those they have; and channel the often abrupt transitions from neighborhood and industrial district to new buzzing scenes filled with amenities and consumption spaces. Archetypical examples are the renovated railroad station with "authentic" stone and steel framing a chic restaurant/bar (cf., Zukin, 1982) or housing community arts groups and farmers' markets. At the same time, groups who provide key inputs into the production of buzz may threaten to withhold their services and cut the supply and quality of buzz attached to a given place. These groups could include artists, photographers, writers, promoters, and performers, among others. Insofar, as the profitability of that place's businesses, the social cohesion among its residents, and the election results of its politicians depend on that buzz continuing, this withdrawal could conceivably constitute a major threat. It would be a buzz strike.[6] Moreover, some places have encouraged buzz inflation, encouraging rapidly growing tourist and club districts; others have pursued "sustainable" growth in buzz, restricting restaurant and liquor licenses in order to more slowly integrate an emerging scene into existing residential neighborhoods and industrial areas. These sorts of policy decisions we suggest offer a critical piece of the interpretation omitted by the more descriptive studies of rent or migration like Gyourko et al. and Cortwright cited earlier.

Such interchanges, boundary work, inflationary cycles, and policy decisions create new ways to influence urban affairs and new problems for policy makers to address. Empirically, these processes likely vary considerably, and investigation into these variations needs to be guided by clear propositions about where and why they might differ. Such as:

- Where local politics are more tightly coupled with national politics, governments may be more likely to support cultural organizations whose buzz extends nationally or internationally.
- In conflicts among residents about integrating a scene into their neighborhood, the moral contribution of local artists' buzz to the local community (i.e., building vs. undermining trust) may become an important political controversy. It should vary with the cultural/scene distance of the arts groups from residents.
- In conflicts between residents and arts professionals over cultural developments (e.g., building a new museum), residents may be concerned about impacts of heightened buzz on neighborhood issues (e.g., traffic and home prices) while artists and arts management professionals (curators, museum directors, etc.) may operate from a more cosmopolitan perspective (e.g., judge local projects in reference to global icons).
- Where conflict revolves around industrial policy to subsidize local scenes, the productivity and wealth generating consequences of area artists' buzz may become central political issues.
- In a patron-client political culture, political leaders will tend to resist generic cultural planning frameworks and instead support specific participants separately to build particular and personal buzz dependencies and loyalties rather than generalized policy resources equally accessible to all. Conflict will revolve around movements pushing for "reform" and seeking to develop an "artist class consciousness."
- When historically countercultural scenes begin to cooperate with established business interests, political organizations, and residential groups, internal critiques may arise from within the scene asserting that their buzz is being, respectively, sold out, co-opted, or domesticated. Internal controversy will revolve around the scene's capacity to deliver its core cultural experiences and integrate new participants as it grows and becomes more interdependent with other domains.

Table 3. Political Contexts Shift the Value of Resources.

	Ideal Types of Political Systems				
	Business dominant	Politically dominant	Egalitarian	Culturally dominant	Residential neighborhood dominant
Resource types					
Money	H	M	L	L	L
Votes	L	M	H	M	M
Community influence	L	M	M	M	H
Political leader access	L	H	L	L	M
Aesthetic buzz	L	L	M	H	L

H, high; M, medium; L, low.
This matrix illustrates how resources shift in their impact in different political contexts. It highlights resources and contexts of the sort we stress in this chapter, separating two types of power: votes and political leader access. Other resources may be more salient in different settings. The differences in impact are due to shifting rules of the game across different contexts. For example, as Chicago's traditional political dominance has declined, so do the impacts of those resources most important for a politically dominant power structure.

In sum, as the rules of the game shift across political systems, so do the impacts of resources: money talks in a business dominant power structure, but votes count more in an egalitarian system. Hypothetical examples of shifts in resource impact are listed in Table 3.[7]

We offer (without demonstrating) these propositions to illustrate the sort of analysis encouraged by pursuing the links between cultural politics and the many concepts from the overlapping literatures we have invoked: resources, exchange, issue areas, inflation, buzz strikes, etc. Many more could be pursued and these could be empirically tested (cf. Silver & Clark, 2014). Our main theoretical concern however is to suggest that cultural practice can be analyzed using such concepts, and that they are no more evanescent or intractable than a taste for a new beer or style of lawn or more standard local politics issues such as zoning and sanitation. Simultaneously, we point cultural political analysts to these overlapping theories since they suggest ways to interpret culture more powerfully and precisely.

BUZZ IN TORONTO: ARTISTS AND CITIZEN GROUPS PLAY KEY ROLES

We conclude by briefly illustrating some of these processes first in Toronto and then in Chicago. In the past decades, Toronto has seen dramatic increases in the centrality and salience of cultural policy in its municipal politics. This account is based on interviews with culture department officials, arts activist organization leaders, Toronto Artscape officials, Toronto Arts Council officials; city staff reports, Ontario Municipal Board documents; and media coverage. A more detailed study of the politics of cultural policy in Toronto is available in Silver (2012).

Against the backdrop of a strong Victorian heritage suspicious of public amusement (Lemon, 1984), large-scale cultural development began in Toronto, and Canada, around the national centennial in 1967. Artist groups, often with counterculture sensibilities, won grants for Homegrown Canadian culture. These supported Toronto's first Marxist theatres, independent art galleries, and new music venues (Churchill, 2010; McKinnie, 2007). Over the next 40 years, many arts advocates found their way into the city's culture department, bringing with them a strong personal commitment to their work. Cultural activists, in other words, with initial and enduring commitments to vital scenes as public goods, brought concerns about buzz creation into City Hall.

Arts and cultural concerns were steadily integrated more deeply into many key civic, economic, political, and community organizations. Proclaiming, "I am an artist and I vote," civil society groups like Artsvote began to exert influence on local elections by holding (highly publicized) mayoral debates and issuing report cards about how arts-friendly candidates for city council are. Toronto Artscape became a major force in developing artist-friendly housing and community development, often extracting significant government subsidies for below-market artist residences. The culture department officially merged with economic development, resulting in a full-time staff member within the latter as an official liaison between the two; it also built informal bridges with the planning department and hired a planner onto its own staff. Buzz was slowly and steadily being officially recognized as a vital urban resource across numerous organizations and actors.

A much publicized controversy in the neighborhood of West Queen West in Toronto between 2005 and 2008 illustrates how these buzz-infused organizations provide resources for activists to intervene in city politics, as well as how local cultural political controversies and creativity often occur in the interplay of buzz with other resources. Starting in the mid to late 1990s, large numbers of mostly young, single artists and cultural workers moved into the former industrial area. Rents were relatively cheap, and, as manufacturing left, the old warehouses provided attractive artist live workspaces, many of which were semi-legally appropriated for that purpose.

Moreover, the area was ripe with the "grit as glamour" that Richard Lloyd (2006) suggests is often attractive to "neo-bohemians" looking for life on the edge. Easy access to the iconic Queen Street scene – a historical center of independent and alternative art worlds – was important as well, for galleries, shows, professional contacts, and identity.

By 2001, the area had the fifth most artists as a share of the local population in Canada and was in the midst of nearly a five percentage point increase in the share of the population working in arts, culture, and recreation between 1996 and 2006 (Statistics Canada data, compiled by authors). The neighborhood has about nine times as many art galleries as the average Toronto postal code, is a center of Toronto's design industry (graphic, interior, software, and more), and has large numbers of tattoo parlors.[8] Concurrently, the share of the population that was married with children dropped down 8 points between 2001 and 2006 alone (Statistics Canada data, compiled by authors). In short, the area became a focal point of artistic and creative work, with a strong orientation toward personal experimentation, youthful self-expression and discovery, and spontaneity.

The buzz of the scene was also attracting new participants and new investment. More new private dwellings were built in the surrounding political ward between 2001 and 2006 than in the previous 10 years. Thousands of new units were under construction in 2012. Rents were on the rise, and core scene participants began to worry about its solvency.

Two concerns were crucial, politically. First, the rapid influx of new residents threatened "buzz inflation" as discussed earlier, where symbols become valued above the experiences that back them. Local media recorded the concern. "Suddenly, the Queen West Triangle was the epicenter of the city's cultural buzz, and everyone wanted a piece of it" (Preville, 2007). "The ratio of 'normal people' to 'artists with cool hair' will be thrown into upheaval" (Whaley, 2007). And another: "Those condo owners will discover that much of the authentic local culture they bought into will have disappeared when they want to sell. It's a bad investment unless the cultural fabric of the neighborhood can be protected and nurtured" (Kuznicki, 2007). These general sorts of worries were shared by city officials as well, who were concerned about maintaining a critical mass of working artists in the area so as to sustain "the [neighborhood's] buzz with respect to being a center of creative expression" (City of Toronto, 2006, p. 8). Here we see strong officials and public acknowledgment of buzz as a valuable resource and explicit concern with buzz inflation as an urban political problem.

One of the most potent symbols of this perceived threat of buzz inflation was in the name and advertising of one of the new condominiums:

The Bohemian Embassy. Referencing a local bar central to Toronto's 1960s bohemian culture in the Yorkville neighborhood (a hangout for Joni Mitchell and others), this name, together with glossy photos of beautiful and decidedly unbohemian people, evoked visceral disgust. A local artist turned this disgust into art, projecting onto a wall near the proposed development an image of a woman dressed like the one in the advertisements, but vomiting.

These graphic reactions detailed the threat, as scene participants saw it. The new developments would drastically reduce the availability of artist workspaces in the area, as existing spaces would be rezoned for residential uses. This would in turn shift the balance of the scene away from a healthy and relatively autonomous mix of buzz production and consumption to a seemingly empty, externally oriented, and inflated buzz consumption. The scene would exist primarily as a weekend pastime for residents whose energies and interests were oriented elsewhere, diluting its expressive and emotional energy. A dwindling core of available workspace would deplete the number of committed full-time participants, and the scene's "artistic heart" would be in danger. Indeed, many artists and core participants had already started moving further west and north before public controversy about these developments emerged in the mid-2000s.

Second, increased developments, in line with our propositions earlier, raised concerns that the very desire to integrate buzz into the fabric of the evolving community would disturb the organic spontaneity of its core identity. No one person planned the neighborhood as an artist colony; people simply started moving into warehouse spaces and making them studios. Galleries burst up here and there, with no blueprint. Being a part of that flowering was part of the aesthetic allure of the scene. The proposed developments, however, to the extent that they did include artist workspaces, did so in a planned "creative mews." But this kind of planning was, for some, an affront to the scene's ethos of improvisation and spontaneity: "arts communities grow organically" (in Foad, 2007).

Scene supporters, artists, local businesses, community groups, and media professionals joined in a campaign to alter the design of the proposed condominium developments. They created an organization, Active 18, named after the area's political ward. One of their central goals was to preserve the neighborhood's offbeat, funky, and independent scene while it grew. Movement supporters pressured City Hall, activating the networks of supporters there that had been building over the years, and were able to win considerable sympathy and support, not only from the culture department but from the mayor's office as well. Using their ability to create buzz as a political weapon, they held press conferences with flashy urban design proposals to demonstrate that they could put on a show as good as the developers. If local artists, businesses, and scene members lacked the economic resources to alter the market dynamics of local development, they could, they thought, move vigorously to mobilize resources they did command (like influence and buzz) to convince political actors to intervene via the resources *they* controlled – power in the form of control over zoning regulations. This in turn, they suggested, would create more economic value by preserving the core activities that had attracted investment into the area in the first place and maintaining work and not only residential uses in the downtown core of the city.

The public rhetorical case was just as crucial. Active 18 was for "good design." This message was in large measure an attempt to square the circle of spontaneity and planning, by advocating a kind of urban design that would at the same time cultivate improvisational expression. They were not simply wild bohemians looking to roam free; they were for a novel overcoming of seeming contradictions. At the same time, Active 18 portrayed themselves not as NIMBYs but called themselves YIMBYs (Yes in My Backyard). They were for development, not against it; but, so they argued, Toronto needed a kind of development that would unleash its creative potential so that its growth in cultural employment could redound to public benefit. That is, their message sought to reframe arts clusters not as the "cultural contradiction of capitalism," but as core and trustworthy pillars of the new economy, increasingly enshrined as such in official city planning documents. Unconventional artists could be useful labor, and for the success of Toronto as a whole, it would be crucial to maintain an urban design in which this kind of work could flourish. Buzz could complement rather than contradict the city's established resource bases.

The case went before the Ontario Municipal Board (OMB), with the city joining with Active 18 in advocating for preserving significant artist workspace in the area. Specifically, the city developed an argument to the effect that developers be required to guarantee "no net loss" of "creative" workspaces. The OMB rejected this argument, on the grounds that a policy intended to protect employment must be based on objective data and more comprehensive analysis, as well as more established planning frameworks. Before the city and Active 18 won a rare appeal (pushed for by Mayor Miller), the city had already settled with developers on two of the three specific proposed developments (to the chagrin of Active 18). With the threat of appeal, and with Toronto Artscape emerging as a powerful broker, the third was settled on terms more favorable to the local arts scene, with

56,000 square feet being sold to Toronto Artscape, who would own and manage the space in perpetuity as affordable artist live work units. Developers would contribute to the repurposing of a nearby and historically significant library as a performing arts hub. They would also contribute additional funds for community arts infrastructure projects, and after some further negotiations, new park space. Though not everything Active 18 wanted – many competing and powerful resources and actors were in play, after all – these are fairly considerable concessions and elite support in a planning environment that was not set up for their benefit,[9] and local arts leaders expressed optimism about the solvency of the scene.[10] The nature of the long-term outcome, however, is still open.

Successful action is more than meeting a specific goal, however; it also creates an enriched platform for further action (Silver, 2011), which in this case meant integrating recognition of the significance of buzz for urban development and sustainability more deeply into the city's policy apparatus. The most significant policy impact of this case may be at this level. Thus, Active 18 continues as a formal organization dedicated to using buzz as an urban resource. This in itself is a significant result, as they are continuing players not only in their own neighborhood but actively training other groups citywide looking to learn the ways of YIMBYism. At the same time, some city officials have accepted arts activist critiques that city agencies were not properly prepared to deal with planning for place-based scene development. They have undertaken new planning initiatives in response, building closer ties between the culture department and the planning department and generating maps and inventories of cultural workers and facilities in order to potentially implement "no net loss" policies. Generating new organizational capacity and integrating cultural policy more deeply into the planning process are two crucial outcomes of political action indeed.

In sum, as the city's economic and social bases increasingly depended on arts and culture, movement activists seized the new opportunity space. The steady integration of culture into the civic, economic, and political fabric of the city provided organizational capacity for using, and official recognition of, buzz as an urban resource. The threat of buzz withdrawal became a political weapon wielded by activists to exercise at least partial influence over city planning, political leadership, and development policy to gain subsidized housing and other benefits. They slowly redefined Toronto's cultural scenes as productive and upstanding contributors to the city's welfare and stability rather than dangerous sources of social deviance. In Toronto's neo-reformist political culture (Boudreau, Keil, & Young, 2009;

Savitch & Kantor, 2002), they were able to parlay the "community benefits" of buzz into power and money.

CHICAGO: ARTS POLICY IS IMPLEMENTED BY CIVIC LEADERS AND CITY HALL, FAR LESS BY ARTISTS AND CITIZENS

Citizens have dramatically increased their interest and participation in the
arts and culture in recent years, but how have arts policies been implemented? Unlike many countries where a ministry of culture leads, in the United
States, arts policy is more state and local, with much local variation. While
Tocqueville showed how citizens could drive many policies in
Massachusetts, he wrote decades before the huge immigrations to U.S.
cities. Migration brought massive differences to different cities and neighborhoods, some of which carry on to the present. Chicago is one of the
most visible illustrations, with minimal white Protestant or Tocquevillian
legacy. It boasted the most powerful political machine in the United States
from about 1933 to 1983, when Harold Washington was elected. Chicago
has fascinated decades of observers, and researchers, but not on culture.
Adding culture is thus especially important.

Art and culture are very new Chicago concerns. In many European locations, like Paris and Berlin, culture was a core policy for centuries. The first
book on Midwest U.S. cities and towns (Longworth, 2007) stresses that
most are in serious decline and minimally stress culture and art. Except
Chicago. How did Chicago change so fast?

Chicago is a new entrant on the stage of global cultural cities, transforming its blue collar and localist heritage. The new combination of participants and resources powerfully documents the rise of amenities and
culture, contrasting with the strong tradition of jobs and contracts as classic resources, led by a Political Machine.[11] Chicago politicians' traditional
concern with such private goods has been joined with an emphasis on public goods like parks and art and flowers, ushering in a new political style
and a new role for culture in the city.

More traditionally associated with hogs ("Chicago: Hog Butcher to the
World"), clientelism ("We Don't Want Nobody Nobody Sent"), and indus-
trialism ("Chicago, City of the Big Shoulders"), Chicago lacks a strong tradition of major civic and city government expenditure and interest in arts,
culture, and amenities. In 1976, Milton Rakove described Chicago as

"Dick Daley's town. Uncultured and parochial ... not an Athens, neither a Rome, nor a London, and never a Paris" (Rakove, 1976, p. 41). In 2003, Mayor Daley II had the street level bus stops and rail entrances redesigned to match those in Paris. What happened in between, how did local politicians drive this process, and how has Chicago politics changed?

We focus here on the role of government and public policy in the cultural transformation of Chicago. This is important as most past work on urban culture and cultural policy has focused more on policy and economics. In Chicago, however, power and politics are paramount. These issues may be more muted elsewhere as policy actors and analysts alike often seek to frame their work as rational deliberation. By contrast, the Chicago case allows us to see personal rivalries, ambitions, and connections that drive local policy up close.

The only major American city with a historically Catholic political majority, Chicago, stands out for its past emphasis on clout, with individual personalities vying for political power and willing to use city resources to sustain and expand political success. To this end, the vast political machine of Mayor Richard J. Daley (Daley I, 1955—1976) wielded the classic tools of patronage jobs and contracts for specific ethnicities and neighborhoods, which have been more important than class. This everyday acceptance of ethnic/national/cultural distinctiveness led to a more anthropological cultural relativism and mutual tolerance – "You deliver your precinct, and I'll deliver mine."

His son, Mayor Richard M. Daley (Daley II, 1989—2011) operated in a world where such clientelist tactics, while not extinguished, were much less effective. But the Chicago tradition of pragmatism, personalism, and localism persisted. Daley II responded to this altered landscape in a vigorous and innovative way, utilizing the arts, entertainment, parks, and amenities to build support among his new, more cosmopolitan, educated, younger, and affluent citizens. And, in good Catholic, nonideological form, Daley learned how to give this constituency what it wanted – flowers, theater, bike paths, green buildings, and music. Simultaneously, traditional ethnic groups "got theirs": Blues, etc. The result is a dramatic transition, from the Political Machine to the Entertainment Machine.

The elder Mayor Daley understood social issues as part of the New Deal legacy. For him they meant concern for the "common man," helping the disadvantaged, providing jobs and support for basic economic needs. His speeches often included a nod of thanks to the New Deal Democratic program, the policies of which he might illustrate with a concrete example chosen for his specific audience, perhaps a hospital or an urban-renewal project for that neighborhood. Here social and fiscal issues strongly over-lapped, consistent with New Deal Democratic ideology of many Chicago citizens (Andersen, 1979; Rundquist, Miranda, & Tunyavong, 1991). Yet if he referred to the big themes of the national New Deal, "Da Mayor" did so plainly, with a grammatical eccentricity that out-of-towners sometimes found amusing. He would also never forget to thank, by name, those who had helped him in that locale, including precinct captains and aldermen. City officials reciprocated by ending their public statements with "God bless Mayor Daley."

Though Daley I did invest in public art,[12] he took a strong stand against the 1960's new social movements and their core concerns with more citizen-responsive, egalitarian, multicultural, and tolerant politics that put environ-mental, feminist, lifestyle, and quality of life issues center stage.

When Mayor Daley passed away in 1976, the Democratic machine began to fragment between competing interests. A fractured party meant more reliance on public support and less on party connections. In this context, the arts would prove useful politically.

Jane Byrne, even though she rose through Daley's machine, ran against Bilandic on a reform agenda. Her victory seemed to validate a cautious and uncomfortable alliance of racial minorities and reformers. But once in office, she reconverted government offices into "funnels for patronage." One of her many reversals involved Bilandic's Chicago Fest. She first sought to cancel Chicago Fest but she pragmatically and "characteristically did a 180-degree turn and adopted the event as her very own, ... [ordering] her Special Events office to come up with spectacles like it" (Davis, 1995, p. 22). And in 1978, she started the percent for art program designating a portion of funds for new and renovated buildings to pay for public art – inspired by national examples. By requiring new buildings to have more sidewalk space, she also made possible sidewalk cafes; they expanded enormously after her administration.

These policies all helped to enliven street life, especially downtown. These were centered first in the tourist and convention areas of the city, and over time broadened to such events as Chicago Fest, which in turn inspired related Lakefront festivities, typically linked with Chicago's ethnic traditions – like the Blues and Gospel Festivals, Latin Music Festivals, and Celtic Festivals. Many included free concerts by top stars in Grant Park, and were much appreciated by low-income Chicagoans. This inaugu-rated a trend, actively pursued by Daley II, of using public music festivals to generate allegiance not by particular employment but through more universal consumption and leisure open to all.

CULTURAL POLICY UNDER HAROLD WASHINGTON: THE CITY OF CHICAGO CULTURAL PLAN

Harold Washington's victory in 1983 shook Chicago to the core. Initially a machine bit player, Washington converted to the cause of reform in large measure due to political expediency. His resources came almost completely from black individuals and businesses, who were traditionally separated from the broader machine structures. In addition, he was elected by a diverse coalition of non-Catholics: Protestant-heritage "lakefront liberals," some Hispanics, Jews, and an overwhelming majority of Chicago's African-Americans.

Washington and his advisors created a reform agenda to match their seemingly prophetic rise to power. One pillar of the agenda was the formation of Chicago's Department of Cultural Affairs, and with it, its first-ever comprehensive cultural plan. The plan was a landmark document. Joining a newly prioritized attention to culture with classic Chicago themes, it aimed to incorporate culture into "all aspects of municipal planning." First and foremost, it was big, stating: "The Chicago Cultural Plan is without precedent in its scope and the grassroots process by which it was crafted. It took shape from the recommendations and observations of thousands of Chicago citizens as well as hundreds of cultural, civic and community groups." But a young attorney from City Hall led much of this effort to meet locally; they were not bottom up, but top down. Second, it stresses the strong charismatic individual in typical Chicago fashion, opening the "Statement of Principles" by averring: "The individual artist is at the foundation of our cultural heritage." Yet, continuing the equally strong Chicago tradition of rooting and tempering individual action in ethno-cultural soil, The Plan itself is presented by its authors as an expression of the collected and multiple cultures of Chicago's neighborhoods and ethnicities.

The Plan proposed a number of specific initiatives. These included streamlining decision making within the Department of Cultural Affairs (DCA), strengthening its role in city governance structures and integrating into Illinois Arts Agencies; commissioning studies about the economic impact of the arts in Chicago; enhancing culture's role in the city's tourist attraction programs; creating cultural incubator programs; offering city buildings at reasonable rates for use by artists as well as rezoning spaces as live-work; increasing grants to arts groups; expanding the Chicago Cultural Center, and many others. The plan was and is an inspiration for many other cities. Still it said almost nothing of citizen or arts organizations; it was non-Tocquevillian.

Very little of it was implemented during Washington's tenure. Indeed, on nearly every front, his agenda was viewed through the Chicago looking glass, as "rewarding a new set of friends and punishing a new set of enemies" (Ferman, 1996, p. 141). Throughout his term, a group of white machine aldermen opposed him at every turn, blocking nearly every reform that could not be implemented by executive order.

DALEY II AND THE RISE OF CULTURE

The 1980s and 1990s marked a monumental shift in Chicago's government perhaps more than in all previous decades of the 20th century. This bold claim may seem surprising. Was the city not governed by a mayor named Daley, as it was 50 years earlier? The two Daleys looked and talked alike – Richard J., the legendary Boss, mayor from 1955 to 1976, and Richard M., in office from 1989 to 2010. How could they be so different?

Chicago's changes were camouflaged by an outdated image of the city, its citizens, and especially its leaders as conservative. What changed? The lifeblood of Carl Sandburg's "City of the Big Shoulders" was heavy industry, production, and growth; its citizens were mostly blue collar. Industrial organization once followed practices of strict seniority, few pay differentials by individual achievement, and promotion from within.

Post-industrialism turns this on its head. National and global competition and precise communication permit contracting out to small firms globally. Local and "particularistic" social relations are partially replaced by more abstract and distant. This break is deeper for Catholics than Protestants, since the role of the priest, parochial schools, and parish life traditionally taught more respect for personal authority and social skills.

Building on mathematical models of risk pioneered at the University of Chicago, the Board of Trade has emerged at the core of a network of futures and options markets that extends around the globe. But if the Board of Trade symbolizes Chicago's core position in global finance, we stress that the city's largest industry is no longer slaughtering, or steel production – or even finance. It is entertainment and tourism (Clark, 2012 provides more statistical detail). Indeed, the most visited park in the entire United States is the Chicago Lakefront; it has far more visitors than the Grand Canyon (although many are from nearby). Often in stark contrast to their preconceptions, visitors are struck by the attractiveness of Chicago's parks, architecture, and boulevards, lined with new flowers, shrubs, benches, public art, and wrought-iron fences. Catering to its new "ethnicities," Chicago hosts Lollapolooza and Pitchfork, two of the world's largest urban pop music festivals.

At the same time, Daley II sought to broaden his political base, to Hispanics, African-Americans, gays, young urban professionals, environmentalists, and many other constituencies. His speeches added references to public goods like "trees, bicycles, culture, and entertainment" (Pasotti, 2010; see also Banuelos, 2009; Feron, 1999). By marching in the Gay Rights Parade, he marked this new commitment. Narrower ethnic-neighborhood visions persist as does classic clientelism. But these are now complemented by a political, civic, and ecological vision of the entire region, where political leaders can work together rather than just fight. Regional civic groups like Open Lands have developed programs targeted to central city neighborhoods, many funded by local businesses.

CULTURAL POLICY AS PRAGMATIC POLITICS

Daley II's family history and personal style made him seem an unlikely candidate to institute these sweeping aesthetics and consumption-driven changes. Yet that history made him into a shrewd politician who would not let ideology interfere with good politics. If he saw that planting flowers and Chicago's theaters made political sense, it was because the rules of the game and the facts on the ground were changing. Important forces had been at work for some years, eroding the machine's popularity. For instance, a detailed study by Thomas Guterbock (1980) of a stalwart machine alderman on the North Side found that many residents did not care about free garbage cans or similar small material incentives. They were quite independent in their thinking and talking about politics.

New organizations and styles that sprang up after the 1970s had diffused more widely, from block clubs and environmental action groups to women, gay, and other new social movements. It was essential to these groups' independent self-image that they not be dominated by a machine hierarchy, but instead be democratically and consensually run by their followers. Globalization, rising cosmopolitanism, education, and media use among typical citizens heightened such concerns. While Mayor Daley II was widely seen as having been carried to office in 1989 by the regular Democratic Party this was not the case, and in a few short years, he increasingly relied on the media instead of the traditional army of precinct captains. Television coverage in the 1980s intruded into the inner sanctum of the Chicago City Hall, the Council Chambers. Visitors to Chicago would comment for instance that they knew all about that night when Mayor Washington's successor was chosen, since they had seen it on TV in Norway! This in turn increased the consciousness by the mayor and council of their worldwide audience, as non-Chicagoans became part of what sociologists call a "reference group." That is, leaders would not just ask, "what do Chicagoans think of this vote and of me," but also "what do others outside Chicago think." Observers in Italy and Spain have similarly reported that foreign television has undermined traditional hierarchies (Clark & Hoffmann-Martinot, 1998, p. 159). As world trade, tourism, and related global forces rise, they have helped change Chicago's political rules.

Media advertising and efficient service delivery increasingly drove politics in Chicago in the 1990s, and contributed to displacing the regular Democratic Party from the lives of individual citizens. If the general analytical trade-off is between the strong political party and the individual citizen, the intermediaries are the neighborhood associations. When the machine was strong, it co-opted or destroyed these (Ferman, 1996 captures this well). Daley II reversed this process by elevating independent neighborhood associations. One way of signaling this was by improving neighborhood parks and sidewalks. The signs announced the change. That is, decades back, the most casual visitor to Chicago was struck by the hundreds of signs all over the city whose bottom line read "Richard J. Daley, Mayor." Under his son, many sparkling new signs proclaimed individual neighborhoods, local associations, and block clubs. But most were mounted by City Hall. These are one visible symbol of a general trend toward more "public goods" rhetoric and policies, such as crime-fighting, education, and tourism (Feron, 1999; St. John, 1999), together with a more neighborhood approach.

Most important for this chapter, however, is that Daley wholeheartedly embraced his new political environment, which required supplementing production concerns with consumption and aesthetic issues. Few of Daley's initial public statements address these issues. The mayor discreetly added occasions like opening night theater performances to his social itinerary. It was easier to sell these types of policy in Chicago via subtlety. Because Mayor Daley II appealed to common Chicagoans in the style and language of his father, some cultural changes may have seemed disconcerting. Take for instance the traditional white police who objected strenuously, although informally, to the mayor's strong and explicit emphasis on minority hiring, a multicultural emphasis in city programs, aesthetics, and service to citizens.

Consider too shifts at Navy Pier. In earlier plans, it was to be supported primarily by commercial sales to individuals, that is, more separable goods. Harold Washington wanted it to be a more public good, a more aesthetically driven edifice with fountains and vistas, open to pedestrians to consume freely. Indeed, Navy Pier became Chicago's number one tourist spot, attracting millions of visitors annually after it was reconstructed in the 1990s. It joined high and low, with cotton candy vendors and a stained-glass window display outside the Chicago Shakespeare Theater.

Seeking to unravel the sources driving amenities by Mayor Daley II, we interviewed such knowledgeable informants as David Doig, active in many amenity policies in the City's planning department before becoming Commissioner of Parks. Asked why, his first answer was "the mayor has been traveling, visiting places like Paris, bringing back specific ideas and policies." Alderman Mary Ann Smith became a citywide leader of aesthetic/consumption issues in the late 1990s, traveling to the West Coast and Scandinavia to bring back slides, which she then showed to citizens. She summarized specific ideas in memos to the Mayor, who endorsed many of them, such as a campaign to add greenery to rooftops in 2000. Her assessment was that it simply took a few years at the beginning of his administration to get the more basic things in order, like a campaign against rats in alleys, and converting brownfields left by old polluting factories, before the more specifically aesthetic might take off (Clark, 2012) (Fig. 4).

These policies are documented dramatically in budgetary commitments.[13] We have assembled apparently for the first time culture and arts spending by the multiple overlapping governments in the Chicago area, which shows a powerful increase through the 1990s, albeit flattening about 2005. This is government spending only, totaling about $80 million when we sum the City, Parks District, and related budgets. Data is complex to assemble as multiple overlapping governments support culture and the arts. The Donnelley Foundation commissioned a report on the arts and culture nonprofits in the Chicago area, which found that they spent a total of some $755 million in 2004 of which $428 million was "unearned." This is not far from the U.S. average, where 13 percent of nonprofit arts agencies funds come from government (National Endowment for the Arts, 2007). By contrast, 52 percent of local culture is funded by local government in French cities (the Ministry of Culture provides less than 15 percent, and private contributions are almost zero). We focus on government spending, but the private–public partnership leverages all sources. Civic leaders, foundations, and businesses are major cultural supporters, and Daley II worked with them actively on culture (Fig. 5).

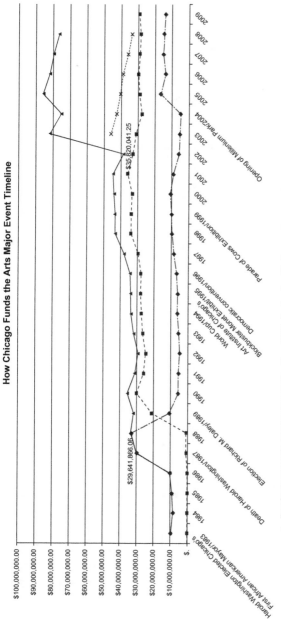

Fig. 4. How Chicago Funds the Arts. *Note:* All Chicago Spending Data was collected and compiled by Nicholas Musillami. All except for Park District Allocations came from the City of Chicago's Annual Appropriation Ordinances, the official agreed upon city budget. Chicago Park District funds came from their annual Audit/Financial Statements available on their website. When annual allocation numbers were not available, gross expenditures were used.

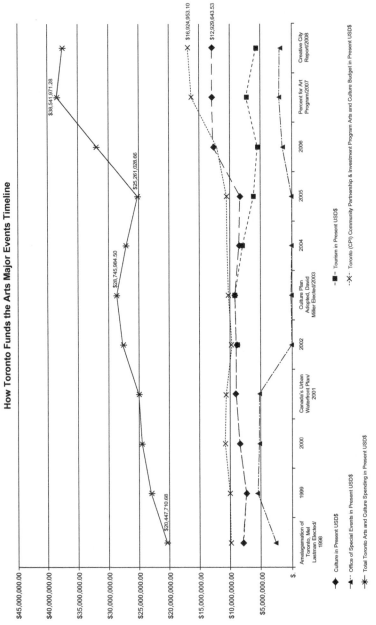

Fig. 5. How Toronto Funds the Arts. *Note*: All Toronto Spending data was collected and compiled by Nicholas Musillami. All data is from Toronto Budgets 1998–2008 available on the City of Toronto Website: http://www.toronto.ca/city_budget/previous_budgets.htm.

MILLENNIUM PARK AND THE CHICAGO WAY OF CULTURAL POLICY

The most dramatic new amenity in Chicago was clearly Millennium Park. It is critical here for several reasons. It was promoted as "Chicago's Eiffel Tower," it redefined the city's global image, and it was a huge ambitious project where public and private resources joined culture in new ways. Millennium Park from a user's perspective illustrates how public arts are used by Chicagoans from all backgrounds and neighborhoods. "The Crown Fountain" by James Plensa features rotating giant images of typical Chicagoans. Every 5 minutes or so they open their mouths and out gushes water. On hot summer days, children of all colors gather underneath waiting for the fountain to spit. "Cloudgate" also known as "the bean" by Anish Kapoor – a giant highly polished stainless steel object shaped like a kidney bean – reflects the city to the viewer in an infinite regress of images, encouraging a view of the city and its residents as in process, flux, and formation – a far cry from the classic images of stability, locality, and familiarity.

The central attractions in Millennium Park all bear the names of their private donors: The Jay Pritzker Pavillion, Boeing Galleries, Harris Theatre For Music and Dance, McDonald's Cycle Center, etc. Donations, along with revenues generated by the below-ground parking garage, were key to building the Park, as Daley promised, to do so without spending a dime of taxpayer money. Timothy Gilfoyle (2006) has documented the inner workings of the massive project. Upholding this "no-taxpayer-money" commitment was one of Daley's primary political concerns and a way of avoiding criticism, especially from the *Chicago Tribune*.

To coordinate Millennium Park's "aesthetic enhancements," Daley tapped John Bryan, CEO of Sara Lee, as his key fund raiser and civic leader. Bryan was an ideal choice – respected by the Chicago corporate elite, he also had strong ties to Chicago's major cultural institutions as Chair of the Art Institute and a Trustee at the University of Chicago. Bryan also had a track-record of success: "he had been an instrumental force in raising money to renovate Chicago's Lyric Opera House and Orchestra Hall, raising 100 million in three years ... This was at the time believed to be the largest amount of money ever given by a business community in support of a local cultural project" (Gilfoyle, 2006). At the same time, Bryan was a prime representative of the new social issues: he "transformed Sara Lee into a corporate model for breaking down gender and racial barriers" (Gilfoyle, 2006). These specifically aesthetic, social, and lifestyle concerns gave Bryan considerable clout with local environmental and neighborhood groups. He joined with the star power of architect Frank Gehry – "acquired" by the Pritzker family's efforts. Here we see masters in the culture of clout at work, applying old tricks within the new rules and among the new local actors.

Bryan was able to raise over $230 million for the project. In the 21st century cultural version of Chicago-style neighborhood/personal politics, he divided up the space into a series of regions (i.e., neighborhoods). Donors were given considerable input into the art and design of their particular spaces, and, more or less, Daley gave Bryan free-rein in this process. Furnari (2010) shows in network analyses how they divided along aesthetic lines, some more civic/citizen engaged, others more physical/garden oriented, even while collaborating. Each brought distinct resources: money, contacts, new public art objects, and multiuse buildings combined synergistically. Here we see the idiom of Washington's Cultural Plan realized on the canvas of globalization.

The list of donors includes many prominent Chicagoans, including Oprah Winfrey. Though the financial coalition was diverse, most gifts came from the finance sector and Chicago's old-guard industrial corporations – that is, from outside traditional growth machine interests like real estate and development. What held this group together, led by Bryan, was their shared membership in most of Chicago's philanthropic, civic, and artistic boards. Indeed, the arts groups in Chicago join many of its top business leaders, who see each other at dinners, fund raisers, symphonies, and art shows. Though clearly these leaders were concerned with growth, they were also motivated to create a world-class facility that would push aesthetic boundaries while Daley was interested in harnessing their connections, talents, and resources to stamp his name on a revitalized and more inviting, open, and multicultural downtown. Before Millennium Park, the most dramatic joining of these was Richard Franke's Chicago Humanities Festival, downtown, on and off campus at the University of Chicago.

In Chicago, one can find, as in the past, more narrow, open business conflicts, such as between new gondoliers and older barge haulers in the Chicago River, where Mayor Daley II mediated and encouraged a view that the river should be open to all users. How many mayors can speak of diversity with these two as examples? What could be a sharper marker that culture has been "institutionalized" into the normal life of normal Chicago politics? And Daley quipped further that he hoped the Chicago River would soon have more excitement than the Seine. New rhetoric, impossible in old Chicago, would have blushed at any comparison to Gay Paree.

CULTURAL POLICY IS A POLITICAL OUTCOME

Over the last half century, culminating in Daley II, Chicago's leaders have thus increasingly adopted policies that reflect three changes: toward more public goods, more managed growth, and more amenities. The Chicago case is thus ideal for highlighting the deeply political character of cultural policy, which analysts and policy makers all too often misrepresent as a pure exercise in nonpolitical planning.[14]

Indeed, Chicago machine politicians were masters of the political sphere, sending precinct captains into neighborhoods in order to know what their clients wanted. The new entertainment machine continues these practices, but also on a different, expressive level. Chicago is now host to not only ethnically rooted music festivals like the Blues or Celtic festivals, but Lollapalooza and the indie music Pitchfork Festival. If Daley I's power hinged on skilled precinct captains who knew what their people wanted, Daley II inaugurated a style of power that hinged on skilled cultural affairs officers sensitive to what indie music fans, environmental activists, jazz aficionados, and foodies liked, plus other elements of increasingly differentiated and refined domain of consumption. Fleury (2007, 2014, p. 180) shows that sensitive managers similarly built the Beaubourg Center into a powerful scene, by so engaging participants, that citizenship is experienced as an identity in public space. Beaubourg attracts as many visitors as the Eiffel Tower and the Louvre combined. Chicago's Millennium Park in this respect is closer to Beaubourg than the Eiffel Tower in joining multiple cultural events in adjacent public spaces, from sculpture to ice skating to opera. Mayor Rahm Emmanuel made producing a new Cultural Plan one of his first and most publicly broadcast policy goals, with new support for local and neighborhood musicians and music venues reportedly at its center.

The news is that citizens are no longer moving to the Paris Latin Quarter or New York's Greenwich Village to find the arts. You can now stay in Iowa City. There are all sorts of artistic, bohemian, colorful, and diverse neighborhoods in small- and mid-sized towns across the United States and elsewhere. These are entertainment machines of a new sort that work alongside the traditional growth machines. Analysts and policy makers can learn from the Chicago case: how cities with weak cultural traditions can dramatically transform themselves, without violence, in more profound ways than some nations where elites have proclaimed revolution.

CONCLUSION

The cases of Toronto and Chicago highlight two modes of active intervention in cultural policy, which complicates standard gentrification stories in which economics trumps politics and culture. Cities with different political culture would show different dynamics. Thus, in neo-clientelist Chicago, powerful patrons — top political and civic leaders — have sought to make the city's buzz dependent on their personal grace and friendship (Clark & Silver, 2013). Strong leaders and active movements, not only the unfolding of economic necessity, have put buzz onto the agenda. Their decisions take place in highly conflictual contexts, where coalition building and narrative framing are essential to what actually gets done. Understanding the resources they can bring to bear on these decisions is vital to understanding how cities are now governed.

It will take some time before academic research can confront these issues in a systematic way. If they are still new for policy makers and activists, they are even newer for urban theorists and analysts. By comparison, it took some 25 years of case studies, survey research, and intellectual debate about growth machines before Ramirez et al. (2008) could produce a systematic and empirically based morphology of mayor governing coalitions. At present, we lack survey results that explicitly probe the influence of cultural groups and initiatives across city governments and agencies. In *The City as an Entertainment Machine* (Clark, 2004, 2011) we analyzed cultural items from past surveys. Though the international surveys of the Fiscal Austerity and Urban Innovation project have moved toward the new issues discussed here, they have only begun to add questions about culture, amenities, and scenes. We have encouraged others in related research in *The Politics of Urban Cultural Policy: Global Perspectives* (Grodach & Silver, 2013), which includes some 18 case studies from around the globe, and elaboration of the Toronto case.

In such moments of intellectual and social ferment, however, theorizing of the sort undertaken here is vital to outline potential questions and connections that may not appear on the agenda of the activist or empirical researcher. This chapter offers a theoretical framework for analyzing cases where politics, cultural policy, economic development, and residential neighborhoods overlap. We build on a truly global movement of arts and culture. Yet it is not isolated from politics, despite much past rhetoric. Expressive culture is becoming deeply engaged in the social and political fabric of urban life. Our framework points at some of the local processes and actors through which the arts and culture can have an impact, proposing a new concept for a newly salient resource – buzz – that has in many contexts endowed new actors with a surprisingly strong influence. Toronto and Chicago provide useful first sites for investigating how this resource operates on the ground. But these cases need to be expanded and deepened, compared to other detailed case studies, and integrated into large-scale surveys that take culture seriously.

NOTES

1. Florida (2010) summarizes and popularizes much of the research confirming this trend; the popularity of his Rise of the Creative Class, as well as of the work of authors like Saskia Sassen and Sharon Zukin, is in part evidence for it.

2. Richard Florida and Alan Scott (2000), for example, though writing from very different perspectives, both link regional and city growth to the rise in culture production, but leave politics out. Similarly, Edward Glaeser and Richard Lloyd – again, very different sorts of writers – link the rise in urbanism to the growth in culture industries, consumer cities, and postindustrial labor conditions, but largely omit political impacts and leader. Clark (2003) ties variations in urban amenities to different political cultures, but pays little attention to the politics and policies of building amenities.

3. For instance, much past work on community power and urban leadership has tended to classify leaders by their (generic) social backgrounds, such as business, political, Catholic, or Italian. This was the most commonly reported data in many historical studies, even Dahl's (1961) history chapters of New Haven. Similarly, Markusen treats "artists" as a relatively homogeneous progressive political cal block against business and professional elites – even though their issue-specific concerns (aesthetic, political, residential, etc.) might be very different. Indeed, as Catungal and Leslie (2009) have shown, political differences may arise from divisions between commercial and "aesthetically pure" artists. McGovern's downtown "creative class" activists were influenced by city politics in Philadelphia, while the similar groups Indergaard studied in New York were less effective; political leaders in Reno were relatively unresponsive to the amenities concerns of the local population, whereas Vancouver, Toronto, and Chicago leaders have stressed these in their cultural policies. The issues may be similar, but the local contexts and coalitions clearly shifted the outcomes. The analytical question is to determine the conditions and factors that account for these shifts.

4. Still the regime label is sufficiently open that it could be broadened to include cultural concerns as we suggest here, just as Ferman (1996) suggested adding framing and political culture to regime analysis.

5. In the formal language of our theory, we refer to the specific buzz of a scene by appending "ies" to the experiential dimensions of scenes. That is, a scene that signals high levels of transgressive experience does so by projecting large volumes of "transgressies," glamorous experiences are signaled by "glammies," and neighborly experiences are signaled by "neighbies." This means that some places can be, so to

speak, all sizzle and no steak (high buzz but low experience) or vice versa (powerful experiences with little buzz signaling them). Our analyses of such buzz, for all 42,000 U.S. zipcodes, are detailed at http://scenes.uchicago.edu. One finding is that glammies are stronger in explaining economic growth than cost of living, crime, and population size. Buzz is not just fluff. Currid and Williams (2009) prove a potentially valuable way to develop empirical measures of buzz.

6. Stinchcombe (1968, p.119) observes that labor strikes were not a usurpation of an existing form of power by a new group but rather were a new way of exercising power, linked with the rise of labor markets and formally free employment. Buzz strikes are a similarly new form of power, linked with the rise of culture.

7. Parsons and Dahl discussed resources which T. N. Clark, J. S. Coleman, and A. L. Stinchcombe codified in exchange matrices showing how resources could shift in prices. This chapter extends the logic one step further by codifying how cultural and aesthetic criteria can shift the value/prices of other distinct resources. See Clark (1973, chapter 4).

8. The figures are based on yellow pages data compiled by the authors. M6J, the postal code in which West Queen West is located, has 27 art galleries, compared to 2.5 in the average Toronto postal code; 5 tattoo parlors compared to 0.5 in the average Toronto postal code.

9. Most notably, the area lacked a secondary plan, understaffing in the Planning and Legal departments made it difficult to move quickly enough to impose many controls on the development process, and the city was often trying to create policy in the course of quasi-legal process before the OMB.

10. "I'm not going anywhere, the other [arts and cultural organization] owners aren't going anywhere. ... It's about making sure that the condos become more than they were intended to be. We have to make sure the people learn to care about the area. My Polly-anna dream is to make sure they do" (Christina Zeidler, in Rau, 2007).

11. As Chicago is the most studied city in the world, it is critical to update these emerging patterns. We make only occasional comparisons and references to the huge past literature on Chicago that features very different rules of decision making; detail of this sort is in Clark (2012).

12. For instance, the Chicago Civic Center as well as public sculptures by Picasso, Calder, and Chagall all were built under Daley I. Daley I also orchestrated the election of Ira Bach as head of City Planning to ensure his place atop the hierarchy and avoid "political bureaucracy" (Miller, 2000, 254). This move allowed Daley to avoid variances, sell alleyways, reroute traffic, etc. all to ensure the interests of private business looking to build massive buildings (Miller, 2000, 255–261). This allowed architects to experiment with their creative freedom and to build in ways previously impossible.

13. We sought to assemble comparable data for Chicago as well as Toronto and other cities, but found the task daunting, and that past efforts have barely done this either. One of the few studies is by Americans for the Arts (2004) of the 50 largest U.S. cities which shows that Chicago spent $24 per capita on the arts. Unfortunately, the study only included one agency in each city, the Department of Cultural Affairs for Chicago, which makes comparisons inconsistent.

14. This is encouraged by the professional standards of organizations like the International City Managers Association and its more specialized counterparts as

well as academic disciplinary specialization. Even "cultural policy" analysts seek to differentiate themselves from public policy and political science. Cf. http://icma.org/en/icma/ethics/code_of_ethics; http://en.wikipedia.org/wiki/Cultural_policy.

ACKNOWLEDGMENTS

The authors thank for their helpful comments Herman Boschken, Meghan Kallman, Sarah Cappeliez, and Stephen Sawyer. Sarah Cappeliez and Nicholas Musillami provided valuable research assistance. This research was supported by the Social Sciences and Humanities Research Council.

REFERENCES

Alexander, J. C. (1987). *Twenty lectures: Sociological theory since World War II*. New York, NY: Columbia University Press.

Andersen, K. (1979). *The creation of a democratic majority, 1928–1936*. Chicago, IL: University of Chicago Press.

Banuelos, N. I. (2009). Promoting a Urbs in Horto: A review of Mayor Richard M. *Daley's speeches on beautification*. Chicago, IL: University of Chicago (Paper for Urban Policy Analysis course).

Barber, A. (2008). *Reno's big gamble: Image and reputation in the biggest little city*. Lawrence, KS: University Press of Kansas.

Bell, D. (1973). *The coming of post-industrial society: A venture in social forecasting*. New York, NY: Basic Books.

Bellow, S. (1975). *Humboldt's gift*. New York, NY: Penguin.

Boltanski, L., & Chiapello, E. (2005). *The new spirit of capitalism*. London: Verso.

Boudreau, J. A., Keil, R., & Young, D. (2009). *Changing Toronto: Governing urban neo-liberalism*. Toronto, ON: University of Toronto Press.

Brenner, N., & Theodore, N. (2005). Neoliberalism and the urban condition. *City*, *9*(1), 101–107.

Catungal, J. P., & Leslie, D. (2009). Placing power in the creative city: Governmentalities and subjectivities in Liberty Village, Toronto. *Environment & Planning A*, *41*(11), 2576–2594.

Churchill, D. S. (2010). American expatriates and the building of alternative social space in Toronto, 1965–1977. *Urban History Review*, *39*(1), 14–31.

City of Toronto. (2006). Request for direction report, south district application 05 199764 SPS 00 TM, official plan and zoning review in the West Queen West Triangle Area 2005 199764 SPS 00 TMWard 18 – Davenport. Online. Retrieved from http://www.toronto.ca/legdocs/2006/agendas/committees/te/te060613/it005.pdf. Accessed on February 12, 2012.

Clark, T. N. (1973). *Community power and policy outputs: A review of urban research*. Beverley Hills, CA: Sage.

Clark, T. N. (2003). The breakdown of class politics. *The American Sociologist*, *34*(1), 17–32.

Clark, T. N. (Ed.). (2011). *The city as an entertainment machine*. Lantham, MD: Lexington Books.

Clark, T. N. (Ed.). (2012). *Trees and real violins: Building post-industrial Chicago*. Book Draft, University of Chicago. Retrieved from www.faui.org/authors/clark.

Clark, T. N., & da Silva, F. C. (2009). Revisiting Tocqueville: Citizenship norms, political repertoires, and cultural participation. In M. Cherkaoui, P. Hamilton, & A. Frenod (Eds.), *Raymond Boudon: A life in sociology* (pp. 1–32). Oxford: Bardwell Press/GEMAS.

Clark, T. N., & Hoffmann-Martinot, V. (Eds.). (1998). *The new political culture*. Boulder, CO: Westview Press.

Clark, T. N., & Silver, D. (2013). Chicago from the political machine to the entertainment machine. In C. Grodach & D. Silver (Eds.), *The politics of urban cultural policy, global perspectives*. London: Routledge.

Clark, T. N. (Ed.). (2004). *The city as an entertainment machine, Research in Urban Policy*, Vol. 9, Oxford: JAI/Elsevier. Lantham, MD: Lexington Books, 2011 (Paperback).

Cortwright, J. (2005). *The young and restless in a knowledge economy*. Chicago, IL: CEOs for Cities.

Currid, E. (2007). *The Warhol economy: How fashion, art, and music drive New York City*. Princeton, NJ: Princeton University Press.

Currid, E., & Williams, S. (2009). The geography of buzz: Art, culture and the social milieu in Los Angeles and New York. *Journal of Economic Geography*, *10*(3), 423–451.

Dahl, R. A. (1961). *Who governs? Democracy and power in an American city*. New Haven, CT: Yale University Press.

Davis, R. (1995). Running Chicago. *Illinois Issues*, (February), 22.

Della Porta, D., Kriesi, H., & Rucht, D. (1999). *Social movements in a globalizing world*. New York, NY: St. Martin's Press.

Ferman, B. (1996). *Challenging the growth machine: Neighborhood politics in Chicago and Pittsburgh*. Lawrence, KS: University Press of Kansas.

Feron, D. (1999). *Working on an image of the city that works*. Master of Arts thesis, Department of Sociology, University of Chicago.

Fleury, L. (2007). *Le cas Beaubourg. Mécénat d'Etat et démocratisation de la culture*. Paris: Armand Colin.

Fleury, L. (2014). *Sociology of culture and cultural practices*. Lanham, MD: Lexington Books.

Florida, R. (2010). *The great reset: How new ways of living and working drive post-crash prosperity*. New York, NY: Harper.

Foad, L. (2007). Selling off Queen West. *Now Magazine*, 26(51), August 23–30.

Furnari, S. (2010). *Multiple networks, brokerage and institutional change in the creation of Millennium Park in Chicago, 1997–2004*. Ph.D. thesis, Bocconi University, Italy.

Gilfoyle, T. (2006). *Millenium Park: Creating a Chicago landmark*. Chicago, IL: University of Chicago Press.

Grazian, D. (2003). *Blue Chicago: The search for authenticity in urban blues clubs*. Chicago, IL: University of Chicago Press.

Grodach, C. (2012). Before and after the creative city: The politics of urban cultural policy in Austin, TX. *Journal of Urban Affairs*, *34*(1), 81–97.

Grodach, C., & Silver, D. (2013). *The politics of urban cultural policy: Global perspectives*. New York, NY: Routledge.

Guterbock, T. (1980). *Machine politics in transition: Party and community in Chicago*. Chicago, IL: University of Chicago.

Gyourko, J., Mayer, C., & Sinai, T. (2006). *Superstar cities*. National Bureau of Economic Research Working Paper Series. Online. Retrieved from http://www.nber.org/papers/w12355.pdf. Accessed on March 30, 2012.

Harvey, D. (1989). From managerialism to entrepreneurialism: The transformation of urban governance in late capitalism. *Geografiska Annaler, 71B*, 3–17.

Hitzler, R., Bucher, T., & Niederbacher, A. (2005). *Leben in Szenen: Formen jugendlicher Vergemeinschaftung heute*. Wiesbaden: VS, Verlag für Sozialwissenschaft.

Indergaard, M. (2009). What to make of New York's new economy? The politics of the creative field. *Urban Studies, 46*(5), 1063–1093.

Jacobs, J. (1969). *Economy of cities*. New York, NY: Random House.

Kuznicki, M. (2007). OMB decision on Queen West: Spark a revolution. Online. Retrieved from http://remarkk.com/2007/01/16/omb-decision-on-queen-west-spark-a-revolution/. Accessed on February 12, 2012.

Lee, L. (2003). Super-gentrification: The case of Brooklyn Heights, New York City. *Urban Studies, 40*(12), 2487–2509.

Lemon, J. (1984). Toronto among North American cities: A historical perspective on the present. In V. Russel (Ed.), *Forging a concensus: Historical essays on Toronto* (pp. 323–352). Toronto, ON: University of Toronto Press.

Lidz, V. (2001). Language and the "family" of generalized symbolic media. In A. J. Treviño (Ed.), *Talcott Parsons today: His theory and legacy in contemporary sociology* (pp. 141–176). Lanham, MD: Rowman & Littlefield Publishers.

Lloyd, R. (2006). *Neo-bohemia: Art and commerce in the postindustrial city*. New York, NY: Routledge.

Logan, J. R., & Molotch, H. (1987). *Urban fortunes: The political economy of place*. Berkeley, CA: University of California Press.

Longworth, R. C. (2007). *Caught in the middle: America's heartland in the age of globalism*. New York, NY: Bloomsbury.

Lowi, T. J. (1964). American business, public policy, case-studies, and political theory. *World Politics, 16*(4), 677–715.

Markusen, A. (2006). Urban development and the politics of the creative class: Evidence from a study of artists. *Environment & Planning A, 38*(10), 1921–1940.

McAdam, D., McCarthy, J. D., & Zald, M. N. (1996). *Comparative perspectives on social movements: Political opportunities, mobilizing structures, and cultural framings*. New York, NY: Cambridge University Press.

McDonald, K. (2006). *Global movements: Action and culture*. Malden, MA: Blackwell.

McGovern, S. J. (2009). Mobilization on the waterfront: The ideological/cultural roots of potential regime change in Philadelphia. *Urban Affairs Review, 44*(5), 663–694.

Miller, R. (2000). City hall and the architecture of power: The rise and fall of the Dearborn Corridor. In J. Zukowski (Ed.), *Chicago architecture and design 1923–1993* (pp. 247–263). Munich: Prestal Verlag.

McKinnie, M. (2007). *City stages: Theatre and urban space in a global city*. Toronto, ON: University of Toronto Press.

National Endowment for the Arts. (2007). *How the United States funds the arts* (2nd ed.). Retrieved from www.nea.gov/pub/how.pdf. Accessed on March 19, 2012.

Parsons, T. (1971). *The system of modern societies*. Englewood Cliffs, NJ: Prentice-Hall.

Pasotti, E. (2009). *Political branding in cities: The decline of machine politics in Bogota, Naples, and Chicago*. New York, NY: Cambridge University.

Pasotti, E. (2010). *Political branding in cities*. Cambridge: Cambridge University Press.

Pink, D. H. (2006). *A whole new mind: Why right-brainers will rule the future*. New York, NY: Riverhead Trade.

Postrel, V. (2004). *The substance of style: How the rise of aesthetic value is remaking commerce, culture, and consciousness.* New York, NY: Harper Collins.

Preville, P. (2007). Bedeviled triangle. *Toronto Life*, June.

Putnam, R. (2000). *Bowling alone: The collapse and revival of American community.* New York, NY: Simon & Schuster.

Rakove, M. (1976). *Don't make no waves, don't back no losers: An insiders' analysis of the Daley Machine.* Bloomington, IN: Indiana University Press.

Ramirez, A. M., Navarro, C. J., & Clark, T. N. (2008). Mayors and local governing coalitions in democratic countries: A cross-national comparison. *Local Government Studies, 34*(2), 147–178.

Rau, K. (2007). Artists win in development deal. Xtra!. Online. Retrieved from http://www.xtra.ca/public/Toronto/Artists_win_in_development_deal-3852.aspx. Accessed on February 12, 2012.

Rundquist, B. S., Miranda, R. A., & Tunyavong, I. (1991). *Race, class, and fiscal policy: Chicagoan's attitudes on taxes and services.* Bloomington, IN: Midwest Political Science Association.

Sassen, S. (1994). *Cities in a world economy.* Thousand Oaks, CA: Pine Forge Press.

Savitch, H. V., & Kantor, P. (2002). *Cities in the international marketplace.* Princeton, NJ: Princeton University Press.

Scott, A. J. (2000). *The cultural economy of cities: Essays on the geography of image-producing industries.* Thousand Oaks, CA: Sage.

Silver, D. (2011). The moodiness of action. *Sociological Theory, 29*(3), 199–222.

Silver, D. (2012). Local politics in the creative city: The case of Toronto. In C. Grodach & D. Silver (Eds.), *The politics of urban cultural policy, global perspectives.* London: Routledge.

Silver, D., Clark, T. N., & Navarro Yáñez, C. J. (2010). Scenes: Social context in an age of contingency. *Social Forces, 88*(5), 2293–2324.

Sliver, D. A., & Clark, T. N. (2014). *Scenes.* Chicago, IL: University of Chicago Press.

Smith, N. (2002). New globalism, new urbanism: Gentrification as global urbanization strategy. *Antipode, 3*(3), 427–450.

St. John, P. (1999). Crime and public goods. Presentation to Urban Social Processes Workshop, University of Chicago and Email Communications, December 12.

Statistics Canada. *Canadian business patterns (1999–2008): Establishment counts by Canada and provinces, industry sector (NAICS, 6-digit)* [computer file]. Ottawa, ON: Statistics Canada. Business Register Division [producer]; Statistics Canada. Data Liberation Initiative [distributor]. Retrieved from http://www.statcan.gc.ca/start-debut-eng.html. Accessed on April 2009.

Stinchcombe, A. L. (1968). *Constructing social theories.* Chicago, IL: University of Chicago Press.

Taylor, C. (2007). *A secular age.* Cambridge, MA: Belknap Press of Harvard University Press.

The Theater Loop. (2009). Online. Retrieved from http://leisureblogs.chicagotribune.com/the_theater_loop/2009/10/new-nea-chief-lauds-daley-arts-policy-says-model-for-nation.html#at. Accessed on March 12, 2012.

Whaley, K. (2007). Condo project on Queen West approved. The Torontoist. Online. Retrieved from http://torontoist.com/2007/01/ condo_project_o/. Accessed on February 2012

Zukin, S. (1982). *Loft living: Culture and capital in urban change.* Baltimore, MD: Johns Hopkins University Press.

Zukin, S. (2010). *Naked city: The death and life of authentic urban places.* New York, NY: Oxford University Press.

CULTURE IS ON THE RISE – WHY? THEORIES OF CULTURAL PARTICIPATION AND EMPIRICAL EVIDENCE

Terry Nichols Clark and Peter Achterberg

ABSTRACT

Several theories suggest transformations in citizen participation. Putnam and many others suggest a decline in participation. By adding issue specificity, we find that the arts and culture are a major exception: they are rising in many countries and contexts.

Keywords: Participation; arts; culture; comparative politics

PAST THEORIZING ON CULTURAL PARTICIPATION

Consider first just three widely discussed theoretical perspectives that could be extended to address cultural issues.

Can Tocqueville Karaoke? Global Contrasts of Citizen Participation, the Arts and Development
Research in Urban Policy, Volume 11, 221–235
Copyright © 2014 by Emerald Group Publishing Limited
All rights of reproduction in any form reserved
ISSN: 1479-3520/doi:10.1108/S1479-352020140000011026

1. Cultural activities are often associated with voluntary associations and civic culture. Much discussion has centered on Robert Putnam's main theme in *Bowling Alone* (Putnam, 2000) and more recently about the decline of trust (2007). These argue that civil society is weakening; membership in voluntary organizations has been dropping, signifying less trust, a loss of community, and turning inward by individuals who are less socially and civically engaged. Putnam cites many surveys for especially U.S. citizens and more traditional organized groups, like Boy Scouts and bowling leagues. *Intriguingly, we find the opposite for cultural organizations. They are on the rise in many studies, and the main activists are young persons – implying a very different dynamic from that of Putnam.*

2. Another classic tradition for the study of voluntary associations is the theory of Verba, Schlozman, Brady, & Nie, (1993 and various updates). They argue that the "normal" pattern is essentially class politics, in the sense that the citizens who participate most in civic life and politics are higher in status and more socially connected. Thus higher education, income, and occupation, but also those more connected: fixed residential location, a stable job, which tends to rise with age, should all lead to higher participation by established older persons. *Again, intriguingly we find disparate results for cultural participation and arts. Younger and less socially connected persons participate more. Status varies by issue.*

3. A third broad, related perspective is that of Ronald Inglehart whose terms have shifted, but his core ideas stress the rise of postmodern values (which one might imagine should include cultural concerns). He theorizes and offers considerable data to show that these general values are more important over time, as countries modernize, and among individuals who are more affluent. (More specifics follow.) *Corollary: The affluent and young will be more interested and concerned with culture. We find some support for this proposition, but find it insufficient, especially regarding individuals in their social context and how these impact cultural activities.*

What is lacking in these three major theoretical statements that they should miss key elements of current social changes? We address this by first reviewing our theory of the New Political Culture (NPC) and then adapting it to consumption, arts, and culture via the new concept of scenes. Several propositions are stated, which are tested with several large data sets.

THE NPC: THE WORLD HAS CHANGED DRAMATICALLY IN THE LAST FEW DECADES

The new "knowledge economy," "creative class," outsourcing combine in globalization, which operates in several domains:

- via finance and economic exchange stressed by the World Bank, and others,
- via communication: computers/broadband/Internet/contracting out, detailed by Manual Castells and Thomas Friedman in *The World is Flat*,
- via politics (human rights, NGOs, and our NPC),
- via a new emphasis on consumption, lifestyle, popular culture often via popular media (Hollywood, Bollywood, BBC, CNN, CDs and DVDs, iPods).

Consider just a few common themes in all four areas, then how these relate to culture. In all four areas — of finance, communication, politics, and consumption — we see the same contours of a NPC. It transcends the older debates about capitalism versus socialism, and left versus right. Instead of old conflicts of rich and poor (or in Korea the two regions) we see new, issue-specific concerns, like feminism and environmental protection and many more, sometimes around Internet groups. In contrast to hierarchy and tradition of the past, we see more individualism and egalitarianism, as expressed

- via free markets, small entrepreneurs, and a mobile workforce in the economy instead of long-term careers, strong unions, and large organizations dependent on clientelist banks or state loans;
- via the Internet and individual communication options like smartphones, social media and personalized selections, blogs, instead of limited choice large television channels or major newspapers;
- via a new focus on the citizen, on neighborhoods, on individual participation, and self-generated bottom-up rather than top-down politics. Traditional political parties and voter turnout are in decline. Localized, issue-specific groups are growing. Decentralization is a huge theme in Korea, to move away from Seoul and from the domination of the national government. Implementation is harder, of course, but one clear institutional change is the local election of mayors. Similarly, the Internet has added a targeted, issue specificity to political campaigns in Korea. These were adapted by the Obama campaigns for two US elections;
- via new types of political leaders like Bill Clinton, Tony Blair, and Gerhard Schroeder among many others who break old rules and ideological categories;

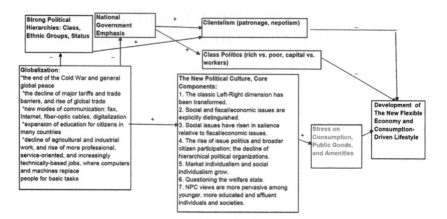

Fig. 1.   Relations among Key Variables in the NPC Framework.

- via individualizing lifestyle, in dress, entertainment, spontaneity, and volatility of choice. This same individualism that can be expressed politically is also expressed daily in people's lives, where they choose clothes, food, hats, and where to spend their time. This extends the individualism to many new domains: in contrast to tourists traveling in a large group to a classic, fixed destination, or traveling to the same vacation home with your family. Instead, young persons increasingly find or search for more uniquely personalized life styles.

This NPC is emerging around the world. We have documented its extent and change in over 15,000 cities and towns in 35 countries in the book entitled *The New Political Culture*. The NPC is explored further in seven other books, on the decline of class politics, the rise of citizens, the emergence of new types of leaders, a case study of Chicago, and political cultures of the world. See www.faui.org, which includes in the *Newsletter* abstracts of 50 books published by our Fiscal Austerity and Urban Innovation Project over the past 20 plus years (Fig. 1).

CONSUMPTION AND AMENITIES RISE IN SALIENCE TO INDIVIDUAL CITIZENS, GROUPS, AND POLITICAL LEADERS

Classic concerns of work and job decline. This is not to say people work less, but a new creativity, a playfulness, an entrepreneurship have come to define the ideal workplace, such that ideal organizations like Microsoft or Google are detailed as having "campus-like creative settings." They are the new models in business magazines like *Fortune* and *Business Week*. Work and leisure are no longer so isolated; leisure concerns penetrate the workplace. Driven by more income, education, and the NPC, culture and tourism are key parts of this transformation. Art is on the walls of many banks; major corporations sponsor theater, music, and public art. Political leaders sense the importance of rising arts and culture concerns among citizens and look for ways to capture these concerns: via public art, music festivals, historic preservation of neighborhoods, museums, and more. Essen, Germany, Naples, Italy, Bogotá, Colombia, and Chicago, USA, are all heavy industrial cities that have dramatically transformed themselves via creative mayors and arts and culture-based policies in the last decade or two. We cite these precisely as they were rapid but deep transformations by strong political leaders, not just a continuation of a long tradition, as one finds in Paris or Beijing. We see more bookstores, Internet sites, coffee shops, and all forms of cultural activities in these cities and all over the world. Participants in our FAUI project have documented deep change in these and other locations.

More generally, this rise of consumption, lifestyle, amenities, and culture is captured in emerging new theories of "postindustrial society" that contrast with more traditional workplace theories of which Marxism is the most extreme. Classic individualism in its pure market form, in the tradition of Locke, Hobbes, and Adam Smith, contrasts sharply in the themes of newer theorizing. Our volume illustrating this transformation and extension of the NPC is *The City as an Entertainment Machine* (Clark, 2003, 2011), whose title stresses the new importance of entertainment, consumption, and culture for cities. It lays out an analytical perspective stressing the importance of amenities as attracting persons to locations that have the most powerful amenities (schools, low crime, clean air, friends and family, restaurants, cultural facilities).

The core argument of the book is summarized in the simple path diagram (Fig. 2), showing how amenities are an addition to land, labor, capital, and human capital. They draw talent.

But this book and the traditions it extends treated separate amenities largely in isolation. This is normal for economists who tend to see the world atomistically. But so do many literary or cultural critics, who focus on an individual painting, or "the work of theater" of Shakespeare or "the text" of a novel or "le livre comme objet." But if we instead ask persons why they visit a museum or theater, and what made the experience important or not, the answers are often much more holistic. They normally

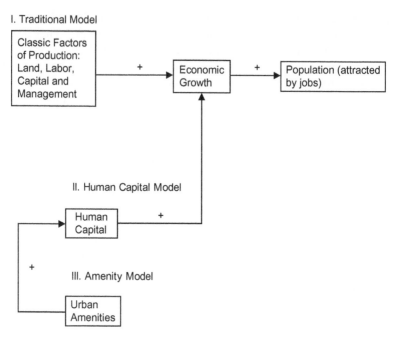

Fig. 2. Three Successive Models of Development.

engage the lifestyle of the visitor or tourist as much as the "site" which the visitor or tourist was "meant" to see. There are many theories of aesthetics, which can be enriched by incorporating a more holistic set of elements that together comprise a scene. Canterbury, England, Andong and Korea, illustrate a powerful "scene" that attracted scholars and pilgrims for centuries.

THE RISE OF CULTURE: EMPIRICAL EVIDENCE

From mayors' agendas for urban renewal to the general population's practices, the arts have become a major area of political interest, economic investment, and self-realization in most developed countries. This global rise of arts and culture has been largely ignored until now for two main reasons. On the one hand, most studies on the arts are case studies whose authors have not sought to explore the broader and the political implications of arts participation. On the other hand, leading quantitative studies of arts and culture participation tend to focus on the traditional arts (live theater, symphony concerts, visiting museums) and omit such new activities as playing in a small band and many digital arts (graphic design, video, web, and interactive design, animation). Still, there is by no means consensus here: rather many if not most writings on the arts suggest a decline rather than growth in recent decades. The main resolution of this conflict is to focus on distinct types of art and culture.

The more established "high" art like classical music concerts, opera, and museum attendance show stability or decline in many countries. This has led to a sense of crisis in many arts organizations, like the U.S. National Endowment for the Arts which commissioned multiple studies. Many showed the classic decline of the "benchmark" high arts, but Novak-Leonard and Brown (2011) showed high participation and growth in some nontraditional activities. And the French Ministry of Culture studies document this pattern with more detail, growth in media related film, music, and more, especially among young persons who create personal entertainment libraries, etc. These have often been missed as they are not classic benchmark items, but many are captured in the World Values Survey item, which permits the respondent to include all arts and culture items in which she participates. We hope to nudge social scientists to catch up to these developments. This critical finding came from working together in Chicago summer 2007. It is presented here with less than full detail to convey how the ideas developed and acknowledge Peter Achterberg. Other chapters push further, esp. chapter 14. The World Values Survey website includes full questionnaires and commentaries on each item.

Fig. 3 shows the results of a simple regression analysis in which the salience of culture as reported by citizens – measured as the share of space political parties in a country in an election year spend on issues such as the need to provide cultural and leisure facilities including arts and sport, the need to spend money on museums, art galleries, etc., the need to encourage worthwhile leisure activities and cultural mass media – develops in time in 22 western countries. The plotted trend line clearly shows an upward trend in the salience of these culture issues.

Splitting out the analysis above for each country separately in Table 1 shows that in 16 countries there is a positive and statistically significant trend in the prominence of culture. Conclusion: political culture is more oriented toward traditional "high" culture – culture is clearly on the rise politically.

If these cultural issues are on the rise, which parties (Table 2) are specifically concerned with these issues?

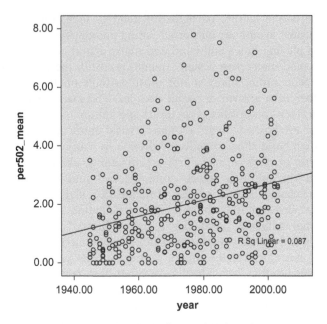

Fig. 3. Trend in the Salience of Culture Issues.

There are no strong differences between the political parties in the degree to which culture issues are salient to them (in the Means column). The mainstream parties all show rises in attention to culture, but the smaller parties show no change (Pearson's r column of Table 1).

To move the level of analysis to another level, we also investigated whether membership of cultural activity groups has increased over time. Table 3 presents the results for the period 1981–2000 using the World Values Survey.

The conclusion: for most countries, the picture that emerges is that cultural group membership is rising indeed. Note, however, that this does not seem to be the case in postcommunist countries.

Since in the literature much attention is given to generational differences in values, behavior, and what else more, in Fig. 4 we analyzed how generations differ in the membership of cultural activity groups.

The above of course leads to the conclusion that Verba and Nie and Putnam are mistaken on one thing: culture is on the rise without any doubt. So theories derived from the work of Inglehart that argue that

Table 1. The Rise of Culture in Some More Detail.

Country	General Mean	Pearson's r	N
Australia	1.23	0.40*	23
Austria	2.52	−0.36	17
Belgium	3.65	0.51*	19
Canada	1.19	0.22	18
Denmark	0.56	0.43*	17
Finland	1.03	0.32~	17
France	1.76	0.60**	15
Germany	1.95	0.51*	15
Great Britain	1.63	0.57*	15
Greece	2.72	0.80**	9
Iceland	1.66	0.36~	16
Ireland	2.71	0.39*	16
Italy	1.59	0.77***	15
Luxembourg	3.20	0.82***	13
Netherlands	3.00	0.05	18
New Zealand	2.01	−0.09	18
Norway	4.45	0.39~	15
Portugal	3.13	0.80**	11
Spain	2.10	0.25	8
Sweden	1.68	0.44*	18
Switzerland	1.57	−0.19	15
United States	0..68	−0.09	14

$\sim p < 0.10$; $*p < 0.05$; $**p < 0.01$; $***p < 0.001$ (one-tailed test for significance).
Note: Source is World Values Surveys in all analyses. The correlation is between cultural salience and time.

Table 2. Concern with Culture for Each Party Family.

Party Family	Mean Salience of Culture	N	Trend
Ecology parties	2.46	22	0.03
Communist parties	2.05	58	0.33**
Social democratic parties	2.16	59	0.50***
Liberal parties	1.93	59	0.49***
Christian democratic parties	2.40	58	0.19
Conservative parties	1.73	59	0.48***
Nationalist parties	2.68	33	−0.26
Agrarian parties	1.81	55	0.24
Ethnic and regional parties	1.65	35	0.25
Special issue parties	1.62	42	0.15

$**p < 0.01$; $***p < 0.001$ (one-tailed test for significance).
$F = 1.891$; $P < 0.051$.

Table 3. Rising Membership of Cultural Activity Groups.

Country	1981	1990	2000	Delta
Netherlands	12.5	34.6	45.2	32.7
United States	13.9	19.7	36.9	23
Sweden	13	12.7	26.7	13.7
Finland	3.1	20.1	14.6	11.5
Canada	9.7	17.7	20.1	10.4
Denmark	6.2	12.5	16.6	10.4
Belgium	10.3	16.2	18.9	8.6
Iceland	7.6	13.8	15.5	7.9
Estonia		11.1	7.9	7.9
South Korea	3.2	11		7.8
Japan	3.8	6	11	7.2
Norway	6.6	13.5		6.9
Italy	3.9	4.9	9.9	6
West Germany	6.1	12		5.9
South Africa	8.2		13.5	5.3
Britain	6.1	9.3	10.4	4.3
Ireland	6.7	10.1	10.9	4.2
Argentina	5.3	5.9	9	3.7
Mexico	6.5	11.5	9.5	3
France	5.6	8.8	8.1	2.5
Spain	4.9	5.3	6.6	1.7
Northern Ireland	6.1	10.9	7.6	1.5
Hungary		2.5	3.6	1.1
Romania		1.6	2.6	1
Austria	13	8	13.2	0.2
Chile		9.3	9.3	0
Bulgaria		4.3	4	−0.3
Portugal		6.2	3.7	−2.5
Brazil		5.4	2.4	−3
Latvia		6.8	3.7	−3.1
Russia		4.9	1.2	−3.7
Lithuania		7.3	2.9	−4.4
China		7.3	2.2	−5.1

culture will become more important in more affluent countries seem tentatively supported are basically validated here. Still while it may be true that a rise in culture is found, this does not imply that the mechanisms underlying this rise of culture are those that are covered by Inglehart's theory. *To sum up the foregoing, culture is on the rise. In the remainder of this chapter, we begin to interpret why.*

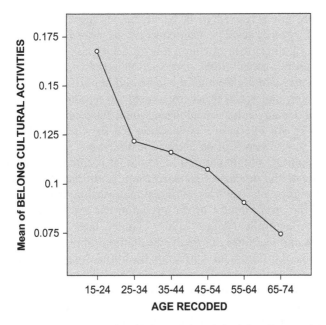

Fig. 4. Generations and Memberships to Cultural Activity Groups ($F = 115.196$; $P < 0.001$; $N = 78,675$).

CONTEXTUALIZING THE RISE OF CULTURE I

Explaining the Rise of Culture

Inglehart's explanation for the rising importance of issues of culture is derived from his theory explaining the upsurge of postmaterialist values. This logic for explaining the salience of postmaterialist issues is primarily materialistic (Houtman, 2003). Based on two hypotheses, the scarcity and the socialization hypothesis, Inglehart argues that those living in wealthy circumstances in their formative years (14 through 16 years of age) regard nonmaterial issues as important. Thus, because postwar generations were brought up in a secure and wealthy environment, they attach less importance to material issues and instead attach more importance to nonmaterial issues, quality of life issues and culture. Following this materialistic logic, it can then be understood that in the more wealthy nations, material problems are not perceived to be as urgent, as most citizens have never experienced material scarcity. Consequently, in more prosperous countries, individuals will direct their attention toward achieving a better quality of life by striving for self-actualization, participation in the arts, and so on.

Yet, one may wonder whether the increased importance of issues of individual freedom and social order are caused by economic development, as Inglehart and many other sociologists would have us believe (Houtman, 2003, p. 167). An alternative explanation for the rise of cultural politics focuses on the processes of secularization that have taken place in many Western countries. Within cultural sociology, it is commonplace to suggest that because of the process of secularization, traditional Christian religion has lost its grips on the lives of individuals within these societies; and because of this, traditional Christian religion has lost its ability to "overarch" society morally (Berger, 1967). Under these circumstances, the obviousness and legitimacy of the traditional moral order of values that is supported by the dominant Christian tradition decays rapidly (Wilson, 1982).

Through this process, behavioral rules and the self-evidence of certain types of behavior are taken less for granted, as the traditional influence of the church, as an authoritative institution, has by and large fallen away. Berger et al. argue that "The typical situation in which the individual finds himself in a traditional society is one where there are highly reliable plausibility structures. Conversely, modern societies are characterized by unstable, incohesive, unreliable plausibility structures. Put differently, in the modern situation certainty is hard to come by" (Berger et al., 1973, pp. 17–19). In these societies, individuals have to increasingly make decisions about their own course of life. The "standard biography" has been replaced by a "do-it-yourself biography" (compare Beck and Beck-Gernsheim, 1996) and more than ever before, individuals have to choose their own life course. Put differently, "Traditions lose their obviousness and part of their relevance. Religious beliefs and ideologies fade out and decreasingly control the lives of people. If they are followed, the rules are laid down in a less precise and less coercive manner. Concrete behavioral rules are traded in for more general behavioral rules" (Elchardus, 2002, pp. 46–47, our translation into English).

Modern life increasingly may thus be characterized as a search for certainty and truth because people increasingly have to choose what they think is worth living for. What is more, they increasingly need to define and redefine their identity. Whether one should be free or not, what they find beautiful and what not, what is valuable and what not are all questions that need constant answers in a world without any clear and dominant tradition guiding people. That issues of culture have become salient can therefore also be understood from the fact that in time societies have turned away from tradition and toward the individual (Heelas, Lasch, & Morris, 1996).

The problem with these general interpretations like postmaterialism or secularization is that they assume, or stress, a single main factor. An alternative approach is to suggest that there are many factors that operate in multicausal manner, and their relative weights and dynamics vary in part with smaller units, like scenes. The strongest version of this leads to historicism, but the mainstream Weberian version is updated for instance in Thompson, Ellis, and Wildavsky (1990). Our scenes approach follows this main tradition in moving to lower level units, below nations where possible, illustrated in Chapter 14.

Empirical Evidence Explaining Culture

In order to simplify the analyses somewhat, we chose to find out whether greater salience of cultural issues goes together with higher membership of

Table 4. The Relationship between the Political Salience of Culture and Individual Level Membership of Culture and Arts Groups.

Country	Correlation Membership and Salience of Culture
Austria	0.73
Belgium	−0.68
Britain	0.99
Canada	0.73
Denmark	0.81
Finland	0.89
France	−0.88
Germany	0.05
Iceland	0.99
Ireland	0.40
Italy	0.99
Netherlands	0.97
Norway	0.99
Portugal	−0.08
Spain	0.71
Sweden	0.54
United States	−0.25

Table 5.   Explaining the Salience of Culture.

Independents	Model 0	Model 1
Constant	0.30	−0.09
GDP		0.89**
Religiosity		−0.73**
Deviance	82.22	70.84
R^2 country level		0.46
R^2 time level		0.20
N	34	34

$*p < 0.05$; $**p < 0.01$.
N.B. for 1981: No data on religiosity are available.

cultural activity groups in a country in order to validate a culture-centrism index. In Table 4 the results are shown.

The membership of cultural groups at the national level is positively correlated with the salience of culture issues at the same level (the mean correlation is 0.47): for this reason we constructed a scale for the centrality of culture in a nation. Below this scale was regressed on GDP and the degree of religiosity (Table 5).

The analysis shows that both religion and prosperity equally contribute to the salience of culture. Both the materialistic logic and the logic focusing on institutional changes thus are confirmed. This analysis however does not contextualize the circumstances in which culture starts to matter to individuals. That is the aim of our theory of scenes, elaborated elsewhere.

REFERENCES

Beck, U., & Beck-Gernsheim, E. (1996). Individualization and "precarious freedoms": Perspectives and controversies of a subject-orientated sociology. In P. Heelas, S. Lash, & P. Morris (Eds.), *Detraditionalization: Critical reflections on authority and identity*. Oxford: Blackwell.

Berger, P., Berger, B., & Kellner, H. (1973). *The homeless mind: Modernization and consciousness*. New York, NY: Random House.

Berger, P. L. (1967). *The sacred canopy: Elements of a sociological theory of religion*. New York, NY: Anchor.

Clark, T. N. (2011). *The city as an entertainment machine*. Lanham, MD: Lexington Books (Elsevier published 2003).

Elchardus, M. (2002). De Dramademocratie. Lannoo.

Heelas, P., Lasch, S., & Morris, P. (Eds.) (1996). *Detraditionalization.* Oxford: Blackwell.

Houtman, D. (2003). *Class and politics in contemporary social science: "Marxism lite" and its blind spot for culture.* New York, NY: Aldine de Gruyter.

Novak-Leonard, J., & Brown, A. (2011). *Beyond attendance: A multi-modal understanding of arts participation.* Washington, DC: National Endowment for the Arts.

Putnam, R. (2000). *Bowling alone: The collapse and revival of American community.* New York, NY: Simon &; Schuster.

Thompson, M., Ellis, R., & Wildavsky, A. (1990). *Cultural theory.* Boulder, CO: Westview.

Verba, S., Schlozman, K. L., & Brady, H. E. (1995). *Voice and equality civic voluntarism in American politics.* Cambridge, MA: Harvard University Press.

Verba, S., Schlozman, K., Brady, H., & Nie, N. (1993). Citizen activity: Who participates? What do they say? *American Political Science Review, 87*(2), 303–318.

Wilson, B. (1982). *Religion in the sociological perspective.* Oxford: Oxford University Press.

HOW CONTEXT TRANSFORMS CITIZEN PARTICIPATION: PROPOSITIONS

Filipe Carreira da Silva and Terry Nichols Clark

ABSTRACT

Eight propositions state how contexts shift citizen participation. Religion, consumption patterns, and varied political repertoires transform participation. Hierarchical, authoritarian contexts foster antiestablishment participation and protest activities. Trust only emerges from some contexts. Participation in the arts and culture vary with other contextual elements.

Keywords: Participation; politics; authority; religion; culture; arts

Jeremiads, that recurrent American genre, tend to be highly popular among social scientists. Its rhetorical effect has proved effective generation after generation. The latest grand lament of a lost golden past in the social sciences has been Robert D. Putnam's *Bowling Alone*, one of most cited monographs in political science since its publication in 1995. With it, thousands of practitioners all over the world devoted themselves to the study of

Can Tocqueville Karaoke? Global Contrasts of Citizen Participation, the Arts and Development
Research in Urban Policy, Volume 11, 237–250
Copyright © 2014 by Emerald Group Publishing Limited
ISSN: 1479-3520/doi:10.1108/S1479-352020140000011027

the causes of the great democratic malaise of our time – the gradual and seemingly inexorable civic decline of mature liberal democracies. People vote less and less, don't join political campaigns as they used to, and associational life is a bleak shadow of what was just a couple of generations ago. Alexis de Tocqueville, for whom the secret of American democracy lay in its vibrant civil society and voluntary associations, would be deeply disappointed at the poor condition of American democracy today, so Putnam's argument goes. Would he? We are not so sure. Of course, we do not intend to correct Putnam's jeremiad with the opposite mistake, utopian enthusiasm. Both pessimism and optimism can prevent one from appreciating crucial possibilities of the phenomena at stake. Pessimism and optimism are dispositions that, although they can and should be studied as such, are not to interfere with scientific inquiry. It was the pessimism of Max Weber, perhaps one of the most distinctive and alluring features of his thinking, which prevented him from appreciating the democratic potential of the rising Bismarkian social state. Similar difficulties are faced by incorrigible optimists (consider Thomas Friedman's proposal of globalization as the solution for many problems). However seductive these rhetorical strategies can be, their limitations soon come to the fore when confronted with alternative modes of scientific inquiry. In this chapter, we propose one such alternative. We argue that not enough attention has been paid to a whole facet of democratic experience that does not conform to Putnam's neo-Tocquevillian understanding of civic virtue.

---

1) "Bowling Alone" proposition (Tocqueville/Putnam):

The higher the level of participation in voluntary associations, the higher are the levels of trust and political legitimacy.

Corollary: As the welfare state retreats, civil society organizations become more important sources of legitimacy and trust.

Putnam's underlying civic standard is the Protestant, town meeting tradition of participation. This is, we will show, a highly specific civic tradition that has become political science's standard for "democracy." As the identification between trust and democracy becomes a taken-for-granted assumption, political scientists grow less and less sensitive to dissent, conflict, passion, irony, glamour, and many other ingredients of political scenes. These, we claim, are as important elements of democratic life as the "generalizable trust" of the New England town meeting civic tradition.

One's trust in others diminishes as personal attributes grow different. Democratic life, however, feeds upon difference, anonymity, and pluralism. In other words, contrary to what this literature wants to make us believe, there is no necessary relation between trust and democracy. The small-scale, religiously and ethnically homogeneous Protestant town meetings provide a model that works (and is desirable) only in certain specific contexts. Indeed, to search for the causes of generalized trust as the antidote for the alleged civic malaise of our highly differentiated, globalized, and multicultural societies is barking up the wrong tree. Instead of imposing one specific civic tradition's model of participation, under the guise of a scientifically neutral model of "good governance," one should try to cope with the global diversity of civic experiences and pay special attention to emergent forms of political engagement.

---

2) "Democracy is more than trust" proposition:

The higher the religious, ethnic, class homogeneity, the higher the levels of generalizable trust.
Corollary: Trust covers only a small part of the democratic experience.

Through the FAUI project, we have been documenting a general shift in citizenship norms since the 1970s. This general value shift explains not only why Putnam's jeremiad is only half the story, but also suggests what the other half is. In the United States and several European countries, an engagement norm of citizenship has been gradually replacing the traditional duty-based one in the past half a century. As a result, the political repertoires of citizens in these societies are becoming increasingly more differentiated. Besides voting, people (younger people, in particular) are more and more engaging in an array of forms of political participation, from blogs and political consumerism to socially dense forms of collective action such as manifestations and rallies.

The following propositions qualify and expand Proposition #1:

3) "Rise of the New Political Culture (NPC)" proposition:

a) In affluent democratic societies, the younger, more urban, and more educated a population is, the more likely it is to embrace a socially liberal yet fiscally conservative agenda.

b) The higher is the prevalence of NPC, the more issue-politics replaces class politics.

c) The higher the prevalence of NPC, the higher the rise of consumption politics and the importance of amenities (for instance, in driving local development).

Corollary: The rejection of hierarchy and welfare paternalism in favor of horizontal, issue-politics increases as societies become more postmaterialist, NPC.

4) "Norms of citizenship" proposition:

In affluent democratic societies, the older and less educated a population is, the more likely it is to endorse a duty-based conception of citizenship; conversely, the younger and more educated a population is, the more likely it is to subscribe to an engagement norm of citizenship.

Corollary: The rejection of hierarchical and low intensity forms of participation increases as NPC spreads.

5) "Political repertoires" proposition:

The younger, more affluent, and more educated, the more likely it is to have a differentiated political repertoire (voting and political campaign tend to be replaced by protest, Internet activism, consumer boycott).

Corollary: In advanced affluent societies, generational change is accompanied by more differentiated and participatory forms of political engagement.

In this book, we suggest that culture needs to be taken seriously by political scientists in two different ways. First, at a macro-level, diversity between cultural traditions needs to be taken into account. The Protestant cultural tradition upon which neo-Tocquevillians draw and implicitly suggest as "the civic one" is simply one among many others. With economic and cultural globalization and increased migratory flows, the parochialism of the neo-Tocquevillian model of participation has become all the more flagrant. Indeed, while it is the case that civic participation can lead, in certain contexts, to increased interpersonal trust levels and reinforced political legitimacy, this is not necessarily so. In other contexts, more participation (including in the arts and culture) does not lead to higher legitimacy and trust. This is exactly where we part company from Putnam and those who advocate a "one solution fits all" kind of approach. If we look beyond the town meeting, Puritan civic tradition within which neo-Tocquevillians like Putnam operate, we soon realize that different traditions promote different mechanisms of political legitimation: in places like Bogotá, Colombia, glamour and irony can be much more powerful sources of civicness and legitimacy than Putnam's celebrated 1950s American bowling leagues. Cultural and local diversity renders the neo-Tocquevillian model implausible and simplistic. Our main question is: How do different types of participation affect trust and legitimacy? How can we begin to make sense of the country/local variance of this relationship?

---

6) Civic religious traditions matter proposition:

The positive relationship between participation and trust suggested in Proposition #3 holds only in affluent democratic Western societies. Moreover, even here, it does not represent a universal pattern: local exceptions abound. In other groups of countries, other types of relationship between participation and trust exist: in certain countries, like South America, low participation and low trust coexist; in others, like Japan, low participation goes hand in hand with high trust; in yet others, like Korea, Portugal, or Austria, high participation coexists with low trust.

Corollary: Civic and religious traditions shape how participation affects trust and legitimacy.

As we will show, if one takes a global view on these general changes in political culture and combines them with detailed local analyses of urban processes of change, a compelling case emerges for one to discard the orthodox Tocqueville/Putnam model of political participation through formal associations. Our proposed alternative points to new forms of participation, leadership, and legitimacy that are not only more globally widespread than the New England Tocqueville/Putnam political model, but are also much more in tune with the emergent patterns of political culture in the past few decades. This is even more so outside the United States, even in the international book he edited, if one reads the chapters closely (Putnam, 2002).

The revivalism of neo-Tocquevillians like Putnam is based upon the claim that political participation has declined since the 1960s as an unintended consequence of a number of socioeconomic developments. In what follows, we show that this claim does not stand up to empirical scrutiny. On the contrary, we suggest the opposite may actually be true. There has not been a decline but an increase in political participation in the last half a century. Such an increase is associated with the expansion of the repertoire of political action, a development that is very much "off the radar screen" of Putnam's model. What has been happening since the 1960s in the United States is nothing less but a shift in the very norms of citizenship: what constitutes political participation, what is generally considered to be the duties of a "good citizen," has dramatically changed since the Eisenhower years.

In brief, one can describe the prevalent conception of citizenship in the mid-twentieth century as duty based. Citizens' duties included electoral participation, payment of taxes, and availability to serve in the military. In turn, citizens expected to have their civil, political, and certain economic and social rights protected. Almond and Verba's (1963[1965]) classic *The Civic Culture* is perhaps the best description of the political culture in which this conception of citizenship originated and developed. They suggest a "threefold classification of participant, subject, and parochial" political cultures, where the highest degree possible of civicness corresponds to someone who devotedly performs his citizenship duties. Such a classification is itself exemplary of the mode of thinking associated with this duty-based idea of citizenship (Almond & Verba, 1963[1965], p. 19). Likewise, Putnam describes the generation that experienced World War II and its aftermath as a "long civic generation," due to its exceptional willingness to work for a political party and vote, to write letters to public officials, or to attend political rallies (Putnam, 2003, p. 45). The inculcation of citizenship duties functional to the political system was an elemental aspect of the political socialization experience in this period. In short, this was a generation for whom the exercise of citizenship was closely related to norms of social order. The style of politics in mid-twentieth century Europe and North America still had strong elements of "class politics" and clientelism: left and right were clearly opposed to one another as hierarchical relations between the citizenry and their representatives predominated. The public questioning of racism, sexism, and homophobia, as well as the assertion of individual rights of self-expression, had to wait for the next generation to take place.

Indeed, all this began to change in the 1960s. The shift in citizenship norms from a class politics paradigm to the NPC is revealed as soon as one considers that the older debates about capitalism versus socialism, and left versus right, have gradually been complemented, if not replaced entirely, by new, issue-specific concerns, like feminism and environmental protection, among others. In contrast to the hierarchy and tradition of the past, individualism and egalitarianism exist more pervasively today. A new focus on the citizen, on neighborhoods, on individual participation, and on self-generated bottom-up rather than top-down politics has also become apparent. A new generation of political leaders, leaders who break old rules and break free from ideological categories, has gradually developed a new style of politics.

Consider the French case. If the style of General Charles de Gaulle was illustrative of the older class politics style, Nicholas Sarkozy broke from it; his celebrity wife Carla Bruni captured NPC values. The French classify their mayors as variously Bobo or not. The shift from class politics and clientelism to NPC is also illustrated by individualizing lifestyles, exemplified in dress, entertainment, spontaneity, and volatility of choice. This same individualism – which can be expressed politically – is also expressed daily in people's lives, in how they choose clothes, or where to spend their free time.

This tendency extends the individualism to many new domains: in contrast to tourists traveling in a large group to a classic, fixed destination, or traveling to the same vacation home as a family; instead young persons increasingly find, or search for, more personalized lifestyles. Music provides yet another excellent illustration of this societal shift in norms and values. One could perhaps regret the fact that classical music is no longer taught to every middle-class child, as seemed more common in the upper middle class world of the 1950s. We suggest alternatively that one should try to understand the political implications of classical music's new, broader scope. To wit: classical music finds itself in more venues than ever before, in concert halls, at festivals, on iPods, examined and reexamined daily through myriad niche interests by millions of people, and we would be remiss to overlook the significance of this broader influence of classical music in revivalist grieving over a lost golden age (Kimmelman, 2008, p. 40).

Underlying this normative shift is the assumption that there are multiple components to citizenship. Traditional components include norms of law abidingness, solidarity, criticism, and deliberation. NPC citizenship norms add others that are more self-expressive and individualistic: political consumerism is one good illustration of this. If class politics was associated with a duty-based notion of citizenship, NPC comes associated with a more egalitarian, individualistic, and expressive conception of what it means to be a citizen. These two basic components of citizenship currently coexist, especially in North America and West Europe. Among different groups, however, their importance varies. Younger people tend to exhibit a stronger positive correlation to NPC citizenship norms (such as forming one's own opinion), whereas older people are more often supportive of ideas like obeying the law (a classic civic duty). The younger and more educated you are, the more likely you are to be dissatisfied with hierarchical, institutionalized forms of participation.

The relationship between values and practices is a particularly complex one. More work is needed to flesh out the exact causal mechanisms operating in this interface. Still, citizenship norms seem to correspond to certain political practices. For instance, it is more likely for someone holding socially liberal views on abortion and gay rights to boycott products for ethical reasons than those who do not. Conversely, someone for whom participation is a civic duty is more likely to vote. Note that both citizenship norms might promote political participation, only of a different kind. People closer to an NPC framework are more likely to participate in more expressive, individualistic, and noninstitutionalized ways, given their dissatisfaction with the formal options of political participation. In turn, those who exhibit a more conventional conception of citizenship will certainly be more inclined to participate through institutionalized channels. Contrary to the conventional view that favors more institutionalized forms of participation (as if these were, from the standpoint of democracy, superior to informal ones), our contention is that they are complementary. To vote is certainly the most efficient way for a group of citizens to choose their representatives in a democratic fashion. Expressing one's views in an Internet forum, however, can be equally important for the maintenance of democracy as a way of life. Moreover, as we will later show, the variety of political repertoires is larger than most political analysts are usually willing to accept. Once we confront the Calvinist civic tradition (strong in New England, the Netherlands, Scotland, and Switzerland for centuries, but now spreading globally) with other political cultures, we soon realize that glamour, irony, and entertainment can be alternative and powerful sources of political legitimacy.

In sum, at the same time as election turnout has been declining, people are engaging in other ways including working with informal groups in their communities, joining contentious activities, and becoming Internet activists and political consumers. In short, there was no decline in political participation in the past four decades in the United States, but rather we experienced an extraordinary expansion of the repertoire of political action. People nowadays still vote and join political parties, but they do so in different ways (less deferential, more egalitarian: the democrat campaign for the 2008 Presidential election of Barack Obama, with its massive voluntary door-to-door mobilization, provides a good illustration of this tendency);

more importantly, they also join Internet groups and boycott products for ethical and political reasons, both expressions of their more self-conscious individuality. But, one might ask, are people today participating more or less than 50 years ago, considering all forms of political activity? This is the question we try to answer next, again drawing on the findings of the FAUI project.

Based upon our previous work, we expect a decline (or, at best, a mainte-nance) of more institutionalized forms of political participation to be accom-panied by an increase of the more individualized forms of participation associated with the NPC. This would be consonant with our main thesis that a new constellation of values and norms has been steadily establishing itself since the 1970s. As generations succeed one another, the prevalence of a class politics citizenship gives way to a more pluralist polity (Keane, 2008) in which NPC citizenship (norms and practices) grows in salience.

The case for a general decline in civic participation lacks empirical support. The trends in political participation show a decline in electoral participation and political campaigns and a rise in all other forms of partici-pation. The political engagement of the American public seems not to have declined in absolute terms but rather, given the enlargement of political repertoires, become more diverse. The normative pattern of what constitutes participation and citizenship has dramatically shifted since the 1960s. Internet activism, for instance, is less than 10 years old and growing expo-nentially. The alleged decline has been in the traditional "class politics" paradigm of the 1950s, the model that Putnam takes for a civic golden era. People may not be participating as before in the professional bowling lea-gues he elects as "civically beneficial," but not for the reasons he suggests (civic anomie). The very foundations of democracy and citizenship have been changing in the United States and abroad in the last few decades toward a more socially liberal, fiscally conservative political culture. With it, new trends of political participation have emerged, along with a more differ-entiated pattern of political participation. Individualistic and expressive forms of political participation are growing significantly, whereas tradi-tional forms like voting are either stable or in decline.

There are, of course, forms of participation that, despite not being explicitly political in their nature and aims, perform nonetheless political functions. Tocqueville was among the first to call attention to the fact that membership in nonpolitical voluntary organizations, from church groups to music associations, could have the unintended positive effect of stimulat-ing democratic virtues. This classic insight has inspired a great deal of research on participation and civil society, including the recent revivalist neo-Tocquevillian strand led by Putnam. In what follows, we explore a largely ignored form of nonpolitical participation that is not only changing the way we do politics today, but it is also transforming how we conceive of citizenship – we refer to cultural participation.

The rise of cultural issues is a critical, specific aspect of the NPC. As the NPC develops, classic concerns of work and job decline, ceding their importance to a new creativity, a playfulness, an entrepreneurship that has come to define the ideal workplace.

But one can ask – why does this matter? Why is culture more important than (or, at least, as important as), say, class or income? What makes it so special? One reason is the dramatic rise of culture since the 1970s in the United States and in many other countries around the world (see Proposition #3). As consumption has been replacing work as a social source of identity, who we are is increasingly defined by which movies we prefer, by which music festivals we go to, our favorite food, or the clothes we wear. Another reason is related to the second way in which culture needs to be reconsidered. Our claim is that political science has much to gain from studying culture at the local, interpersonal level. Only at this level can we truly appreciate what the rise of culture means and begin to grasp what the consequences might be.

Arts participation is often studied from the perspective of the participants themselves. In this sense, cultural participation is a private good. It fosters creativity, critical thinking, and even self-discovery and empowerment. This is what one benefits from going to a museum or from learning salsa in the local arts learning center. In this book, however, we study arts participation as a public good; specifically, we are interested in analyzing the civic and political benefits of participation in cultural organizations. As a public good, arts participation has repercussions that extend well beyond the individual. The expressive and creative nature of artistic experience (Dewey) connects with the critical, antihierarchical, and individualizing forms of political legitimacy. By empowering individuals, voluntary participation in cultural organizations changes the way individuals act in their capacity as citizens. Endowed with rights and duties, citizens are not merely private persons: they are public persons in the sense that they are politically represented by others. Empowered by cultural participation, citizens seem to be more able to translate their private acts (say, joining a local theater company) into public acts of citizenship (discussing politics with friends, for instance). In other words, arts participation seems to promote certain kinds of competences that are essential to political participation: acquiring a critical perspective and developing one's taste (aesthetic judgment) seems to be positively correlated with the exercise of one's citizenship rights and duties (political judgment). It is in this crucial aspect that arts participation fosters political legitimacy. In a plurality of ways (of which more follow), arts participation benefits not only the individual in question, but also the whole community, which benefits from a self-empowered critical citizenry.

This book documents and explains the several ways democratic politics can benefit from the arts and culture. Our data suggests the existence of a positive effect of arts participation upon democracy, in some locations. Our main goal is not only to explain why this is so, but also why this virtuous relation is far from being a universal social rule. It varies according to many factors, from the impact of global cultural and religious traditions and social institutions to the local "scenes" in which social action is performed.

---

7) "Types of participation matter" proposition:

a) Different types of participation (social, political, cultural, sports, community, etc.) lead to different civic benefits, including positive, negative, or nonsignificant ones.

b) Following Proposition #4, the more collective and hierarchical the type of membership (party, union, and church as opposed to (i) crowd, collective, physically proximate and socially dense participation and (ii) personally separate, at home, PC-based, individualistic form of participation), the less the political mobilization.

Corollary: Some types of participation are Tocquevillian (i.e., promote trust in the political system), others are not (i.e., are expressions of protest against the system), but the latter, in turn, lead to higher political mobilization. Both are vital to democracy: trust is important to political stability and legitimacy; protest is a litmus test of free, liberal democracies.

Arts participation as a driver of civic participation and political legitimacy is perhaps the single most important neglected aspect of political participation research today. The rise of culture as a theme and as a form of practical engagement that we document here for the first time in a systematic fashion is all the more noteworthy as it has been consistently ignored by most political scientists. One needs to broaden our analytic lens to be able to appreciate this crucial development. We do this by deconstructing the Protestant civic tradition (see Proposition #6), as well as by taking into account other forms of participation, legitimacy, and understandings of what it is to be a good citizen (see Propositions #4 and #5). Conceptual and methodological innovations are also needed. The concept of "scene" is a major innovation toward moving beyond traditional structural factors such as class or income, while retaining the explanatory power and comparative potential that fine-grained ethnographies typically lack.

---

8) Arts and scenes proposition:

The rise of the arts and culture, as well as its political implications, as a specific issue area, shifts dramatically depending on how they are locally embedded in different types of "scenes." Scenes vary on such dimensions as local authenticity or transgression and self-expression. Thus, a movie theater in a Disneyland theme park or child-oriented suburb is different from a movie theater in a second neighborhood surrounded by "adult" bookstores, bars, and prostitutes.

Corollary: Crucial to the rising arts participation, which promotes the most trust and legitimacy, is the meaning they have for the individuals performing them – to study how such meaning is produced and how it varies, scenes are a powerful analytical instrument.

An alternative to the Tocqueville/Putnam tradition is a more sensitive cultural palette that might help us repaint some of the traditional (New England-inspired) institutions to make them more tractable to persons who find their intricacies off-putting. Additionally, altogether different institutions may be crafted or ridden to capture the energies of persons whose cultural backgrounds are closer to the matador than the civics teacher. One source of inspiration one can draw upon is concrete, successful cases of new modes of securing political legitimacy other than voting or citizen participation.

A word on our methodological strategy is now in order. One could call it a "social-scientific methodological cubism," that is, a methodological approach to social objects that claims that instead of studying them from one single perspective (the "observer," i.e., the scientist) one should instead create a multifaceted portrait of the object in question – each facet being the result of a given methodology (ethnography, cross-national survey data analysis, etc.) and of a given analytical scale (micro, meso, or macro). The combined result is the traversing of analytical scales and of methodologies that can pave the way to the replacement of the Cartesian representational epistemology, already derided by Dewey as the "spectator theory of knowledge" but that is still associated with mainstream social-scientific inquiry today, by a more pragmatic sociological understanding.

This strategy allows us to go beyond the "civil" neo-Tocquevillian model of participation to include the entire spectrum of modes of political engagement. Two examples suffice to illustrate our point. First, consider the "uncivil" modes of violent protest and social revolt – Paris 1789. Second, take the highly personal, individualistic, and ecstatic sort of experience in Pentecostalism that started in Los Angeles (LA) (with lots of music and media in services) and is taking over Latin America. Both are directed against elites, but the latter tends to aim at a transformed personal/private/religious/emotional space, whereas the former tends to be more political and public, in the streets.

We are particularly interested in scenes where art and culture join with distinct quasi-political values to generate emotionally powerful consequences for the participants and spectators. We feature those that have often been identified with Paris, but which also play in Seoul. Some have elements of a Tocquevillian nature, in that they engage their participants and teach them the tools of mini politics via personal learning and participation. But many, we deliberately seek out precisely as they differ from Tocqueville's American civic groups which included a shared sensitivity to common values and the public good, thus fostering commitment through enhanced trust and confidence in leadership generally.

Rather, we turn our camera on others too often ignored by political theorists precisely as they can teach the "wrong" things. Our goal is not moral elevation of the reader, but a deeper understanding of the distinctive types of scenes that may indeed instruct their participants in lessons that may be antidemocratic, discourage trust and confidence, and inspire hatred and political jealousy and sometimes violence. These are needed to complement the proper games and stories taught to "good children" by Tocqueville and political soccer moms of the world. Why needed? Because if we as observers or journalists or social scientists want to understand the dynamics of politics and culture today, we cannot censor out what is happening if it is not politically correct. Indeed, as Durkheim showed us, the deepest values in a society are illuminated if we focus on deviations, crimes, the immoral actions that are the most horrific and more deeply sanctioned by courts and magistrates. Social and political values can even be potentially calibrated, Durkheim held, by inspecting the civil code, the magnitude of different sanctions for different acts, then classifying them in ways that we can see what most of us noncriminals hold as our deepest commitments (in his *The Division of Labor* and *Suicide*). The guillotine still carries such symbolic power that it is not allowed on French soil. The tourist must thus visit Switzerland to view an authentic French guillotine. This is exactly as Durkheim would have it.

REFERENCES

Almond, G. A., & Verba, S. (1963[1965]). *The civic culture: Political attitudes and democracy in five nations*. Princeton: Princeton University Pres.

Keane, J. (2008). Acts of European citizenship. In E. F. Isin & G. M. Nielsen (Eds.), *Acts of citizenship*. London: Zed Books.

Kimmelman, M. (2008). The "mash of myriad sounds". *The New York Review of Books, 40*(14), 40−44.

Putnam, R. D. (Ed.) (2002). *Democracies in flux: The evolution of social capital in contemporary society*. Oxford: Oxford University Press.

Putnam, R. (2003). *Bowling alone*. New York, NY: Simon and Schuster.

Weber, M. (1968). *On Charisma and institution building*. Chicago, IL: University of Chicago Press.

THE CONTEXTUAL EFFECT OF LOCAL SCENES ON CULTURAL PRACTICES: THE CASE OF SPAIN

Clemente J. Navarro Yáñez and María Jesús Rodríguez-García

ABSTRACT

The analysis of cultural consumption centers on the influence of individual characteristics (mainly social class). However, this chapter proposes that this relationship is contextual. More specifically, this relationship varies according to the nature of local cultural scenes where people live. In order to show the contextual impact of cultural scenes, we analyze a representative survey among a Spanish population. Three main conclusions are drawn. First, two main dimensions explain the patterns of cultural consumption by the Spanish population: the classical distinction between popular and high culture, and the distinction between conventional and unconventional cultural practices. Second, other characteristics, beside social class, are important to explain the implication of population in different patterns of cultural consumption, for instance, age; young people are oriented toward more unconventional practices regardless of their social class. Third, local cultural scenes matter: the difference

Can Tocqueville Karaoke? Global Contrasts of Citizen Participation, the Arts and Development
Research in Urban Policy, Volume 11, 251–267
Copyright © 2014 by Emerald Group Publishing Limited
ISSN: 1479-3520/doi:10.1108/S1479-352020140000011028

between cultural practices of different groups (for instance, young and old people) is reduced in municipalities oriented toward unconventionality, showing an "assimilation contextual effect." This contextual effect also has some impact upon local cultural policies that we mention briefly.

The analysis of lifestyles and cultural consumption has focused mainly on determining the impact of individual attributes on the types of practices developed by individuals. However, the effect of the access or exposure to certain opportunities of cultural consumption is less frequently analyzed, or even whether this exposure has different effects according to different social groups. The analysis of this issue is one of the objectives of the "Cultural Scene" research program, which is being developed under the project "Cultural Dynamics of Cities." In this chapter, we try to determine whether existing cultural scenes in different municipalities influence how Spanish residents develop their cultural practices, with data from a nationally representative survey.

Keywords: Spain; cultural consumption; cultural scenes; class; assimilation

LIFESTYLE AND CULTURAL PRACTICES: SOCIAL DIFFERENCES AND OPPORTUNITIES FOR CULTURAL CONSUMPTION

The study of cultural consumption often focuses on analyzing the impact of social inequalities. Here, there are three major perspectives. First, some suggest that social inequalities constitute the main factor defining lifestyles, which manifest as patterns of cultural consumption. One of the best known proposals is that of Bourdieu (1979) which states that higher-status groups pursue consumption related to "high culture" or "fine culture"[1] in opposition to "popular culture" or "culture of masses" characteristic of lower-status groups (Katz-Gerro, 2002). Second, the thesis of cultural omnivorism argues that the "upper classes" do not have an aversion to consumption practices that characterize "popular culture," but rather engage in both popular and high culture. Thus, those of higher-status groups develop a wider range of cultural consumption than lower-status groups (Peterson, 1992; Peterson & Kern, 1996; Warde, Martens, & Olsen, 1999; Wilensky, 1964).

This does not imply the end of "cultural hierarchies," but that higher-status groups have a wider variety of tastes (Fernández & Heikkilä, 2011). Third, others maintain that individuals choose from a wide range of cultural consumption opportunities offered by postindustrial societies, using different practices to build and express their identity. We take this to indicate the absence of a direct relationship between social inequality and lifestyle (Bauman, 1998).

But how is the relationship between status and cultural practices affected by the experience of, access to, or existence of different opportunities for cultural consumption? For example, is the inclusion of social inequalities – Bourdieu's "habitus" – in the field of cultural consumption constant regardless of where individuals live? This is a question that occupies our research from the perspective of cultural scenes,[2] and the answer seems to be negative (Clark, 2004/2011). The main thesis is that the character of cultural consumption opportunities that exist in a territory – a city, for example – influence the consumption patterns of its inhabitants. These consumption patterns, as indices of different lifestyles, are structured both socially and territorially, that is, the development of a particular set of cultural practices is a result of exposure or proximity to certain types of cultural consumption opportunities.

From the perspective of cultural scenes, territories can be understood (or read) through their existing cultural consumption opportunities; not by their magnitude but by the lifestyles they promote in terms of values and identities. We do this by measuring the orientation of the existing cultural scenes from 15 subdimensions: traditionalism, charisma, expression, glamour, exhibitionism, neighborliness, localism, and ethnicity, among others. The combination of these dimensions accounts for different cultural scenes (Silver, Clark, & Navarro, 2010). In Spain's case, a key dimension that distinguishes the cultural scene of specific municipalities is the difference between conventional and unconventional. The first includes the values and identities of tradition, formality, and neighborliness or localism; the second is more focused on expressiveness, charisma, glamour, and exhibitionism (Rodríguez-García, Mateos, & Navarro, 2012; Navarro, Mateos, & Rodríguez-García, 2012) (Fig. 1).

Next, we ask how these differences in cultural scenes could affect practices of cultural consumption. On the one hand, there may be a direct contextual effect: exposure to unconventional cultural scenes promotes the development of cultural practices linked to them. However, there could also exist indirect contextual effects (or cross-level effects) so that the impact is different for different social groups. In principle, three possible

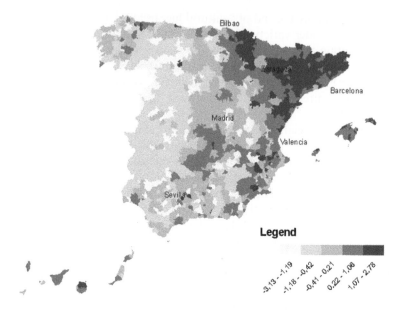

Fig. 1. The Geography of Cultural Scenes in Spain (2001): Conventional Scenes versus Unconventional Scenes. *Note*: Light is more conventional. *Source*: DCC Project. www.upo.es/cspl/scenes

effects could be established. First, a "reinforcing effect": the nature of the cultural scene in a locality promotes practices that are common among groups that are aligned with the mores, customs, and values of those scenes; for example, groups of high cultural capital in unconventional scenes (Andy Warhol's "Factory" in the 1960s New York City art scene). Second, a "refusal effect": the cultural scene inhibits the production of cultural capital by those who do not develop cultural practices that are appropriate for these scenes; for example, people with low cultural capital in unconventional scenes (Reaganaut Businessmen attempting to gentrify the Castro district of San Francisco). Third, an "assimilation effect": the nature of cultural scenes encourages certain groups to develop cultural practices that are uncommon to them; for example, those with lacking cultural capital develop high culture practices which fit the character in the environment of unconventional scenes (The "Race Man" in post-"Great Migration" Chicago, Drake, & Cayton, 1970). (See Table 1 for our hypotheses.)

Table 1. Possible Contextual Effects of Cultural Scenes (Hypotheses).

Contextual effects	H1. Direct		Effect when the cultural scene is unconventional in municipalities More unconventional cultural practices regardless of individual characteristics
	H2. Indirect	H21. Reinforcement	Residents' reproduction of cultural character provides further expression of common practices
		H22. Refusal	Those who do not develop unconventional practices tend to reinforce conventional practices
		H23. Assimilation	Those who do not begin with unconventional practices tend to develop unconventional practices

DESIGN AND ANALYSIS

In order to analyze these contextual effects, the character of local scenes in Spain has been measured according to Navarro (2012), and a representative survey of the Spanish population, up to 18 years and older, has been used to measure individual cultural practices (study CIS2634, 2006). The total sample included 8,265 respondents, proportionally distributed throughout 554 municipalities, with an average of 15 interviews per municipality. This is a sample size and design that allows contextual analysis by performing multilevel analysis.[3]

Specifically, the survey provides information about patterns of cultural consumption and socioeconomic questions commonly used to analyze them. Cultural consumption patterns are examined using three questions about behavior or cultural practices related to television programs, music, and the kind of clothes respondents prefer (Table 2). Multiple correspondence analysis is applied to determine the relationship between respondents' choices in answering these three question, in order to identify different dimensions and patterns of cultural consumption as indexes of lifestyles. Then, we used these dimensions as dependent variables in multilevel regression models. These included two types of independent variables. The first is comprised of basic demographic characteristics associated with lifestyle: gender, age, educational level (measured as years of education),

Table 2.   Cultural Consumption Practices Analyzed.

Television	Music	Clothes
News or cultural programs	Classical, jazz, protest	Normal and proper
Movies and entertainment	(political)	Fashionable, flashy
magazines	Modern (pop, rock)	Convenient and
Sports	Electronic/Urban	comfortable
Other programs	Spanish-folk, flamenco	
None	None/No preference	

Source: CIS2634 (2006).

and occupational status. The second is an ordinal scale that combines employment status and occupation to identify five distinct groups: unemployed workers, manual workers (blue collar), skilled workers (white collar), service-industry personnel, and, finally, managers and professionals.

The orientation of the cultural scene is measured through indicators of how a municipality is dominated by either conventional versus unconventional amenities (Navarro et al., 2012). In addition, we add two weights to the scores: municipal size, and density of cultural consumption opportunities (measured by the number of cultural amenities per inhabitant). Municipal size plays a role in the number of, and diversity of opportunities for cultural consumption, which would account for the extension of certain unconventional practices (Fischer, 1984). Nevertheless, scenes are comprised of more than just volume or density of cultural consumption opportunities. We find evidence of a relationship between the size of a municipality, the population density within, and the character of the cultural scene. The relationship is strongest between size and density, and less so between these variables and the conventionality score of the scene in a municipality (Navarro et al., 2012).

RESULTS AND DISCUSSION

Lifestyles and Patterns of Cultural Consumption

When we analyzed this data, a number of lifestyle patterns emerged. First, some cultural practices are much more widespread than others (see Fig. 2): news and cultural programs (40%), or movies and series on television (33%) are responsible for the vast majority of television consumption; pop and rock music (33.8%), followed by Spanish folk music (24%) and

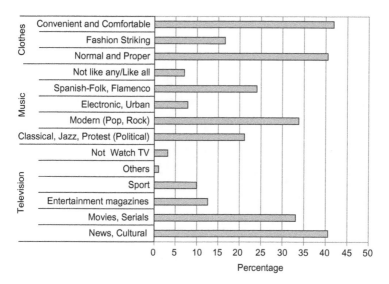

Fig. 2. The Extent of Cultural Practices in Spain (2006). *Source*: CIS2634.

classical music (21%) account for nearly 80% of all reported taste in music. Meanwhile, respondents are divided between those who prefer regular and correct clothing (40%) versus convenient and comfortable clothing (42%). From a descriptive perspective, this means that some cultural practices are central to the lifestyles of a significant proportion of the Spanish population.

Multiple correspondence analysis shows that these practices could be summarized into two main dimensions (Fig. 3). One dimension differentiates practices according to their "aesthetic distance"[4] against conventionality. There are those who like electronic, urban, or modern rock and pop music, fashionable clothing, and prefer to watch movies and series on television – as opposed to those who prefer more conventional cultural practices (see the horizontal axis in Fig. 3). However, the latter may be distinguished into two types according to the second dimension (the vertical axis Fig. 3): the first type listens to Spanish folk music, wears customary (i.e., appropriate) clothes, and watches television shows (soap opera, reality shows, etc.) while the second type prefers classical music and jazz, news and cultural programs, and comfortable clothing. The second axis appears to refer quite clearly to criteria indicative of the distinction between "high culture" and "popular culture" (Bourdieu, 1988; Grignon & Passeron, 1992).

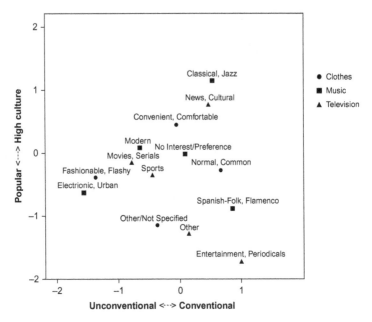

Fig. 3. Cultural Practices and Lifestyles in Spain (2006). Multiple Correspondence
Analysis. Categories in the First Two Factorial Axes.

What social traits are associated with these dimensions of lifestyles? We
performed ANOVAs, comparing gender, age groups, education levels, and
socioeconomic status as independent variables, and the two dimensions of
cultural practices as dependent variables (scores of respondents in the two
axes resulting from correspondence analysis). The results show a clear relationship not only with socioeconomic status, but also with other variables
(see Fig. 4). There is also a downward trend in the two dimensions related
to age and level of education, and, to a lesser extent, occupational status
and gender. These analyses show the importance of socioeconomic status,
but especially of cultural capital (as measured by education) and differences
by age group. More specifically, it appears that professionals, respondents
with more education, and middle-aged people develop more "high culture"
practices, while young people are clearly oriented toward unconventional
cultural practices.

To assess the relative impact of each variable on these two dimensions,
we performed OLS regression analysis (see Table 3). All variables included
show significant coefficients. This suggests that cultural practices are not

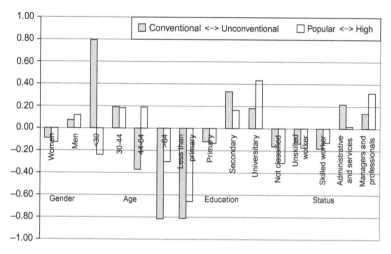

Fig. 4. The Social Bases of Cultural Consumption Patterns in Spain (2006). The Value 0 Is the Average of the Distribution of the Two Dimensions. *Source*: CIS2634 (2006).

Table 3. The Social Bases of Cultural Consumption Patterns in Spain (2006) OLS Regression.

	Conventional <-> Unconventional	Popular <-> High
Constant	1.255	−1.164
Gender (man)	0.062	0.183
Age	−0.032	0.010
Education (years)	0.008	0.044
Socioeconomic status	0.020	0.084
R^2	0.319	0.080

Source: CIS2664.
Note: All coefficients significant at $p < 0.05$.

only related to social status or cultural capital, but also related to social traits that account for social change, and specifically the importance of age. Younger people develop a less conventional lifestyle, although maintaining closer ties to popular culture, rather than high culture practices.

Thus, in addition to the well-known relationship between socioeconomic status and lifestyles, cultural practices are also closely related to age (Ollivier, 2008), especially when trying to differentiate between styles that are more or less conventional. If the difference between high and popular practices seems to be articulated according to status and cultural capital, the difference between conventional and unconventional practices depends, above all, on age.

The Contextual Effects of Cultural Scenes

In addition to the preceding lifestyle analysis, our hypotheses suggest that cultural scenes should have an effect. Municipalities where unconventional cultural scenes predominate should promote unconventional cultural practices, such as those we have measured in the first dimension, as well as patterns linked to high culture and distinction, as measured through our second dimension.

We performed multilevel analysis to explore the relative impact of contextual features in the municipalities. The two dimensions of cultural practices defined above remain the dependent variables. Socioeconomic and demographic characteristics are included as independent variables as well as the unconventional orientation of scenes, volume, and density of cultural consumption opportunities. Analyses show overall the existence of contextual effects according to the character of the cultural scene (Table 4). When a city's cultural scene tends toward an unconventional orientation, unconventional cultural practices increase (model 1), as do "high cultural" practices (model 2). The spread of unconventional practices is also explained by the density of cultural consumption opportunities, but not the size of the municipality. Individual traits that explain the development of unconventional practices (compared with conventional ones) are gender and age (especially among men and young people), while for the second dimension (popular vs. high practices) level of education and social status are significant explanatory factors. That is, the reproduction of high (or popular) practices is more dependent on the socioeconomic status of residents, while unconventional practice patterns appear to be associated more with age, as we saw in the regression analyses presented above. The difference here is we added that, in both cases, such cultural practices are encouraged by the character of the cultural scene of the municipality in which respondents reside (hypothesis 1).

According to our second hypothesis, the contextual influence of the cultural scene would be different for different social groups. Thus, we expect

Table 4. The Contextual Effect of the Scenes on Cultural Practices: Direct Contextual Effects. Multilevel Regression Models.

	Model 1	Model 2
	Conventional <-> Unconventional	Popular <-> Fine
Constant	**1.277**	**−1.162**
Cultural scene (unconventional)	**0.019**	**0.026**
Municipal size	−0.002	−0.019
Amenities density	**0.020**	0.025
Social class	*0.015*	**0.77**
Gender	**0.064**	**0.186**
Age	**−0.032**	**0.009**
Education	*0.005*	**0.044**
V. inter-municipal	**0.025**	0.043
V. inter-individual	0.690	0.899
ICC	0.035	0.046
Expl. Var. level-1	32.801	11.466
Expl. Var. level-2	33.731	13.608
Deviance	18293.303	20277.562
Difference	550.000	550.000
Difference in Deviance	−5589.151	1984.59
N (municipalities)	554.000	
N (interviews)	8265.000	

Note: In bold: significant at $p < 0.05$; italics: significant at $p < 0.10$.

that young people show a greater tendency toward unconventional cultural practices, but especially in contexts that are favorable to them, reflecting a contextual reinforcement effect. What can be expected for older people? A refusal effect might emerge if this group develops more conventional practices in opposition to a context of unconventional scenes. On the other hand, an assimilation effect could exist if older people increase their participation in unconventional practices when they are situated in unconventional scenes. The same could be said for groups that reflect the social base of more "high culture" practices (as opposed to popular practices).

A demonstrative example is education level. Highly educated residents of a municipality with unconventional scenes would experience contextual reinforcement effects. Since education correlates to unconventional cultural practices, those residents would reproduce the local cultural mores because it's easier for them to do so − because they have more cultural capital, plus the reflection of their mores in their local scene. They would therefore contribute to an increase in expressions of those same mores within the locality. On the other hand, a refusal effect would be expected for those with less education for the opposite reasons. Likewise, we would look for an assimilation effect – more unconventional practices – for those with the same education level living in more conventional scenes. Additional steps were taken to investigate the impact of these subcultural effects – those of reinforcement, rejection, and assimilation. To verify their existence we introduced cross-level interaction terms. We analyzed the impact of age on the orientation of scene characteristics, focusing on the distinction between conventional and unconventional contexts. Further, we constructed models to investigate how contexts affect popular and high practices. Finally, we substituted respondents' level of education and investigated its impact on scene orientation. In both cases, these indirect contextual effects are shown to have an impact. We found that level of education has a strong relationship to scene orientation, especially for practices involving cultural distinction – that is, when an individual engages in typical practices of cultural consumption in order to express identification with a certain scene or group. In the first case, the interactive effect is significant at $p < 0.06$ and, for the second, at $p < 0.05$ (Table 5).

What do these effects indicate? In both cases, the analyses imply an assimilation effect: the differences between groups are reduced when residents live in the environment of an unconventional scene. For instance, we see that as a scene scores higher for unconventional dimensions there is less difference in the characteristics of the cultural practices engaged in by residents – and that this assimilation occurs for residents in the 25th and 50th percentile for level of education (Fig. 5), but this trend is much higher among those with less education. It would seem that residents with a relative deficit of cultural capital are more likely to experience assimilation effects in response to the dominant cultural scene in their city.

BRIEF CONCLUSIONS:
CULTURAL SCENES' CONTEXTUAL
EFFECTS AND SOME POLICY IMPLICATIONS

Our analysis shows that cultural scenes have a direct contextual effect on the typological patterns of cultural consumption among the Spanish population. Namely, unconventional practices are more prolific when the

Table 5.   The Contextual Effect of the Scenes on Cultural Practices: Indirect Contextual Effects (Cross-Level Effects) Multilevel Regression Models.

	Model 1	Model 2
	Conventional <-> Unconventional	Popular <-> Fine
Constant	**1.276**	**−1.162**
Scenes (unconventional)	−0.002	**0.074**
Municipal size	−0.004	−0.019
Amenities density	**0.022**	0.024
Social class	*0.014*	**0.077**
Gender	**0.064**	**0.186**
Age	**−0.032**	0.009
Education	*0.005*	**0.044**
Scenes*Age	*0.001*	
Scenes*Education		**−0.005**
V. inter-municipal	0.025	**0.044**
V. inter-individual	0.689	0.899
ICC	0.035	0.047
Explained Variance level-1	32.895	11.372
Explained Variance level-2	33.827	13.604
Deviance	18301.15	20281.51
Difference	550	550
Difference in deviance	−5581.302	−3600.944
N (municipalities)	554	554
n (interviews)	7318	7318

Note: In bold: significant at $p < 0.05$; italics: significant at $p > 0.10$.

cultural scene in a municipality is oriented toward "unconventional" opportunities for cultural consumption (i.e., a direct contextual effect). Furthermore, such contexts produce some assimilation effect among different social groups (i.e., a cross-level contextual effect). Put another way, groups with characteristics that aren't entirely in line with the customs or practices of a local scene will sometimes engage in practices of consumption that promote assimilation and there are certain demographic traits that correlate to increased levels of these effects.

In sum, we have been able to show that the character of the cultural scenes of municipalities affects the cultural practices of their inhabitants. But how can this contextual effect be explained? And, more specifically, what does the effect of assimilation reveal? Two possible explanatory mechanisms can be proposed, each with significant policy implications.

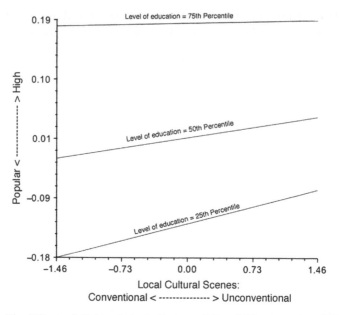

Fig. 5. The Effect of Cultural Assimilation of Local Unconventional Scenes in Spain (2006). More Unconventional Scenes Means Less Differences between Groups According to Levels of Study.

First, assimilation may be produced by an "imitation processes," that is, adherence to certain lifestyles that are seen in the street, in the way people dress, on billboards, in the news, or in certain spaces of cultural consumption. This is often an assumption underlying ambitious cultural and sports institutions or programs, which are predicated on the belief that proximity to certain practices, lifestyles, and actors (i.e., artists and athletes) will result in cultural diffusion to local inhabitants.

Second, assimilation may emerge because of social interaction. The groups that typically develop popular cultural practices tend to develop other more unconventional practices because they live in, interact with, visit areas, and talk with people who are linked to unconventional practices. It would then be interpersonal influence, and not merely imitation, which makes assimilation possible. In this case, activities that celebrate the creation of culturally engaging spaces would provide a critical basis for assimilation, since these encourage residents to interact directly with each other. As a result, some redoubling of culturally distinctive practices should be picked up by the assimilating group. This supposition holds that individuals learn from individuals, from people they meet face-to-face on their daily round, instead of from contrived cultural media.

These two hypotheses are in partial tension, with the former assuming a directionality originating from *structures* of cultural reproduction and the latter assuming a more adaptive capacity of *individuals* to experience and react to culturally orienting practices exhibited by their co-residents. This is a rather difficult tension to reconcile, and many a social theorist has attempted to do so. Are individuals merely responding to their experiential histories? Does one's class and background dictate his every behavior? If the demographics considered above dealt exclusively with social capital traits – income, race, gender, education – then we would have a clearer, and much narrower, answer to a very different question. As it stands, we are interested in cultural capital *and* in the effects of context so that we can further understand the impact of the cultural scene on inhabitants of municipalities in Spain. We, therefore, have a less clear, but more nuanced answer.

What of adaptation? The analyses above point to a combination of cultural practices which promote the adherence of individuals to the cultural scenes which dominate their immediate spatial areas: the place they live, the place they work, and the places they create and consume culture and society. It appears that the interaction of residents plays a significant role in the development of general cultural practices and that this effect counteracts what would be expected from structural theories of the development of cultural practice. In Spain, we see that individuals engage in cultural practices in ways that are novel to their backgrounds. Only about half the variation in lifestyle and culture, as measured by how individuals consume things like music, fashion, and movies, is explained by characteristics defined by cultural capital. For instance, younger, more educated, women with higher incomes favor traditional habits of dress and classical music. This is absolutely worth mentioning, since this seems to violate the assumption that young people with money are transgressive. This may be part of a northern versus southern European difference. If this doesn't point directly to a contextual effect, on some cross-level orientation, it should indicate that, as researchers, we should entertain theories that engage the importance of context in the consumption and reproduction of culture.

From these differing explanations of assimilation come two different perspectives that can serve to orient policies governing cultural agendas in municipalities. One approach would be "instrumental," a strategy that focuses on major events and the construction of cultural spaces. The other would be "mechanistic," placing the onus of socialization on personal interaction with policy that seeks to cultivate the spaces[5] where interactions already take place and promoting the behaviors that enable them. In either case, our analysis highlights the importance of understanding what types of opportunities for cultural consumption exist within specific municipalities – that is, the local cultural scene – and how those patterns of opportunity expand with distinct lifestyles. Investigating the mechanisms underlying these effects will improve our understanding of them, toward a better knowledge of how public policy strategies focusing on culture should be developed in cities.

NOTES

1. "Culto" is a nuanced term in Spanish, being used idiomatically in the sense of a "cult movie," a house of "worship," or in the sense of formality, cultivation, and literacy of "culture." We translate it as "high culture" to compare popular and high cultural consumption, the inclusion of listening to Jazz music in high cultural dimensions notwithstanding.
2. The "Cultural Dynamic of Cities" Project (CSO2008-04288) has been funded by the Spanish National Research Programme (Department of Science and Innovation, Government of Spain). More details in www.upo.es/cspl/scenes.
3. More details about the survey at www.cis.es.
4. Aesthetic distance is the adhesion of an individual's choices to the mores of social groups to which they belong, with their membership as a consideration of their demographic characteristics.
5. Places dense in proximity equipment, following Navarro and Clark (2012).

REFERENCES

Bauman, Z. (1998). *Globalization: The human consequences.* New York, NY: Columbia University Press.
Bourdieu, P. (1979). *La distinction.* Paris: Minuit.
Bourdieu, P. (1988). *Homo academicus.* Stanford, CA: Stanford University Press.
CIS. (2006). *Clases sociales y estructura social.* Estudio No. 2634, Centro de Investigaciones Sociológicas.
Clark, T. N. (Ed.). (2004/2011). *The city as an entertainment machine, research in urban policy* (Vol. 9). Oxford: JAI/Elsevier, 2004; Lantham, MD: Lexington Books, 2011. Paperback.
Drake, S. C., & Cayton, H. R. (1970). *Black metropolis, a study of Negro Life in a Northern City.* Chicago: University of Chicago Press.
Fernández, C. J., & Heikkilä, R. (2011). El debate sobre omnivorismo cultural. Una aproximación a nuevas tendencias en sociología del consumo. *Revista Internacional de Sociología, 69*(3), 585–606.

Fisher, C. S. (1984). *The urban experience.* (2nd ed.). San Diego: Harcourt Brace Jovanovich.

Grignon, C., & Passeron, J. C. (1992). *Lo culto y lo popular.* Madrid: La Piqueta.

Katz-Gerro, T. (2002). Highbrow cultural consumption and class distinction in Italy, Israel, West Germany, Sweden, and the United States. *Social Forces, 81*(1), 207–229.

Navarro, C. J. (2012). El análisis de las dimensiones culturales de la ciudad. In C. J. Navarro (Ed.), *Las dimensiones culturales de la ciudad* (pp. 46–76). Madrid: Catarata.

Navarro, C. J., & Clark, T. N. (2012). Cultural policy in European cities. *European Societies, 14*(5), 636–659.

Navarro, C. J., Mateos, C., & Rodríguez-García, M. J. (2012). Cultural scenes and creative class in Spanish municipalities. *European Urban and Regional Studies*, doi:10.1177/0969776412448188.

Ollivier, M. (2008). Modes of openness to cultural diversity. *Poetics, 36*, 120–147.

Peterson, R. A. (1992). Understanding audience segmentation: From elite and mass to omnivore and univore. *Poetics, 21*, 243–258.

Peterson, R. A., & Kern, R. M. (1996). Changing highbrow taste: From snob to omnivore. *American Journal of Sociology, 61*, 901–907.

Rodríguez-García, M. J., Mateos, C., & Navarro, C. J. (2012). Escenas culturales: Convencionalismo, distanciamiento estético y diversidad. In C. J. Navarro (Ed.), *Las dimensiones culturales de la ciudad* (pp. 96–118). Madrid: Catarata.

Silver, D., Clark, T. N., & Navarro, C. J. (2010). Scenes: Social context in an age of contingency. *Social Forces, 88*(5), 2283–2324.

Warde, A., Martens, L., & Olsen, W. (1999). Consumption and the problem of variety: Cultural omnivorousness, social distinction and dining out. *Sociology, 33*(1), 105–127.

Wilensky, H. L. (1964). Mass society and mass culture: Interdependence or independence. *American Sociological Review, 29*(2), 173–197.

GLOBAL CONTEXTS OF POLITICS AND ARTS PARTICIPATION

Terry Nichols Clark, Filipe Carreira da Silva and Susana L. Farinha Cabaço

ABSTRACT

Does civic participation, especially in the arts, increase democracy? This chapter extends this neo-Tocquevillian question in three ways. First, to capture broader political and economic transformations, we consider different types of participation; results change by separate participation arenas. Some are declining, but a dramatic finding is the rise of arts and culture. Second, to assess impacts of participation, we include multiple dimensions of democratic politics, including distinct norms of citizenship and their associated political repertoires. Third, by analyzing global International Social Survey Program and World Values Survey data, we identify dramatic subcultural differences: the Tocquevillian model is positive, negative, or zero in seven different subcultures and contexts that we explicate, from class politics and clientelism to Protestant and Orthodox Christian civilizational traditions.

Keywords: Participation; arts; culture; subcultures; politics

Can Tocqueville Karaoke? Global Contrasts of Citizen Participation, the Arts and Development
Research in Urban Policy, Volume 11, 269–303
Copyright © 2014 by Emerald Group Publishing Limited
All rights of reproduction in any form reserved
ISSN: 1479-3520/doi:10.1108/S1479-352020140000011029

We introduce context via three political cultures (class politics, clientelism, the "new political culture") and four cultural traditions (Eastern religions, Orthodox Christianism, Catholicism, and Protestantism). Each transforms the relations between arts participation and its impacts. Detailing how and why is the task of this chapter.

The world is changing, arguably more rapidly and profoundly in recent decades than since the Industrial Revolution. Manufacturing is in deep decline; the percent of manual laborers has fallen by over half in most industrial countries since the 1950s. This in turn has transformed the political party system, as unions decline and left parties seek new social bases. All sorts of new civic groups emerge with global NGOs, the Internet, blogs, and new media/engagement strategies. Yet most thinking and theorizing about society and politics lags. Most of our models of civic groups, participation, and democracy come from an industrial era where class politics and party conflict dominated analysis. As we think more globally, and look at broader patterns to help reframe the North American/European experience, what is "established" grows less clear.

Approximately at the same time as the postindustrial political transformation in the West, the post1989 transition to democracy in Eastern Europe led analysts to ask a question most ignored in the West – what are the conditions for democracy to flourish? To answer this, political scientists rediscovered Alexis de Tocqueville. Chief among them was Robert D. Putnam, who in *Bowling Alone* enshrined Tocqueville as "patron saint" of the social capital approach to emphasize the civic virtues of participation in voluntary social organizations (Putnam, 2000). The influence of this Tocqueville/Putnam model has been substantial. "Trust" and "social capital" have become buzzwords of early twenty-first century political science. Social capital has been critiqued in many ways, but one main point here is that its use encouraged analysts to lump together all forms of organizational membership – unions, churches, and political parties. Thus, "participation" or "membership" in the exemplary research usually sums up activities of each of these sorts (Verba, Schlozman, Brady, & Nie, 1993; Zukin, Keeter, Andolina, Jenkins, & Delli Carpini, 2006).

Yet, if we break out participation into its components, we find dramatic differences from the "bowling alone" story. Voting and participation in general politics have declined in many countries since the 1980s, as has been widely reported. But barely noted is the rise of the arts and culture in these same years, even though some World Values Survey (WVS) items suggest massive increases in arts and culture participation in various countries.[1] This is all the more surprising given its ubiquitous character.

The rise of arts and culture, far from being an anomaly, is part and parcel of a much broader and deeper set of changes in an emerging form of politics lived by many, especially younger persons. It is a strategic research site where our litmus test results flag much more profound changes, if we look. Culture can be about politics as well as personal identity. It can be part of one's job, but is more likely part of consumption — in a world where political candidates in their campaigns and actions stress consumption issues increasingly. Arts and culture may have some direct economic implications, but is more generally about meaning and value. For some in a secular but idea- and image-driven world, music and books and their related activities replace the Church and God, and the functions of religion in earlier eras. For young persons breaking with their families and religious and work backgrounds, a charismatic singer like Madonna or Bruce Springsteen is more than entertainment. A reading group discussing Nietzsche, Marx, or Baudrillard can transform its members' thinking. While sympathetic toward the hermeneutically inspired "cultural turn" in American sociology, we seek to complement it with cross-national survey-based data, as this is the only way to capture broad, global sociopolitical changes.

Analysts have sought to capture these profound sociopolitical changes with labels like postindustrial society, the knowledge economy, the third way, neo-liberalism, the creative class or economy, the consumer society, postmodernism, and more. What these have in common is stressing that the rules of many past models no long seem to work, or demand qualification. How do any others specifically link the growing salience of culture and the arts in the past few decades (see Fig. 1) with structural

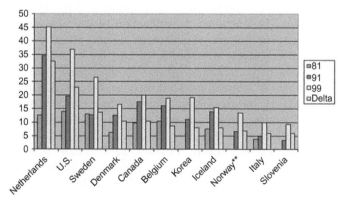

Fig. 1. Rising Membership of Cultural Activity Groups. *Source*: WVS.

socioeconomic changes in developed societies around the world? The answers are clearly diverse but we introduce just one effort to join these changes in systematic manner, based on our past work. Many others are possible, and we hope to encourage alternative interpretations that may extend our effort here.

Our past work documented elements of this structural socioeconomic change as the rise of the "new political culture" (henceforth NPC). Citizens changed first in these respects, and leaders and analysts widely ignored these deep changes; many still do. But no longer do clientelism and class politics dominate politics as they did a few decades back. They are challenged by all manner of "reformers," some of whom relate to this "new political culture." Many local and national political leaders came to adopt an NPC agenda in Europe, Asia, and Latin America, like Bill Clinton or Tony Blair or Antanas Mockus. In the 1990s, with the acceleration of economic globalization and the digital revolution (encompassing technological innovations such as the Internet, mobile phones, and personal computers), the shift from production to consumption started to capture the attention of social scientists. Two research questions, in particular, have been pursued. First, how and why is the growing prevalence of NPC associated with the replacement of class politics by issue politics? Second, how and why is the development of the NPC associated with the rise of consumption politics and the importance of amenities (for instance, in driving local development)? Behind these questions is the hypothesis that the rejection of hierarchy and welfare paternalism in favor of horizontal, issue politics increase as societies become more postmaterialist, NPC.

The chapter is organized as follows. We start by describing the analytical model, where we explain the main assumptions and research hypotheses behind this study. This includes a justification of our conceptual choices (section 2). Next, we present our research design. Here, we discuss the main methodological issues we faced in conducting data analyses (section 3). We then present our findings (section 4). Specifically, we discuss the impact of our seven "contextual variables" in the relationship between cultural membership and democratic politics: these include three political cultures (class politics, clientelism, and the "new political culture") and four cultural traditions (Eastern religions, Orthodox Christianism, Catholicism, and Protestantism). Finally, we conclude the chapter by pointing out some of the most important implications of the current rise of culture, both for the purposes of policy-making and for the social-scientific research of politics.

ANALYTICAL MODEL

As noted above, the simpler patterns that have been widely used (like the decline in voting or bowling alone) do not hold consistently if we break out participation into separate issue areas, age groups, and countries. To make sense of these apparent disparities demands a subtler analytical model. If we look closely, we find that arts and culture are powerfully tied to other aspects of democratic life. But specifics vary by political cultures that follow disparate rules of the game. To clarify these patterns, we have extended past modeling about democratic politics to investigate impacts of culture, as follows. We include the core independent and dependent variables used by past analysts of citizen participation, but with two critical additions. First, we break out arts and culture participation from other content-types of social participation – religious, community, and professional voluntary organizations – and compare its impacts to those of the other types. Second, we explore how these effects shift across political cultures. These two changes generate dramatic differences from most past work.

The central path we explore is how arts and cultural participation, here defined as membership in organizations by type as surveyed in the WVSs (more follows), impacts democratic politics. In turn, our conception of democratic politics includes political practices (protest, vote), norms of citizenship (citizens' beliefs about what makes one a "good citizen"), and attitudes (social and political trust). We hypothesize that the impact of cultural membership on each of these components of democratic politics will not be homogeneous; rather, it will vary by context. We analyze the impact of cultural engagement on democratic politics in several ways. First, we consider direct effects of the standard socioeconomic variables (sex, age, education, income, and left-right self-positioning). Second, we compare the impact of cultural participation with the impact of other types of voluntary organizations, religious, professional, and community. Next, we analyze how these patterns shift across contexts, political cultures, and traditions (shown at the bottom of Fig. 2 as interacting with the direct effects). These illuminate how participating in a cultural organization shifts in meaning and impact on democratic politics when we move from one context to another. The main data is from successive cross-sectional national surveys of citizens (more follows). As a result, while we sometimes use causal language to simplify exposition, most relations are literally associations.

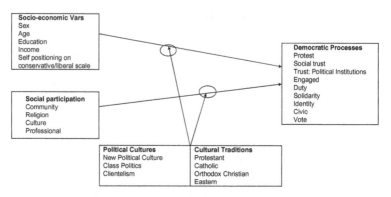

Fig. 2.   Path Diagram of Core Model.

Dependent Variables

Let us begin by explaining our conception of democratic politics.[2] Much civil society research has developed under the influence of Putnam's well-known jeremiad: civic participation is said to be in decline since the 1960s, with serious implications for the health of democracy. We suggest that this decline covers only part of what has happened in the last half a century. Another part of the change is a structural differentiation of political participation patterns accompanying the generational shift, societal value change, and socioeconomic modernization in dozens of countries around the world since the 1960s. Political repertoires of younger cohorts are larger than those of their predecessors (e.g., Tilly, 2006, pp. 30–59). Our stress on expanded democratic repertoires joins the structural differentiation to overcome a narrow and conservative understanding that informed part of the communitarian revival of Tocqueville in the 1990s. For example, even Welzel, Inglehart, and Deutsch's (2005) recent discussion of elite-challenging repertoires shows a bias toward protest activities. Strikes, which enjoy constitutional protection in virtually all consolidated democracies, are excluded from their model under the grounds of their alleged "violent" nature.

To make our conception of democratic politics more empirically realistic and theoretically sound, we consider three broad categories of democratic political participation. First, we include voting and political campaigning,[3] the traditional mechanisms of political participation in representative democracies whose symbolic and noninstrumental functions have become recently reappreciated. Second, we explore the work of Putnam, Kenneth Newton, Francis Fukuyama, and others in considering citizens' attitudes of trust in each other (social or interpersonal trust) and in the government and other institutions (political trust).[4] Third, we analyze elite-challenging modes of political mobilization.[5] This last category includes nonconventional political actions such as participation in demonstrations, signing petitions, writing political commentary in blogs, or boycotting certain products for ethical reasons. Together with voting and trust, protest is one of the three dimensions of democratic politics our model seeks to explain. If we no longer consider the New England, town-meeting model of civic participation as the sole yardstick of democratic politics, but we include all three types just listed, we find no general decline in political participation. While some forms of political action become less popular (e.g., voting in certain countries), others are growing, and still others have emerged in recent years (e.g., political blogs or online petitions) (Dalton, 2007). Whereas we try to overcome the conservative bias of the Tocqueville/Putnam model by enlarging what counts as democratic participation to include protest activities along with trust and voting, we try to avoid its parochialism by enlarging the scope of norms of citizenship with which it operates.

Norms of citizenship encompass the values and representations individuals have of their relation with democratic authorities qua citizens. What are the civic virtues that one should exhibit to be considered an exemplary citizen? The existing literature, both in political theory and empirical political science, is often insensitive to the variety of normative understandings regarding citizenship. For example, neo-republicanism often suggests that there is one ideal set of civic virtues: in the civic republican tradition back to Cicero, Harrington, and Machiavelli, contemporary political theorists try to deduce the civic virtues that the citizens of contemporary nation-states should strive toward (e.g., Pettit, 2000). In the empirical tradition, albeit less philosophically sophisticated than their fellow political theorists, political scientists are arguably more sensitive to the heterogeneous nature of the normative fabric of citizenship. Hence, empirically oriented political scientists such as Russell J. Dalton (2008) and Bas Denters, Oskar Gabriel, and Mariano Torcal (2007) identify several different norms of citizenship in the United States and Europe. We adopt some of those norms here. Specifically, our model includes the "duty-based,"[6] "engagement,"[7] and "solidarity"[8] norms of citizenship. In addition, we use a second cleavage that has received some theoretical treatment in recent years (Habermas, 1994, 2001). We refer to the distinction between identity politics and the rule of law, that is, between "thick" and "thin" norms of citizenship

(Lewis-Epstein & Levanon, 2005). Concomitantly, we distinguish between "identity-based" norms of citizenship and "legal-civic" ones.[9] By adding an ethnic versus civic axis to our model, we wish to add an important corrective to analyses largely based on socioeconomic (civic) norms (Erickson & Nosanchuk, 1990).

Contextual and Independent Variables

In what follows, we discuss the several contextual and independent variables in our model of the impact of cultural membership in democratic politics, as well as the axioms behind each of them. The model's first axiom concerns socioeconomic development. Democratic politics is associated with higher levels of income and education and younger individuals. To be able to form an opinion and express it coherently, to show interest in affairs that transcend the immediate private sphere, and to make political claims in public, are all instances of political conduct that presuppose an educated, motivated, and informed citizenry. The shift from class politics to the "new political culture," or postmaterialism in Ronald Inglehart's (1977) parlance, was driven by the economic and social development of democratic countries in the second half of the twentieth century. As societies become more affluent and democratic regimes consolidate, materialist concerns with existential security are joined by other postmaterialist ones such as quality of life, social tolerance, and self-expression. This "new political culture" provides a unique blend of social liberalism, tolerance, and anti-clientelism with fiscal conservatism. As a result, clientelism and hierarchical institutions are increasingly rejected: as the 2009 example of Japan's traditional political system breakdown illustrates, concerns with equality and transparency are gradually rising on political agendas around the world. Three of the model's contextual variables are thus political cultures associated with socioeconomic modernization processes: class politics (or materialism),[10] clientelism,[11] and the "new political culture" (or postmaterialism).[12]

The central element of our second axiom, cultural traditions, help us understand the shaping influence of broad, civilization value systems on political behavior and beliefs. In line with the "multiple modernities" paradigm developed by Shmuel N. Eisenstadt (2002) and his associates, these cultural traditions can be traced back to the religious culture that historically has dominated each country we are studying. We use this as a measure of the multiple civilizational configurations that compose the world today (e.g., Norris & Inglehart, 2004). Our model includes four of these cultural-civilizational traditions, namely Protestantism, Catholicism, Orthodox Christianity, and Eastern religions.[13] The expectation is that the greater the influence of principles such as individual autonomy and personal expression in a certain cultural tradition, the more likely it is for it to be associated with norms of citizenship and types of political participation that emphasize critical engagement and creative self-realization. To be more concrete: we expect, for instance, cultural membership in Protestant countries to be more highly correlated with the engagement norm of citizenship and protest types of participation than in countries where the dominant cultural tradition is Catholicism, Orthodox Christianity, or an Eastern religion such as Buddhism or Confucianism.

Our third axiom refers to the political benefits of individual membership in voluntary associations. We focus on this particular mode of civic involvement (and not, say, on active participation, volunteering, or donation of money) for theoretical and methodological reasons. There are several explanations for the positive impact of cultural membership on democratic politics. One is suggested by practice theory. In Distinction, Pierre Bourdieu notes the virtuous relationship between types of newspaper reading and political engagement, as Mike Savage and his colleagues in *Culture, Class, Distinction* aptly recall (Bennett et al., 2009, pp. 95–96, 106). This was not, however, Bourdieu's primary interest. Rather, Bourdieu's main goal is to articulate a theory of social stratification based on aesthetic taste: "art and cultural consumption are predisposed, consciously and deliberately or not, to fulfill a social function of legitimating social differences" (1979, p. 7). Bourdieu's elite-mass model of cultural taste has not gone unchallenged, however.

First, as Laurent Fleury notes, by according to the experience of the working classes the kind of attention previously reserved to the culture of the highly literate and by taking an interest in design, advertising, audiovisual products, the transmission and exploitation of knowledge, as well as recreational activities, leisure, and tourism, "cultural studies" played a part in promoting the ubiquity of the "cultural" (Fleury, 2014, p. 49; Passeron, Mayol, & Macé, 2003).

Second, Bourdieu has been challenged by the work of Peterson and Simkus on "culture omnivores" (Peterson & Simkus, 1992), which showed that people of higher social status were not averse to participation in activities associated with popular culture. Indeed, high-status people were adding practices and cultural forms to their cultural repertoire at an accelerating rate: they were omnivores because they were developing a taste for everything. Research on cultural omnivores focuses on the individuals and their practices, while our past work has focused instead on their political culture (NPC). Despite the different analytical focuses, we are both tapping into the same rising pattern: cultural omnivores, who tend to adopt an NPC, "tend to be more politically engaged" (Chan, 2013). Consistent with DiMaggio (1996), Chan uses the British Household Panel Survey to suggest that "omnivores are quite distinctive in their social and political attitudes. Compared with visual arts inactives, omnivores are more trusting and risk-taking. They are also more supportive of the supranational European Union, and they tend to eschew subnational and ethnic identities, which suggests a more open and cosmopolitan outlook. Omnivores are more egalitarian in their gender role attitudes, and they are more liberal on homosexuality. Omnivores are greener regarding the environment and climate change which can be interpreted as them having more trust in scientific authority" (Chan, 2013, p. 29). However, Chan, apart from the observation that it is related to social status (but not social class), provides no explanation for these political effects of being a cultural omnivore.

A different line of inquiry into the political effects of cultural consumption lies in the intersection between American pragmatism and Frankfurt school critical theory, namely Axel Honneth's attempt to reconnect Mead and Hegel in the form of a theory of recognition. François Matarasso (1997), the author of the influential albeit methodologically controversial 1997 *Use or Ornament? The Social Impact of Participation in the Arts*, has recently suggested Axel Honneth's theory of recognition provides an explanation for his findings (2010, p. 5).

To better appreciate the pragmatic origins of Honneth's proposal, consider Belfiore's and Bennett's *The Social Impact of the Arts. An Intellectual History*. From classic Greece and turn of the century American pragmatism, they review many theories that suggest the arts' positive impact in promoting "man's sense of well-being and his health, as well as his happiness" (2008, p. 102). They cite contemporary studies that show a link between cultural participation and longevity. While these studies have not established a causal relation between cultural participation and the beneficial physiological processes associated with longevity, they suggest nonetheless that if democracy is not merely a form of government, but a "way of life, social and individual" (Dewey, [1937] 2008, LW11: 217), then it depends on the widespread participation of a community in a dialogue over its ends, the quality of which would depend upon the quality of that community's democratic culture. To improve democratic culture, the pragmatist would explore ways to improve public deliberation and civic participation, which would include education and the arts. In short, cultural participation promotes the sort of active, creative training by "spectators" which democracy needs to flourish if it is conceived of as a way of life.

A final possible explanation for the positive effects of cultural membership on democratic politics is that the political is itself aesthetic in nature. The idea that the political is aesthetic has been explored by authors such as Hannah Arendt (1982) in *Lectures on Kant's Political Philosophy*, where she describes the human condition of action as the "political" that is both existential and aesthetic, and Jacques Rancière (2004) in *Disagreement*. By contrast, echoing Nietzsche, Max Weber suggests that aesthetics is close to eroticism and largely follows subjective, deep dynamics relatively distinct from the economy and politics.

Consider empirical studies on the relationship between cultural membership and political participation. Several authors suggest that the more intense forms of civic participation are more strongly correlated with political action (Rosenblum, 1998; Wilson, 2000), and this is the variable for which we had more information regarding the countries under study. Our claim, following Tocqueville, is that social participation fosters political participation. However, *pace* Putnam but still following Tocqueville, we qualify this claim: we presuppose that not all types of voluntary organizations are equally beneficial to democratic life. Some, in fact, can be harmful (Tocqueville, 1945), while others might be irrelevant (Erickson & Nosanchuk, 1990). The dynamics between different types of civic organizations is important to our purposes as we wish to find out the extent to which each of these types is correlated with the several dimensions of democratic life. Our model distinguishes four content-types of voluntary organizations, namely religious, professional, communitarian, and cultural[14] (Fig. 3). Each of these four types constitutes an independent variable in our block on

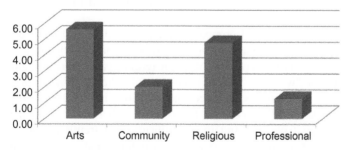

Fig. 3. Membership in Voluntary Organizations (WVS 1981–2004, Variation, Mean).

"social participation" (see Fig. 2). Our aim is to see whether membership in distinct types of voluntary associations is associated with different citizenship norms and stimulates different political practices. Inspired by a wealth of evidence suggesting that arts organizations are among the most potent "schools of democracy," we want to test whether membership in cultural associations has a significant, distinct impact in democratic politics from membership in other types of voluntary associations.

RESEARCH DESIGN AND DATA COLLECTION

Our analysis aimed to produce a rigorous quantitative documentation of the context-mediated impact of cultural membership in democratic politics. To test our model, we have used data from leading international surveys: the WVS (1999–2004 waves) and the International Social Survey Program (ISSP, 2004). The sample of our study is composed of cross-section observations for 42 democratic countries during the period 1999–2004. We test our model with ordinary least squares (OLS) and hierarchical linear modeling (HLM) regressions. To capture intervening factors at the country level, we used the Gini index, education (gross enrollment ratio), and cultural trade as percentage of the GDP (see Fig. 2).[15]

Most arts participation studies are local case studies, small-N comparisons, or national level analysis (usually conducted by national authorities, such as Ministries of Culture). In turn, civil society and participation research, as far as we know, has failed to systematically explore the impact of membership in cultural organizations in democratic politics. The present research, by contrast, uses cross-national survey data because this is the only way to reconnect these two lines of inquiry – membership in cultural voluntary organizations and democratic practices and values – on a global level.

The collection of valid comparative data faced several challenges. The first concerned the availability of data: despite the growth in survey data collection in "non-western" countries in recent years, there is significantly more data for "western" societies. To measure change in arts and culture, the number of countries was reduced to those in the 1999–2004 WVS waves (and the ISSP 2004 wave for voting). Other challenges include the potential impact of time and the identification of trends in the data; the operationalization of "thick" concepts as political cultures (e.g., the "new political culture") and cultural traditions (e.g., Protestantism); and the more general reciprocity[16] and omitted-variable bias. In addition, there are diverse potential threats to the reliability of measurement (e.g., Jackman, 2008). We also faced operationalization challenges of all secondary analyses: limitations in geographical scope, time period, and, more importantly, the wording of each survey item. A case in point is one of our key variables: membership in cultural or artistic voluntary organizations. The only available item in the WVS is question A066, which reads *"Please look carefully at the following voluntary organizations and activities and say ... which if any do you belong to? [the list included] Education, Arts, Music or Cultural Activities."* Aware of the potential measurement error due to the inclusion of educational organizations like Parent Teacher Associations (PTA) in this item, we recomputed the results for parents and nonparents of school-age children. There were minimal differences.[17]

FINDINGS

We test our model of the impact of cultural membership in democratic politics in two successive steps. First, we run multilevel regression analyses in order to estimate the impact of the individual and contextual levels in predicting participation, attitudes, and norms of citizenship in democratic countries around the world. The results corroborate our expectations: for the general model, arts participation is the best predictor of protest activities among voluntary organization membership, alongside the educational level attained (see Tables 1 and 3). This pattern holds for the political cultures and cultural traditions analyzed, especially in the "new political culture" and Protestant contexts (Table 4). This is the first dramatic result that illustrates the core point of the chapter: the arts have far more impact than past work has identified, and it is new and powerful.[18] Any new variable that rivals education is major news for survey researchers generally.

The second dramatic finding from our empirical work is most simply illustrated in a set of nine small bar charts that contrast the impact of arts participation across contexts (Fig. 4).[19] These contexts are political cultures and world areas (specifically the seven at the base of Fig. 2, like class politics and clientelism). These show clearly that the impacts of the arts vary substantially across our contexts, four of which are graphed in Fig. 4. These are the core findings that we interpret in the rest of the chapter, discussing how and why the arts vary so powerfully across the different contexts. In what follows, we focus on each specific context successively,

Table 1.　Multilevel Regression Analysis: Predictors of Democratic Politics (NPC Context).

	Participation	Attitudes		Norms of Citizenship			
	Protest	Trust: political institutions	Social trust	Engaged	Duty	Solidarity	Civic
Level 1							
Sex (female)	−0.042***	0.049	0.075*	0.014	0.012	−0.041	0
Age	0	−0.026	0.066*	−0.016	−0.007	0.028	0.012*
Educational level	0.125***	0.001	0.040	−0.07	−0.003	0.070	0.007
Income	0.030***	−0.013	0.038	−0.09	−0.002	0.002	0.005
Community	0.009*	−0.002	−0.010	−0.004	0.011*	−0.004	−0.004*
Religious	−0.013*	0.007	−0.035	0.005	−0.003	−0.001	−0.003
Arts	0.048***	0.046	0.012	0.006	−0.005	0	0.003
Professional	0.027***	0.002	−0.009	0.003	0.007*	−0.004	−0.005*
Level 2							
Gini index	−0.08*	0.163	0.058	−0.005	−0.031	−0.091	0
Education (gross enrollment ratio)	0.15***	−0.127	−0.025	0.014	−0.016	0.049	−0.001
Cultural trade as % of GDP	0.02	0.033	0.034	−0.001	0.015	−0.014	−0.003
Intercept	1.324	0.623	0.836	1.998	2.576	2.421	1.583
Standard error	(0.141)	(0.859)	(0.117)	(0.130)	(0.527)	(1.620)	(0.219)
Intra-class correlation	0.18	0.51	0.002	0.04	0.27	0.57	0.02
Variance component (level 1)	0.201	0.575	1.566	1.998	0.696	1.720	0.667

Note: The values presented are standardized regression coefficients. Level 1 = individual citizen/respondents, data source: WVS (1999–2004 wave). Level 2 = Aggregate (nation) level, data source: United Nations Development Programme and UNESCO. Software: HLM 6.02. $*p < 0.05$; $**p < 0.01$; $***p < 0.001$. $N_{1 \ minimum} = 42,625$ citizen respondents in 42 countries.

beginning with the three political cultures – class politics, clientelism, and the NPC – and moving on to the cultural traditions, from countries whose dominant religious traditions are one of the Eastern religions, to countries with a predominant Orthodox Christian, Catholic, and Protestant orientation.

The Appendix shows details of the multilevel regression analysis, plotting standardized regression coefficients of arts participation, by context. We computed both OLS and multilevel estimates, which are generally similar. We often refer to the regressions of the impact of four types of

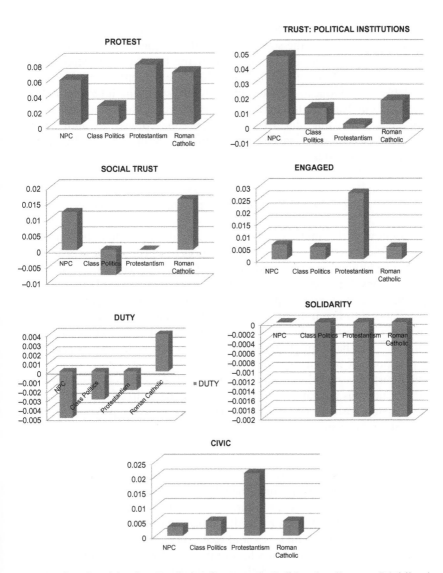

Fig. 4. Arts Participation Predicting Democratic Politics, by Context (Multilevel Regression Analysis). *Note*: WVS data (1999–2004). The values in the plots represent standard multilevel regression coefficients.

social participation on each component of democratic politics (dependent variables), controlling the socioeconomic descriptors (Table 4). Space limits prohibit presenting all 14 tables from the two types of estimates and seven contexts. Two of the 14 full tables are presented; the others are available upon request. Methodologically, we stress the interaction effects shown in our basic path diagram (Fig. 3), especially how and why results, especially concerning the arts, vary from one context to another. We comment on the most salient and distinctive results, especially as they vary across contexts.

Three Types of Political Culture: Different Arts Impact

We begin with the analysis of how political cultures mediate the impact of cultural membership in democratic practices and values. As noted above, political cultures are not associated with a particular set of countries. Rather, they traverse countries, regions, and cities. Individuals may well adhere to a certain kind of political culture despite (or, sometimes, because) they happen to live in a setting where other values are dominant. For this reason, we measure political cultures with survey items posed to individual citizens.[20] The basic question (null hypothesis) here is: to assess the political implications of my membership in a cultural organization, does it matter which sort of basic values regarding social and economic change I subscribe to? Our findings indicate impact (Fig. 4). In some political cultures, cultural membership fosters certain democratic practices and civic norms, while promoting different ones in others.

Class Politics

Consider the class politics context. This context is ideal-typically characterized by hierarchical institutions (the Church, political parties, and unions), materialist values (related to security and economic development), and a model of citizenship defined by the fulfillment of civic duties such as serving in the military and paying taxes, and receiving class-party-driven state benefits. Our aim here is to discuss how and why belonging to a cultural organization influences political beliefs and conduct in this specific context. We build on recent work on class politics such as Evans (1999), Clark and Lipset (2001), and Achterberg (2006).

The most interesting finding here is that cultural membership increases voting turnout (Table 3). This is the only context in which this happens. Why does arts participation in class politics contexts lead one to vote, while it suppresses voting in other contexts? A political cultural explanation is that in class politics contexts the "rules of the game" distinctly favor turnout more than in other contexts. The role of collective organizations in mobilizing turnout seems key: unions, stronger political parties, and civic groups are closely tied to political parties. These are the classic organizations that mobilize voters in cities and countries with stronger class politics, like the Scandinavian countries, and in the past, most Southern European countries and Latin America (e.g., Verba, Nie, & Kim, 1978). These organizations remind their members that voting is important, discuss elections in meetings and newsletters, often monitor who has not voted on election day, visit individuals to remind them to vote, and drive them personally to the polls. This highly labor-intensive campaign work is ideologically consistent with the collective ethos of labor/left party/collective church traditions. These have traditionally also been the largest and best staffed organizations involved in electoral politics. They are stronger on the left/popular side than among conservative parties in most class politics societies (Clark & Hoffman-Martinot, 1998). Here, more institutional forms of political participation, like voting and political campaigning, are conceived of as legitimate, effective means of exercising and claiming citizenship rights, no less than protest activities themselves: hence the positive association of cultural membership with both voting and protest in class politics contexts (Table 2).

If, in materialist class politics contexts, cultural membership seems to foster turnout, the same is not true of other aspects of democratic politics. One such dimension is trust, both in other persons and in the government: in both cases, the impact of arts participation is not significant. Similarly, class politics contexts seem to act as a sort of "buffer zone," which limits the impact of cultural membership on the norms of citizenship: under class politics, this impact is weaker than in most other contexts. By contrast, the impact of more hierarchical civic organizations such as the Church is strong in this context: it is a significant predictor of both the duty-based and of the identity norms of citizenship, as well as of social and political trust. Cultural membership in class politics contexts, dominated by hierarchical institutions and materialist concerns, seems to have somewhat mixed political consequences − if it fosters voting (and, to a lesser extent, protest), its impact in other dimensions of democratic life is negligible compared to other predictors.

Clientelism
Empirically often overlapping class politics, clientelism is a second political culture whose mediating influence between arts participation and

Table 2. Multilevel Regression Analysis: Predictors of Democratic Politics (Class Politics Context).

	Participation	Attitudes		Norms of Citizenship			
	Protest	Trust: political institutions	Social trust	Engaged	Duty	Solidarity	Civic
Level 1							
Sex (female)	−0.058***	0.061*	0.038	0.021	0.042**	−0.007	−0.031
Age	0	−0.032*	0.027	−0.005	0.029***	−0.011	−0.002
Educational level	0.159***	0.004	0.041	−0.002	0.019*	0.001	−0.001
Income	0.044***	−0.016	0.012	−0.006	0.023*	−0.029*	−0.006
Community	0.012*	−0.011	−0.001	−0.010	0.002	−0.004	−0.011
Religious	−0.018*	0.037	−0.024	0.007	−0.002	−0.011	−0.011
Arts	0.024***	0.011	−0.008	0.005	−0.003	−0.002	0.005
Professional	0.012*	−0.009	−0.013	−0.001	0.007	0.005	−0.009*
Level 2							
Gini index	−0.023*	0.036	0.022	−0.051	−0.015	−0.022	0.018
Education (gross enrollment ratio)	0.08	−0.012	−0.050	0.072	−0.017	0.165	−0.017
Cultural trade as % of GDP	0.05	0.035	0.070	0.015	0.043	−0.001	−0.009
Intercept	1.639	1.257	0.918	1.837	2.094	1.785	1.698
Standard error)	(0.157)	(1.035)	(0.143)	(0.137)	(0.334)	(1.764)	(0.222)
Intra-class correlation	0.18	0.61	0.02	0.04	0.27	0.64	0.20
Variance component (level 1)	0.201	0.558	1.569	0.475	0.689	1.694	0.667

Note: The values presented are standardized regression coefficients. Level 1 = individual citizen/respondents, data source: WVS (1999–2004 wave). Level 2 = Aggregate (nation) level, data source: United Nations Development Programme and UNESCO. Software: HLM 6.02. *$p < 0.05$; **$p < 0.01$; ***$p < 0.001$. $N_{1\ minimum} = 42,625$ citizen respondents in 42 countries.

democracy we wish to test.[21] Arts participation here has markedly different political consequences than in NPC and class politics. Two results immediately distinguish clientelism. First, cultural membership is here associated with duty-based and identity models of citizenship. In the other cultural contexts, artistic voluntary participation tends to "prevent" one from equating citizenship with serving in the military or paying taxes, a duty-based understanding of the civic bond. However, in a clientelist political culture, this relation becomes positive – here if one is a member of, say, a book club, one is more likely to endorse duty-based norms of citizenship. Confirming the general legitimacy of duty in this political culture, the duty-based norm is affirmed by respondents higher in education, income and membership in professional associations. In addition, this is the only context in which belonging to an arts association is positively correlated with an identitary understanding of the political bond.[22] This flows, we believe, from the strength of personalistic ties in a clientelist context, affirming its impact even as deeply as one's personal identity. Second, if one belongs to an arts organization in a clientelist context, it is not more but *less* likely that the citizen will take part in manifestations or other protest activities, and endorse a norm of citizenship associated with rights-claiming (Table 4).[23]

These two results combined are nothing short of remarkable. Attesting to the importance of context, these are clear examples of how the same social practice (belonging to a cultural organization) can entail profoundly different political implications. These findings powerfully reinforce our general point that the experience of belonging to a cultural organization acquires distinct political meanings in different contexts: of all political cultures discussed in this chapter, clientelism is the only one in which the impact of cultural membership on protest activities, as well as on the engagement and the legal-civic norms of citizenship, is negative. This reverses in the next context.

"New Political Culture"
In an "new political culture" context, not only is the impact of cultural membership on protest activities positive, its impact is also the strongest among all political cultures (Table 4).[24] Why? Recall that the NPC is an emerging political culture that combines socially liberal attitudes (say, a pro-choice position) with a fiscally conservative agenda. As such, the citizen-oriented individualism associated with postmaterialism tends to reject the hierarchical and bureaucratic state apparatus. This egalitarian individualism seems to be a contributing factor for the predisposition of individuals engaged in cultural activities, more than in class politics or clientelist contexts, to engage in elite-challenging activities. In other words, if one is critical of big government and supports gay marriage, while being a member of a poetry reading club, this will probably translate into political terms as a predisposition to, say, sign petitions and to adopt a rights-claiming attitude. Interestingly, it will not foster as much trust in other persons as in the government. These findings not only corroborate past work suggesting that social and political trust are different attitudes explained by

different variables (e.g., Coleman, 1988; Newton, 2001), but also reflect the nature of this specific political culture, that is, a combination of socially liberal attitudes with fiscal conservatism that is particularly salient in large, cosmopolitan urban settings (e.g., Boschken, 2003).

Four Cultural Traditions/Civilizations

Our focus so far on political cultures could lead some to consider either that behind our model lies some sort of evolutionary framework, guiding the analyst from the class politics and clientelism of the past to the NPC of today's global cities and cosmopolitan democrats, or that we are solely concerned with the socioeconomic processes of societal change. Both inferences would be wrong. Although we do not deny the profound impact of socioeconomic change in individuals' attitudes and practices, we also attend to possible effects of "civilizations," broad sociocultural religious patterns. In addition, we do not equate modernization with westernization, that is, the gradual diffusion of western values and institutional solutions across the globe. Our understanding of modernization processes, on the contrary, is that of a plurality of appropriations and reinventions of the original, western European modern project. These responses to modernity can be seen as expressions of different civilizations. This is why, in addition to political cultures associated with socioeconomic change, our model includes cultural-civilizational traditions. Their religious-cultural cores are not reducible to socioeconomic concerns (Eisenstadt, 2008). Here, cultural traditions refer to the religious-based cultures that have been historically predominant in each country. As such, cultural traditions refer to specific groups of countries.[25] Our findings in the next sections thus concern the mediating role of some of major cultural traditions for the impact of arts membership on democratic politics (Fig. 4 and Table 4).

Eastern Religions
A major cultural tradition is formed by eastern religions, which include, among others, Buddhism, Taoism, and Confucianism.[26] In the countries where these cultural traditions are predominant (South Korea, Japan), or at least occupy a prominent position (India), the central finding is the individualist and engaged political repercussions of arts participation. Korean reading club members, for instance, are more likely to engage in protest activities and endorse a model of citizenship that emphasizes engagement. And the more educated they are, the more likely this is to occur.[27]

Furthermore, cultural membership seems to be part of an expanded scope of individuality at the expense of solidarity. First, cultural membership in this context decreases one's solidarity toward the worst-off. Second, and more important, of all cultural traditions, this is the only one in which to belong to a choral society or a theater group is unrelated to increased trust in other individuals. In these countries, the sources of social trust are elsewhere, namely in a left-wing ideological stance, higher income, and being older.

Orthodox Countries
Moving now to majority Orthodox Christian countries, namely Hungary, Bulgaria, Romania, Moldova, and the Ukraine, one cannot ignore the fact that all were under communist rule for much of the second half of the twentieth century. The most striking result concerning the political impact of cultural membership here is its passive outlook – something not to be found in any other context. There is no correlation between, say, being a member of a chorus in Romania and endorsing a rights-claiming conception of citizenship rights. Similarly, cultural membership has the least impact on protest activities. Furthermore, signaling perhaps a divorce between arts participation and institutional politics in this context, the only kind of trust promoted by this specific sort of social participation is social, not political trust (Table 4). The impact of religious membership, in turn, is almost residual in these Orthodox countries: there is only a weak negative correlation between this sort of social participation and the duty-based norm of citizenship, perhaps attesting to the more complex role of religion combined with the communist past.

Catholic Countries
Consider next the two cultural traditions historically most influential in western democracies – Roman Catholicism and Protestantism. In majority Catholic countries, a cultural tradition that includes Southern European and Latin American countries,[28] the political impact of cultural membership assumes yet another configuration. The most salient finding is the anti-hierarchical and libertarian political meaning, absent in NPC or Protestant contexts. Two results illustrate. First, cultural membership is negatively correlated with voting (Table 3).[29] This is noteworthy insofar as this is the only context in our study where this occurs: in all other contexts, cultural membership fosters voting and political campaign work. And only in NPC contexts is belonging to an arts association more strongly correlated with joining a demonstration or signing a petition than in Catholic countries

Table 3. Social Participation Predicting Representative Democracy
Component (OLS Regression).

	NPC	Class Politics	Protestant	Catholic
Sex (female)	−0.035***	−0.007	0.041***	−0.056***
	(−6.254)	(−1.376)	(−6.370)	(−8.498)
Age	0.255***	0.274***	0.193***	0.156***
	(43.799)	(48.824)	(18.214)	(16.435)
Highest level of education attained	0.081***	0.094***	−0.002	0.021*
	(12.681)	(15.493)	(−0.250)	(2.267)
Income	−0.004	−0.010	0.049***	0.001
	(−0.672)	(−1.095)	(8.809)	(0.224)
Self-positioning in political scale	0.005	0.038***	−0.080***	−0.096***
	(0.730)	(6.041)	(−5.363)	(−7.604)
Religious	−0.020***	−0.001	−0.036***	−0.018*
	(−3.338)	(−0.177)	(−3.513)	(−2.041)
Arts	0.048***	0.074***	0.051***	−0.028***
	(7.818)	(12.548)	(5.133)	(−3.211)
Constant	1.488	1.379	1.739	1.755
Adj. *R*-square	0.075	0.104	0.021	0.008

Source: ISSP, 2004.
Note: The dependent variable is an index of ISSP variables: vote in last elections and attend
political meetings and rally. The values presented are standardized coefficients for OLS regression analysis. $*p < 0.05$; $**p < 0.01$; $***p < 0.001$. T-statistics in parentheses. Pairwise deletion
was applied to missing values. Vote is an index composed by the following variables: voted in
last election and political action: attend political meetings or rally.

(Table 4).[30] Second, turning to political beliefs, cultural membership is
negatively correlated with the duty-based norm of citizenship: if I belong
to, say, a theater group in Spain, I will more likely reject equating citizenship with paying taxes and identify it instead with street demonstrations.[31]

These are among the most interesting and unexpected findings our
model has produced. We have already seen how contexts such as the NPC,
class politics, or clientelism shape the political consequences of cultural
membership. The significant differences found among all these contexts
share one thing − they are consistent with the cultural patterns[32] prevalent
in each context. But Catholicism seems to enhance a different contextual
effect: the political impact of cultural membership is not consistent with the
broad cultural traits of the Roman Catholic Church, but a *reaction* to
them. Following this interpretation (not unique to us, except for the arts
data), the antihierarchical and libertarian political consequences of cultural

Table 4. Impact of Cultural Membership on Democratic Politics (OLS Regression).

	Participation	Attitudes		Norms of Citizenship			
	Protest	Social trust	Political trust	Engaged	Duty	Solidarity	Civic
Arts members in NPC context	0.088***	0.058***	0.004	0.061***	−0.027***	−0.020	0.023***
Arts members in Class Politics context	0.055***	0.005	0.014	0.028***	−0.004	−0.029	0
Arts members in Clientelistic context	−0.029***	−0.034***	−0.006	−0.037***	0.023***	0.098***	−0.022***
Arts members in Protestant context	0.029***	0.056***	0.028***	0.023***	−0.057***	−0.056***	0.026***
Arts members in Catholic context	0.057***	0.046***	0.006	0.025***	−0.047***	−0.044***	0.034***
Arts members in Orthodox context	0.013***	0.011***	−0.003	0.001	−0.014***	0.009	0.005*
Arts members in Eastern context	0.018***	0.004	−0.005	0.008***	−0.004	−0.021***	0.009***

Note: The values presented are standardized coefficients for OLS regression analysis. $*p < 0.05$; $**p < 0.01$; $***p < 0.001$. WVS, 1999–2004 wave. Control variables in the model: sex, age, highest level of education attained, income, ideological self-positioning, membership in community organizations, membership in religious organizations, membership in professional organizations.

membership is an indication that members in cultural associations in countries like Spain, Portugal, or Poland find in these organizations an outlet
providing a critical distance from the socially conservatism of the Catholic
tradition.

Protestant Countries

Several Catholic effects reverse in majority Protestant countries.[33] Here,
support for protest activities,[34] for engagement and legal-civic norms of
citizenship, and for social and political trust,[35] arts participation shows
positive impacts – all in line with Protestantism's cultural legacy. That is,
principles like individual autonomy and personal expression not only support norms of citizenship and types of political participation emphasizing
critical engagement and creative self-realization, but they give this cultural
tradition a distinctive flair. It differs from NPC contexts, for example, in
that individuals in Protestant countries joining cultural organizations are
even less likely to associate citizenship with serving in the military or paying taxes. And it differs from class politics in that political impacts of cultural membership are substantially stronger. Imagine a literary club
member in the Netherlands. Our findings suggest that he would be significantly inclined to conceive of citizenship as claiming rights. He would also
strongly reject civic models associated with fulfilling duties or showing solidarity for the most vulnerable members of society.[36] But now consider that
our imaginary Dutch bibliophile has a materialist, class politics orientation.
In this case, as we have seen above in considering the "buffer zone" effect
of class politics, the political impact of his cultural membership would be
much weaker. To sum up, belonging to a literary club or a choral society in
a Protestant country makes one more prone to trust other fellow citizens
and the government, to object to models of citizenship based either on the
fulfillment of duties or in solidaristic values, while supporting protest activities and norms of citizenship based on a legal-civic, rights-claiming understanding of the good citizen.

   This makes the Protestant cultural tradition different from all the others
considered so far. In Catholic countries, cultural membership is associated
with antihierarchical attitudes and practices; in Orthodox countries, it promotes social trust; in Eastern religious countries, it has individualistic and
engaged political implications; in NPC contexts, it is linked to protest activities and the engagement norm; in class politics contexts, to voting and
political campaign; in clientelist settings, to the duty-based and identity citizenship norms. One type of social participation, seven cultural contexts,

seven different political consequences: in a word, culture matters. Culture matters, first of all, because it is on the rise globally. Culture matters also because of all types of voluntary associations here considered, cultural membership has the most significant political impacts. And culture matters further in that these political impacts are significantly mediated by different political cultures and cultural-civilizational traditions. These last two findings combined seem to vindicate our efforts at building a theoretical model of the political meaning of the rise of culture: that is, how and why, in multiple contexts around the globe, is arts membership associated with democratic values and practices.

CONCLUSION

This chapter documents the rise of culture and arts participation as a dramatic exception to the widely held view that we are increasingly bowling alone, that is, that civic activity is declining. In the Netherlands, the United States, Canada, and Scandinavia, arts and culture participation has tripled or doubled from 1981 to 2004. Our finding derives from examining civic participation items for issue-specificity, rather than implicitly assuming that issues are not distinct (the working rule of most participation research). We next explored interrelations between arts and culture participation and several measures of democratic politics, finding that they vary considerably by context. This sharply contradicts and qualifies the generality of the Tocqueville/Putnam hypothesis. The core of the chapter interprets differences by context. As far as we know, this is the first attempt to identify and discuss the political consequences of arts participation on a global scale.

The implications for democratic politics of nonpolitical associational life are a classic theme in the social sciences. Using survey-based cross-national data, we analyzed specifically the impact of being a member of a cultural organization on various indicators of democratic politics – from practices like voting or protest, attitudes toward political institutions, to beliefs regarding citizenship. Our specific findings bolster the hypothesis that the recent rise of culture has important political consequences. These consequences, however, are neither limited to a certain component of democratic politics – say, the representative democracy component versus elite-challenging activities – nor are they homogeneous across contexts (transnational or country-level). Our model has shown how the impact of cultural membership on the different components of democratic politics is profoundly shaped by the concrete cultural contexts in which individuals live. While in some it drives one away from traditional party politics, in others it has the exact opposite effect, leading one to vote and participate in political campaigns.

Besides significant political implications, the rise of culture also has important policy implications. As local governments around the world have shown since the mid-1970s, policy innovation in the arts and culture is a powerful political instrument: from the strategic electoral use of humor and irony to ambitious municipal plans of urban renovation associated with cultural events or institutions, in such disparate locations as Bogota (Colombia), Naples (Italy), or Chicago (USA), there is overwhelming evidence of the rise of culture in local policy-making.[37] Bogotá, Naples, and Chicago are among the many sources of a new style of leadership and citizenship, new modes for engaging citizens that often conflict with the Tocqueville/Putnam tradition. Rather than focusing on the Kiwanis Club or the League of Women Voters, mayors in Naples, Chicago, and especially Bogotá have developed a highly popular symbolic leadership, joined in specific actions, as alternative modes of governance that work (instead of the classic civic group). These alternative modes of urban governance work in part since they are founded on a base of distrust, alienation, and cynicism that makes the Tocqueville model distinctly more difficult to construct. In the last few years, we have collaborated with several Latin Americans, Italians, and Spaniards to document and generalize the lessons from Bogota, Naples, and even Chicago in a manner that they might be applicable to situations such as the civic vacuum found in Mexico City as well as some LA (and Chicago) neighborhoods. From this perspective, UN-supported initiatives like the 2004 "Agenda 21 for culture" are but a high-level, institutional response to the accumulated experience of dozens of local government initiatives around the world that had been using arts and culture to foster social, economic, and political development for decades.

Culture and arts participation should be taken seriously for all the above reasons. More people have life experiences shaped by it; as "schools of democracy," to paraphrase Tocqueville, cultural organizations nurture a wider range of civic virtues than most other types of associations surveyed, at least the standard types in the WVSs; and one can only begin to understand the political significance of the rise of culture if cultural diversity is adequately accounted for. There are then good reasons to place culture high on the research agenda of the social sciences.

NOTES

1. Data from World Values Survey (WVS) of national samples of citizens in each country. Question: A066. "Please look carefully at the following of voluntary organizations and activities and say ... which if any do you belong to? Education, Arts, Music or Cultural Activities." In Canada, a study on citizens' preferences regarding federal spending points in the same direction, by finding that one of the few items that shows significant change between 1994 and 2010 is support for "arts and culture," which climbed from 15 to 30 percent. See *Focus Canada 2010 – Final Report*. Environics Institute (2010, p. 20).

2. We thus restrict our analysis to democratic countries. Our list of 42 democratic countries is based on the Polity Score. Details of the indicators that constitute the index and the criteria for the classification of countries, according to the information are available at http://www.systemicpeace.org/polity/polity4.htm.

3. "Representative democracy" is an index composed of the following variables: "voted in last election" and "political action: attend political meetings or rally." *Source*: International Social Survey Programme (ISSP) (2004).

4. "Social trust" is an index composed by the variables: most people can be trusted; do you think people try to take advantage of you (1 "can't be too careful," 2 "most people can be trusted"). Trust in political institutions corresponds to the variable confidence in the government (1 "none at all" to 4 "a great deal"). *Source*: WVS (1999–2004). See, e.g., Rothstein and Stolle (2008); Stolle and Rochon (1998).

5. "Protest" is an index composed by the following variables: political action–sign petition; joining boycotts; attending lawful demonstrations; joining unofficial strikes; occupying buildings and factories. They have 3-point scale: 1 "would never do"; 2 "might do"; 3 "have done." *Source*: WVS, 1999–2004.

6. The "duty-based" norm is an index composed by the following WVS variables: give authorities information to help justice; future changes: greater respect for authority; national goals: maintaining order in nation; and also by ISSP 2004 variables: good citizen: always vote in elections, never try to evade taxes, always obey laws, serve in the military. Indexes in the WVS and ISSP were constructed with quite similar items. The same basic analyses were repeated with both surveys, explained further below, esp. in the Methodological Appendix.

7. The "engagement" norm is an index composed by the following WVS variables: politics important in life; reasons to help: in the interest of society; discuss political matters with friends, and also by ISSP 2004 variables: good citizen: keep watch in government; active in associations; understand other opinions; choose products with ethical concerns; help less-privileged in the country/in the world.

8. The "solidarity" norm is an index composed by the following WVS variables: importance of eliminating big income inequalities; reasons for voluntary work: solidarity with poor and disadvantaged, and by ISSP 2004 variables: rights in democracy: government respect minorities; access to adequate standard of living; tolerance of disagreement.

9. In the case of the ethnic/civic norm axis (identity and civic norms), we only have information in the WVS on one variable. In the absence of other options, we

maintain it in our analysis. In the ISSP 2004, there was not information available on this normative dimension. The WVS variable is: how proud of nationality (civic norm: not very/not at all proud).

10. Class/Party Politics is an index composed by the WVS variables: work orientations: compared with leisure; materialism orientations; society aimed: extensive welfare versus low taxes.

11. Clientelism is measured by Worldwide Governance Indicators, which include: control of corruption; rule of law; regulatory quality; government effectiveness; political stability and absence of violence; voice and accountability. More information available here: http://web.worldbank.org/WBSITE/EXTERNAL/WBI/EXTWBIGOVANTCOR/0,,menuPK:1740542~pagePK:64168427~piPK:64168435~theSitePK:1740530,00.html.

12. New Political Culture (NPC) is an index composed by the WVS variables: being with people with different ideas; choose products with environmental concerns; postmaterialism 4-item scale (maintain order; greater democracy; curb inflation; greater freedom of speech), in which items 1 and 3 express a materialist orientation whereas 2 and 4 indicate postmaterialist values.

13. In the case of cultural traditions (Protestant, Catholic, Orthodox Christianity, and Eastern religions), each respondent is linked to each one of these four types depending on the dominant cultural tradition in his/her country.

14. In the case of WVS, the variables accounting for "voluntary organizations membership" are: belong to community, religious, arts, and professional voluntary organizations: 1 "not mentioned," 2 "belong"; membership in religious and cultural voluntary organizations in the case of ISSP 2004. We compare cultural organizations with community, religious, and professional associations because these were the main types of social organizations chosen by Putnam to illustrate his claims in *Bowling Alone*. See Putnam (2000, pp. 48–92).

15. To account for the hierarchical nature of our data, we employed multilevel regression analysis using, for the national level, United Nations Development Programme data for the Gini index, Education gross enrollment ratio, cultural trade as percentage of the GDP (see http://unstats.un.org/unsd/default.htm) and WVS data (membership in voluntary organizations and socio-demographic variables as controls) for the individual level. The statistical tests applied to the model used WVS data (1999–2004 wave). A slightly different model was implemented on voting as ISSP only has information regarding religious and arts groups (not on community and professional voluntary associations). Except for this difference, the same model was applied to voting. As Fig. 2 indicates, we included socioeconomic variables as direct effects and as moderator variables (one at a time in seven separately estimated models), three political cultures ("new political culture," class/party politics, clientelism), and four cultural traditions (Protestantism, Catholicism, Orthodox Christianity, and Eastern religions).

16. We are aware of the potential reciprocity bias that exists in the general model we are testing – our general model analyzes if social participation impacts democratic politics, but the inverted relation might also hold. We tested this possibility and, in fact, the levels of political participation, trust, and the adherence to norms of citizenship predict membership in voluntary organizations. The variation

explained by these models – measured by the adjusted R^2 – is inferior to our model of interest). See Appendix, part 5.

17. In addition, in order to test for the possible contamination of the measurement of arts participation by educational organizations we have run OLS regressions using the Citizenship, Democracy and Involvement Survey, and WVS data. We compared the results of our predictors of interest – only for the United States (the CID questionnaire was only applied in the United States): "member: cultural or hobby activities organization" (CID, 2005) and "belong to education, arts, music or cultural activities" (WVS, 1999–2004). The date of the CID survey was 2005: http://www.uscidsurvey.org/. The findings show that the results for the model with the item without reference to education (CID) do not diverge significantly from the WVS: both are positive and significant predicting, for example, protest (Cf. King, Murray, Salomon, & Tandon, 2004).

18. In Table 4, a clear pattern emerges from the results: arts participation is a significant predictor of political participation, attitudes, and norms of citizenship in most contexts analyzed. Note also the coefficients for arts participation predicting Protest in Table 1 (NPC context) and Table 2 (Class Politics context). In Table 3, we present the results for the representative democracy component. Arts participation is the only indicator that shows significant regression coefficients throughout the contexts.

19. We also implemented a test of between-subjects effects to see if each context had a different effect on each of our dependent variables. Result: they indicated a significant context effect (e.g., impact of different political cultures on protest: F (2,52979)=31,86, $p < .001$).

20. Except in the case of clientelism.

21. Clientelism is a context constructed not from information obtained by means of cross-national surveys (which did not include "clientelist" items), as in the case of the other contexts, but from national information gathered by the World Bank. See Methodological Appendix.

22. Standardized regression coefficients (arts membership in clientelist context predicting solidarity norm of citizenship): $\beta = 0.098$ ($p < 0.001$).

23. Standardized regression coefficients (arts membership in clientelist context predicting protest, engaged norm of citizenship): $\beta = -0.029$ ($p < 0.001$), $\beta = -0.037$ ($p < 0.001$).

24. NPC contexts show significantly higher impacts of cultural membership than of the other types of apolitical associations on protest activities. This holds true for the three political cultures: NPC, class politics, and clientelist, where cultural membership is a better predictor of protest than any other type of organizational participation (religious, community, or professional).

25. Using religion as a prime historical indicator of traditional basic values and culture is classic in social science, from Max Weber's works on sociology of religion (1958, 1964) to Talcott Parsons (1951), to Henri Mendras (1997), and even Daniel Bell (1973).

26. Due to data availability, this last context is analyzed only for three countries (India, Japan, and South Korea). Future waves of the WVS and similar cross-national surveys should try to enlarge the number of countries from this part of the world.

27. "More educated" refers here to the positive and statistically significant regression coefficient correspondent to the direct effect of the variable predicting the dependent variables (concerning the highest level of education attained by the respondent).

28. The complete list of majority Catholic countries included in our analysis is Argentina, Austria, Belgium, Canada, Chile, Croatia, Czech Republic, El Salvador, France, Hungary, Ireland, Luxembourg, Malta, Mexico, Peru, Poland, Portugal, Slovakia, Slovenia, Spain, and Uruguay.

29. Standardized regression coefficients (cultural membership predicting voting): $\beta = -0.028$ ($p < 0.001$).

30. Standardized regression coefficients (cultural membership predicting protest): $\beta = 0.057$ ($p < 0.001$).

31. Standardized regression coefficients (cultural membership predicting duty and engaged norm): $\beta = -0.047$ ($p < 0.001$) and 0.025 ($p < 0.001$).

32. "Cultural determinants" refer to structural features of each context, in the sense of Raymond Boudon's "operative" definition of structure. See Boudon (1971).

33. The complete list of majority Protestant countries in our analysis is Australia, Estonia, Finland, Germany, Iceland, the Netherlands, New Zealand, Norway, Switzerland, Great Britain, and USA.

34. Still, it has to be said that the sources of political trust are conservative and hierarchical, i.e., low income, right-wing self-positioning, and belonging to a religious organization most increase trust.

35. Standardized regression coefficients (cultural membership predicting protest activities, social trust, and engagement norm of citizenship): $\beta = 0.029$ ($p < 0.001$), $\beta = 0.056$ ($p < 0.001$), and 0.023 ($p < 0.001$).

36. Standardized regression coefficients (cultural membership predicting duty and solidarity norms of citizenship): $\beta = -0.057$ ($p < 0.001$), $\beta = -0.056$ ($p < 0.001$).

37. The international importance of arts and culture in contemporary urban policy is discussed in Grodach and Silver (2013, p. 13).

REFERENCES

Achterberg, P. (2006). *Considering cultural conflict. Class politics and cultural politics in western societies.* Maastricht: Shaker Publishers.

Arendt, H. (1982). *Lectures on Kant's political philosophy.* Chicago, IL: The University of Chicago Press.

Belfiore, E., & Bennett, O. (2008). *The social impact of the arts. An intellectual history.* London: Palgrave-Macmillan.

Bell, D. (1973). *The coming of post-industrial society.* New York, NY: Basic Books.

Bennett, T., Savage, M., Silva, E., Warde, A., Gayo-Cal, M., Wright, D. (2009). *Culture, class, distinction.* Abingdon: Routledge.

Boshcken, H. (2003). Global cities, systemic power, and upper-middle-class influence. *Urban Affairs Review, 38,* 808–830.

Boudon, R. (1971). *The uses of structuralism.* London: Heinemann.

Bourdieu, P. ([1979] 1984). *Distinction.* Cambridge, MA: Harvard University Press.

Chan, T. W. (2013). Understanding cultural omnivores: Social and political attitudes. Retrieved from http://users.ox.ac.uk/˜sfos0006/papers/att3.pdf

Clark, T. N., & Hoffmann-Martinot, V. (Eds.). (1998). *The new political culture.* Boulder, CO: Westview Press.

Clark, T. N., & Lipset, S. M. (Eds.). (2001). *The breakdown of class politics: A debate on post-industrial stratification.* Baltimore, MD: Johns Hopkins University Press.

Coleman, J. (1988). Social capital in the creation of human capital. *American Journal of Sociology, 94,* 95−120.

Dalton, R. (2007). *Democratic challenges, democratic choices: The Erosion of political support in advanced industrial democracies.* Oxford: Oxford University Press.

Dalton, R. (2008). *The good citizen. How a younger generation is reshaping American politics.* Washington, DC: CQ Press.

Denters, B., Gabriel, O., & Torcal, M. (2007). Norms of good citizenship. In J. van Deth, J. Montero, & A. Westholm (Eds.), *Citizenship and involvement in European democracies. A Comparative Analysis* (pp. 88−108). London: Routledge.

Dewey, J. ([1937] 2008). Democracy and educational administration. In J. A. Boydston (Ed.), *The later works of John Dewey, 1925−1953. Volume 11, 1935−1937. Essays, reviews, trotsky inquiry, miscellany, and liberalism and social action* (pp. 207−225). Carbondale, IL: Southern Illinois University.

DiMaggio, P. (1996). Are art-museum visitors different from other people? The relationship between attendance and social and political attitudes in the United States. *Poetics, 24,* 161−180.

Eisenstadt, S. N. (2002). *Multiple modernities.* New Brunswick, NJ: Transaction Books.

Eisenstadt, S. (2008). *The great revolutions and the civilizations of modernity.* Leiden: Brill.

Erickson, B., & Nosanchuk, T. (1990). How an apolitical association politicizes. *Canadian Review of Sociology and Anthropology, 27,* 206−219.

Evans, G. (1999). *The end of class politics? Class voting in comparative context.* Oxford: Oxford University Press.

Fleury, L. (2014). *Sociology of culture and cultural practices.* Lanham: Lexington Books.

Grodach, C., & Silver, D. (2013). The politics of urban cultural policy. In C. Grodach & D. Silver (Eds.), *Global perspectives.* Routledge Studies in Human Geography.

Habermas, J. (1994). Struggles for recognition in the democratic constitutional state. In A. Gutmann (Ed.), *Multiculturalism* (pp. 107−148). Princeton, NJ: Princeton University Press.

Habermas, J. (2001). Constitutional democracy? A paradoxical union of contradictory principles? *Political Theory, 29,* 766−781.

Inglehart, R. (1977). *The silent revolution: Changing values and political styles among western publics.* Princeton, NJ: Princeton University Press.

Jackman, S. (2008). General lessons on measurement. In J. Box-Steffensmeier, H. Brady, & D. Collier (Eds.), *The oxford handbook of political methodology.* Oxford: Oxford University Press.

Lewin-Epstein, N., & Levanon, A. (2005). National identity and xenophobia in an ethnically divided society. *International Journal on Multicultural Societies, 7,* 90−118.

King, G., Murray, C., Salomon, J., & Tandon, A. (2004). Enhancing the validity and cross-cultural comparability of measurement in survey research. *American Political Science Review, 98,* 191−207.

300 TERRY NICHOLS CLARK ET AL.

Matarasso, F. (1997). *Use or ornament? On the social impact of participation in the arts.* Stroud: Comedia.

Matarasso, F. (2010). *Full, free and equal: On the social impact of participation in the arts.* In http:web.me.com/matarasso

Mendras, H. (1997). *L'Europe des européens.* Paris, Gallimard.

Newton, K. (2001). Trust, social capital, civil society and democracy. *International Political Science Review, 22,* 201–214.

Norris, P., & Inglehart, R. (2004). *Sacred and secular. Religion and politics worldwide* (p. 44). Cambridge: Cambridge University Press.

Parsons, T. (1951). *The social system.* Glencoe, IL: Free Press.

Passeron, J.-C., Mayol, P., & Macé, É. (2003). *Culture(s): Entre fragmentation et recomposi-tions.* Paris: CNDP.

Peterson, R., & Simkus, A. (1992). How musical tastes mark occupational status groups. In M. Lamont & M. Fournier (Eds.), *Cultivating differences: Symbolic boundaries and the making of inequality* (pp. 152–186). Chicago, IL: University of Chicago Press.

Pettit, P. (2000). *Republicanism. A theory of freedom and government.* Oxford: Oxford University Press.

Putnam, R. D. (2000). *Bowling alone.* New York, NY: Simon & Schuster.

Rancière, J. (2004). *Disagreement: Politics and philosophy.* Minneapolis, MN: University of Minnesota Press.

Rosenblum, N. (1998). *Membership and morals: The personal uses of pluralism in America.* Princeton, NJ: Princeton University Press.

Rothstein, B., & Stolle, D. (2008). The state and social capital: An institutional theory of generalized trust. *Comparative Politics, 40,* 441–459.

Stolle, D., & Rochon, T. (1998). Are all associations alike? Member diversity, associational type, and the creation of social capital. *American Behavioral Scientist, 42,* 47–65.

The Environics Institute. Focus Canada 2010 – Final Report. Environics Institute (2010, p. 20). Toronto, ON.

Tilly, C. (2006). *Regimes and repertoires* (pp. 30–59). Chicago, IL: Chicago University Press.

Tocqueville, A. (1945). *Democracy in America* (p. 205). New York, NY: Vintage Books.

Verba, S., Nie, N., & Kim, J.-O. (1978). *Participation and political equality: A seven-nation comparison.* New York, NY: Cambridge University Press.

Verba, S., Schlozman, K., Brady, H., & Nie, N. (1993). Citizen activity: Who participates? What do they say? *American Political Science Review, 87*(2), 303–318.

Welzel, C., Inglehart, R., & Deutsch, F. (2005). Social capital, voluntary associations and col-lective action: Which aspects of social capital have the greatest "civic" payoff? *Journal of Civil Society, 1,* 121–146.

Wilson, J. (2000). Volunteering. *Annual Review of Sociology, 26,* 215–240.

Zukin, C., Keeter, S., Andolina, M., Jenkins, K., & Delli Carpini, M. (2006). *A new civic engagement? Political participation, civic life, and the changing American Citizen.* Oxford: Oxford University Press.

METHODOLOGICAL APPENDIX

The WVS (1999–2004 wave) is the main source of the data used in our statistical analysis. However, for a few variables data were limited, so we used the ISSP 2004 data, as detailed below. We consistently used the same model including as moderator variables: political cultures, that is, NPC, class/party politics, clientelism and cultural traditions, as shown in the path diagram.

1. *Dependent variables* (components of democratic politics)
   Protest is an index composed of the following variables: political action - signing petitions; joining boycotts; attending lawful demonstrations; joining unofficial strikes; occupying buildings and factories. They have 3-point scale: 1 "would never do"; 2 "might do"; 3 "have done." Social trust is an index composed of two variables: most people can be trusted; do you think people try to take advantage of you and a 2-point scale: (1 "can't be too careful," 2 "most people can be trusted"). Trust in political institutions corresponds to the variable confidence in the government on a scale from (1 "none at all" to 4 "a great deal"). We have four more variables which correspond to norms of citizenship. Engaged norm is an index composed of the following WVS variables: importance of politics in life; reasons to help: in the interest of society; discuss political matters with friends, and also by ISSP 2004 variables: a good citizen: keeps watch on government; is active in associations; understands others' opinions; chooses products with ethical concern; helps less-privileged in the country/in the world. Duty norm is an index composed of the following WVS variables: give authorities information to help justice; future changes: greater respect for authority; national goals: maintaining order in nation; and from ISSP 2004: a good citizen: always votes in elections; never tries to evade taxes; always obeys laws; serves in the military. Solidarity norm is an index composed of the following WVS variables: importance of eliminating big income inequalities; reasons for voluntary work: solidarity with poor and disadvantaged, and ISSP 2004 variables: rights in democracy: government respects minorities; access to an adequate standard of living; tolerance of disagreement. In the case of the ethnic/civic norm axis (identity and civic norms) the WVS included only one variable which we analyzed. The ISSP 2004 included no information on this normative dimension. The WVS variable is: how proud are you of your nationality (identity norm: very/quite proud; civic norm: not very/not at all proud).

2. *Explanatory variables*
We included standard variables for political attitudinal analyses as in much past work (sex, age, education, income, left-right self-positioning); voluntary organization membership (belong to community, religious, arts, and professional voluntary organizations: 1 "not mentioned," 2 "belong").

3. *Cases* in analysis
The New Political Culture and Class Politics were measured by constructing indexes for individual respondents, as detailed above. The other cultural dimensions were constructed for nations, since individual data were not available or sensitive enough to analyze. See notes 2 to 15 for specifics.
The list of democratic countries is based on their Polity Score. Below are details of the indicators that constitute the index and criteria for classification of countries, according to the information available at http://www.systemicpeace.org/polity/polity4.htm:

> The Polity conceptual scheme is unique in that it examines *concomitant qualities of democratic and autocratic authority* in governing institutions, rather than discrete and mutually exclusive forms of governance. This perspective envisions a spectrum of governing authority that spans from *fully institutionalized autocracies* through *mixed, or incoherent, authority regimes* (termed "anocracies") to *fully institutionalized democracies*.

4. *Moderator variables* introducing interaction effects — political cultures and cultural traditions
NPC: Index composed of the WVS variables: being with people with different ideas (a121); choose products with environmental concern (b011); postmaterialism 4-item scale (y002).

CP: Class/Party Politics (index composed of the WVS variables: work orientations: compared with leisure; materialism orientations (y002_r); society aimed: extensive welfare versus low taxes (e067_r)).

CL: Clientelism (measured by Worldwide Governance Indicators): control of corruption; rule of law; regulatory quality; government effectiveness; political stability and absence of violence; voice and accountability. More information available here: http://web.worldbank.org/WBSITE/ EXTERNAL/WBI/EXTWBIGOVANTCOR/0,,menuPK:1740542~page PK:64168427~piPK:64168435~theSitePK:1740530,00.html.
    Cultural traditions (Protestant, Catholic, Orthodox, and Eastern religions) — each respondent is linked to these five types depending on the

dominant cultural tradition in his or her country. These traditions use the nation as the unit of analysis, whose score is assigned to each individual, whereas the NPC, class and clientelism indexes use the individual as the unit.

5. Time sensitivity, changes, and interactions among variables. We worked with University of Chicago graduate students, Rita Costa and then Jonah Kushner, each for over a year on multiple models exploring sensitivity of these results to changes over time, and related shifts with small changes in the models. The general patterns that we report held strong, but there are still for instance county-specific variations. The N's drop for single countries, making it difficult to disentangle consistent patterns, and differences within countries are clear. The WVS items were not consistently repeated, making it necessary to compare only certain sets of Waves and years. This led to our general use of political cultures for most analyses. Here is an example of results that shifted slightly over time:

Duty: Models using arts participation with no interactions and arts participation interacted with new political culture suggest that arts participation is negatively associated with deference to political authority. However, the magnitudes of arts-participation coefficients in both models decrease between Waves 1 and 2 and between Waves 2 and 4, suggesting that the strength of this relationship has decreased over time.

ACKNOWLEDGMENTS

Thanks to the many colleagues who contributed their time, energy, research, and writing to this volume. Collaborative work among participants in the Fiscal Austerity and Urban Innovation Project and Scenes Project has taken place for many years and in many contexts. Many memos on activities, data for shared downloading, free reports, videos, news coverage, and more are on several websites (www.faui.org, http://www.tnc-newsletter.blogspot.com/, and http://scenes.uchicago.edu/). Contact the participants about possible data and report access if you would like more. We have published over 50 books together in these overlapping projects. This volume is a tribute to the ongoing cross-national research that has been greatly enhanced by these interactions. Related works and download addresses are at the end of Chapter 2.

The various coauthors also recognize the many colleagues, research assistants, and students whose support and engagement have helped to move this research forward at many institutions around the world.

The numerous chapters and pieces here were assembled by the dedicated team at the University of Chicago, especially Daniel Story and Kathy Hamai whose coordination and editing were key. Terry Clark wrote the section introductions.

Specific acknowledgments are in each chapter.

Portions of chapters draw on material in earlier reports. We include with permission material from: Wonho Jang, Terry Clark, Miree Byun. *Scenes Dynamics in Global Cities.* Seoul: Seoul Development Institute, 2011, Seokho Kim, *Korean Journal of Sociology*, June 2011. Silver and Clark, *Canadian Journal of Sociology*, 2013; Silva, Clark, Cabaço *International Journal of Politics, Culture, and Society*, 2013.

ABOUT THE AUTHORS

Peter Achterberg is an Associate Professor of Sociology and a member of the Centre for Rotterdam Cultural Sociology (CROCUS) at Erasmus University, the Netherlands. With a background in political sociology, Peter developed interest in studying cultural, political, and religious change in the West. Much of his work deals with the question of how people attribute meaning to the changing world surrounding them, whether these meanings have consequences for their behavior, and how these meanings can be explained. His research agenda is focused on three interrelated questions: Do cultural processes such as individualization and globalization erode the legitimacy of social institutions (such as the welfare state, political parties, scientific and judicial institutions, and so on)? How do these processes lead to the formation of new cultures, traditions, and institutions (rising populism, changing welfare cultures, religious revival among the young, etc.)? And, what are the consequences of these cultural changes for social behavior and interaction (political and science communication, social conformity, etc.)? He has a strong focus on combining theory with empirical facts but does not have a strong preference for either qualitative or quantitative research. Recently, Peter has used survey experiments on nationally representative samples. http://www.researchgate.net/profile/Peter_Achterberg2/publications/.

Chad D. Anderson is a Guest Professor of Public Administration at Incheon National University, South Korea. He researches urban administration, cultural administration, and human and labor relations.

Miree Byun (Ph.D. in Sociology) is a Director of the Department of Future and Social Policy Research at Seoul Institute. Seoul Institute is the think tank for the Seoul Metropolitan Government. A graduate of Seoul National University, her research area lies in social changes, Information Technology policy, and urban monitoring for enhancing the quality of citizens' lives. Her work focuses on international comparative study of government policy for urban competitiveness. She has also researched the e-governance and organizational changes on the ubiquitous city. She spent a year at the National Center for Digital Government at the University of

Massachusetts Amherst as a visiting scholar and is a member of the Committee on Administrative Service of Seoul.

Filipe Carreira da Silva is a Research Fellow at the Institute of Social Sciences of the University of Lisbon and a Visiting Fellow at Selwyn College of the University of Cambridge. A graduate of Lisbon University Institute, the University of Lisbon, and the University of Cambridge, da Silva is a social theorist specializing in American philosophical pragmatism, twentieth century cultural and critical theory, and historical comparative sociology. He has been a Junior Research Fellow and Lecturer at the University of Cambridge and a Fulbright postdoctoral scholar at Harvard University. In 2010, da Silva earned the Distinguished Scholarly Publication Award from the American Sociological Association with his first book, *Mead and Modernity: Science, Selfhood and Democratic Politics*. He worked with Donald N. Levine and Terry Nichols Clark from 2003 to 2009 at the University of Chicago.

Terry Nichols Clark is a Professor of Sociology at the University of Chicago. He holds M.A. and Ph.D. degrees from Columbia University, and has taught at Columbia, Harvard, Yale, the Sorbonne, University of Florence, and UCLA. He has published some 30 books. He coordinates the Fiscal Austerity and Urban Innovation Project, surveying 1,200 cities in the United States and more in 38 other countries. www.faui.org. He works on analyzing neighborhood cultural scenes as drivers of urban development. http://www.tnc-newsletter.blogspot.com/.

Daniel J. DellaPosta is a Ph.D. student in the Department of Sociology at Cornell University, prior to which he received a B.A. in Sociology at the University of Chicago. His previous work has introduced and tested a multilevel model of intergroup contact and competitive threat that explains anti-immigrant voting in France at both the municipal and regional levels.

Arkaida Dini worked as a school teacher in France, then pursued doctoral study at the University of Paris and the University of Chicago.

Susana L. Farinha Cabaço is a Ph.D. student at the Department of Government, University of Essex, UK. Her doctoral project concentrates on multilateral political party assistance in emerging democracies, supervised by Dr. Robert Johns. She was awarded a doctoral scholarship from the Portuguese Science and Technology Foundation. Previously, she completed a degree in Sociology and a Master's in Comparative Politics (with a thesis on the use of conditionality in the promotion of democracy), at the Institute for Social Sciences, University of Lisbon, and collaborated on research projects on Urban and Cultural Sociology and social attitudes (European Social Survey). Currently, her research interests concern the study of democratizations, democracy promotion, political party institutionalization, and international political party assistance.

Wonho Jang is a Professor of Urban Sociology at the University of Seoul, where his research focuses on urban and political sociology. His academic interests include the evolution of Japanese political culture, urban policy, and social statistics. Jang received his Ph.D. in Sociology at the University of Chicago, and is the Director of Academic Affairs for the World Association for Hallyu Studies.

Seokho Kim is an Assistant Professor at Sungkyunkwan University. He received his Master's Degree in Sociology from Sungkyunkwan University in Korea and his Ph.D. in Sociology from the University of Chicago, where he was also a research assistant at the National Opinion Research Center. Kim is on the Editorial Board of the Korean Journal of Sociology, and has written on demographic shifts in religion and nationalism. His doctoral thesis examined voluntary associations, social inequality, and participatory democracy.

Yoshiaki Kobayashi is a Professor of Law and Political Science at Keio University. He has been President of the Japan Political Science Association and Japan Electoral Studies Association. His publications include *Malfunctioning Democracy in Japan: Quantitative Analysis in a Civil Society* (2012), 28 other books, and 300 papers in English, Spanish, French, and Japanese.

Jong Youl Lee is a Professor of Public Administration, Chair of the Department of Public Administration, and Director of the Institute of Social Sciences at Incheon National University, South Korea. He researches urban administration, policy studies, cultural administration, and risk management.

Cristina Mateos Mora is an Assistant Professor of Sociology at the Universidad Pablo de Olavide, a researcher at the Centre for Local Political Sociology and Policies, and a member of the Local Government Observatory (Andalusian Studies Centre). Her research interests include gender, civic involvement, and political participation. She has had recent publications in *Ciudad y Territorio, Revista Internacional de Organizaciones,*

European Urban and Regional Research, Reforma y Democracia. She is a member of the Cultural Scenes Project and the International Metropolitan Observatory, Seville. Her Ph.D. analyses the contextual effects of cultural scenes on civic involvement at the neighborhood level in Spain.

Clemente J. Navarro Yáñez is a Professor of Political Sociology at the Universidad Pablo de Olavide, the Head of the Centre for Local Political Sociology and Policies, and the Local Government Observatory (Andalusian Studies Centre). He has been a visiting professor at various universities, such as Florence, Rio de Janeiro, Buenos Aires, Autónoma de Chile, Consiglio Nazionalle della Ricerca, and University of Chicago. He has had recent publications in *European Societies, European Urban and Regional Research, Public Administration Review*, and Cities. His research interests include multilevel governance, local policies and politics, and, especially, public participation policy. Navarro coordinates the Cultural Scenes and Urban Development International Network together with Terry Clark and Daniel Silver. As head of the Cultural Scenes Project in Spain (http://www.upo.es/cspl/scenes/), his main results have been published in "La dinámica cultural de las ciudades" (Catarata). http://www.upo.es/cspl/scenes.

María Jesús Rodríguez-García is a Lecturer in Sociology at the Universidad Pablo de Olavide, Spain, and a researcher at the Centre for Local Political Sociology and Policies. She has been a visiting scholar at the École des Hautes Études en Sciences Sociales (CNRS, France), San Luis (Argentina), Chicago (USA), and the Institut des Sciences Sociales du Politique (CNRS, France). Her research interests include local welfare systems, gender and family policies, and, especially, coproduction and social innovation processes regarding these issues. Rodríguez-García is a main researcher of the "Gender, Participation, and Local Welfare Systems" Project, member of the Cultural Scenes Project, and the International Metropolitan Observatory. She has had recent publications in *Revista Internacional de Sociología, Revista Española de Ciencia Política, Reforma y Democracia, European Urban and Regional Studies, Revista Española de Investigaciones Sociológicas*, as well as the book *Género, políticas de igualdad y bienestar* (Miño y Dávila).

Stephen Sawyer is the Chair of the History department and Founder of the Urban Studies program at the American University of Paris. He also teaches at the University of Paris and École Libre des Sciences Politiques. He taught previously at the University of Chicago Center in Paris and École

Normale Supérieure. A specialist in urban studies and political history with an emphasis on the role of cities in territorial and state construction in the Atlantic world, Sawyer earned his Ph.D. at the University of Chicago in 2008. He has published over 45 articles and book reviews in such journals as *Les Annales*, *The Journal of Modern History*, *The European History Quarterly*, and *The Tocqueville Review*. In 2009, he was awarded a grant for a project from the city of Paris on mapping cultural scenes in metropolitan Paris, which he completed with a research team in 2011: http://dl.dropbox.com/u/5559963/Paris.May%2019.2011.Rapport%20Final%20 CARTOGRAPHIE%20CULTURELLE%20FINALE%202011.pdf.zip.

Daniel Silver is an Assistant Professor of Sociology at the University of Toronto. He received his Ph.D. from the Committee on Social Thought at the University of Chicago. His research spans social theory, urban and community sociology, and the sociology of culture.

Di Wu is a Lecturer at the Management School of the University of Chinese Academy of Sciences, Beijing. He has published *The Research on Urban Residential Choice and Housing Price's Spatial Difference in China: Based on the Theory of Scenes [M]*. Beijing: Economy & Management Publishing House. 2013. 07. ISBN: 7509625149. (in Chinese) He received the Award for National Outstanding Post-doctoral Academic Achievement in China.

Joseph E. Yi is an Assistant Professor of Political Science at Hanyang University (Seoul, Korea). His publications include *God and Karate on the Southside* (Lexington Books, 2009), "Tiger Moms and Liberal Elephants of Southern California" (SOCIETY, April 2013), "Atomized Terror and Democratic Citizenship" (Political Quarterly, September 2013), and "Same-Sex Marriage, Majority-World Christians, and the Challenge of Democratic Engagement" (SOCIETY, forthcoming). Yi received his doctorate in political science at the University of Chicago and studies liberal democracy, civil society, and multiculturalism in the USA and South Korea. He welcomes correspondence (josephyi@uchicago.edu).

INDEX